MW01252799

Politics and Economics of Latin America Series

PANAMA: POLITICS AND ECONOMICS

Politics and Economics of Latin America Series

Current Politics and Economics of Latin America, Volume I
Frank H. Columbus, (Editor)
2001. ISBN 1-56072-884-1

Politics and Economics of Latin America Volume 2
Frank H. Columbus, (Editor)
2002. ISBN: 1-59033-254-7

Politics and Economics of Latin America, Volume 3
Frank H. Columbus, (Editor)
2003. ISBN: 1-59033-619-4

Venezuela: Political Conditions and U.S. Policy
Lance H. Chisolm , (Editor)
2009. ISBN: 978-1-60692-681-9

Panama: Politics and Economics
Ricardo Colson , (Editor)
2009. ISBN: 978-1-60692-403-7

Politics and Economics of Latin America Series

PANAMA: POLITICS AND ECONOMICS

RICARDO COLSON
EDITOR

Nova Science Publishers, Inc.

New York

GUELPH HUMBER LIBRARY
205 Humber College Blvd
Toronto, ON   M9W 5L7

Copyright © 2009 by Nova Science Publishers, Inc.

All rights reserved. No part of this book may be reproduced, stored in a retrieval system or transmitted in any form or by any means: electronic, electrostatic, magnetic, tape, mechanical photocopying, recording or otherwise without the written permission of the Publisher.

For permission to use material from this book please contact us:
Telephone 631-231-7269; Fax 631-231-8175
Web Site: http://www.novapublishers.com

NOTICE TO THE READER

The Publisher has taken reasonable care in the preparation of this book, but makes no expressed or implied warranty of any kind and assumes no responsibility for any errors or omissions. No liability is assumed for incidental or consequential damages in connection with or arising out of information contained in this book. The Publisher shall not be liable for any special, consequential, or exemplary damages resulting, in whole or in part, from the readers' use of, or reliance upon, this material. Any parts of this book based on government reports are so indicated and copyright is claimed for those parts to the extent applicable to compilations of such works.

Independent verification should be sought for any data, advice or recommendations contained in this book. In addition, no responsibility is assumed by the publisher for any injury and/or damage to persons or property arising from any methods, products, instructions, ideas or otherwise contained in this publication.

This publication is designed to provide accurate and authoritative information with regard to the subject matter covered herein. It is sold with the clear understanding that the Publisher is not engaged in rendering legal or any other professional services. If legal or any other expert assistance is required, the services of a competent person should be sought. FROM A DECLARATION OF PARTICIPANTS JOINTLY ADOPTED BY A COMMITTEE OF THE AMERICAN BAR ASSOCIATION AND A COMMITTEE OF PUBLISHERS.

LIBRARY OF CONGRESS CATALOGING-IN-PUBLICATION DATA

Panama : politics and economics / editor, Ricardo Colson.
    p. cm.
  Includes bibliographical references and index.
  ISBN 978-1-60692-403-7 (hardcover : alk. paper)
  1. Panama--Economic policy. 2. Panama--Foreign economic relations--United States. 3. United States--Foreign economic relations--Panama. 4. Panama--Politics and government--1981- I. Colson, Ricardo.
  HC147.P425 2009
  330.97287--dc22

                                                                        2009027751

Published by Nova Science Publishers, Inc. ✚ *New York*

CONTENTS

PREFACE

On June 28, 2007, the United States and Panama signed a free trade agreement (FTA) after two and half years and ten rounds of negotiations. This book discusses the proposed U.S.-Panama Free Trade Agreement, including the adoption of enforceable labor standards, compulsory adherence to select multilateral environmental agreements (MEAs) and facilitation of developing country access to generic drugs. This book also examines the political and economic conditions of Panama and their relationship to U.S. policies.

Chapter 1 - This report assesses the likely impact of the U.S.-Panama Trade Promotion Agreement (TPA) on the U.S. economy as a whole and on specific industry sectors, including the impact the agreement would have on U.S. gross domestic product (GDP); exports and imports; aggregate employment and employment opportunities; the production, employment, and competitive position of industries likely to be significantly affected by the TPA; and the interests of U.S. consumers.

Panamanian exporters generally face substantially lower tariffs in the U.S. market than do U.S. exporters in the Panamanian market because most U.S. imports from Panama enter free of duty either unconditionally or under trade preference programs. Because of this tariff asymmetry, the primary impacts of the TPA likely would be improved U.S. access to the Panamanian market and an increase in U.S. exports to Panama. Nevertheless, the overall impact of the U.S.-Panama TPA on the U.S. economy would likely be small because of the small size of the Panamanian market relative to total U.S. trade and production.

The partial equilibrium model used by the Commission indicates that full implementation of the market access provisions (elimination of tariffs and tariff-rate quotas (TRQs)) of the TPA would likely cause U.S. exports to Panama of the products selected for analysis in this report to increase by between 9 and 145 percent.

The Commission analyzed the impact of both the immediate and the phased elimination of tariffs and TRQs by the TPA using sector-specific analysis of selected U.S. product sectors. The sectors analyzed were meat (beef, pork, and poultry), grain (corn and rice), frozen potato products (e.g., frozen French fries), certain processed foods, sugar and sugar-containing products, passenger cars and light trucks, and certain machinery. For most of these sectors, the TPA would provide small but positive benefits for U.S. exports.

The TPA would likely generate a small increase in U.S. services exports to Panama. Finally, the TPA also could increase trade and investment through trade facilitation, such as the reduction of impediments in customs processing; an improved regulatory environment, such as enhanced investor protections; and increased regulatory transparency. The effects of such measures on bilateral trade and investment flows could become more significant in the medium and long term.

Chapter 2 - On June 28, 2007, the United States and Panama signed a free trade agreement (FTA) after two and half years and ten rounds of negotiations. Negotiations were formally concluded on December 16, 2006, with an understanding that further changes to labor, environment, and intellectual property rights (IPR) chapters would be made pursuant to detailed congressional input. These changes were agreed to in late June 2007, clearing the way for the proposed FTA's signing in time to be considered under Trade Promotion Authority (TPA), which expired on July 1, 2007. TPA allows Congress to consider trade implementing bills under expedited procedures. Panama's legislature approved the FTA on 58 to 4 on July 11, 2007. The 110th Congress may take up implementing legislation in 2008.

Significant changes from previous bilateral FTAs include the adoption of enforceable labor standards, compulsory adherence to select multilateral environmental agreements (MEAs), and facilitation of developing country access to generic drugs. In each case, the proposed U.S.-Panama FTA goes beyond provisions in existing multilateral trade rules and even those contemplated in the Doha Development Round negotiations.

There is one highly sensitive issue that remains to be resolved. In September 2007, the Panamanian National Assembly elected Pedro Miguel González Pinzón to a one-year term as President of legislative body. Although a deputy in the National Assembly since 1999, he is known in the United States for his alleged role in the June 10, 1992 murder of a U.S. serviceman in Panama. A Panamanian court acquitted him of the charge in 1995, but the United States does not recognize the verdict and maintains an outstanding warrant for his arrest. His continued presence as National Assembly President has been one factor delaying consideration of the FTA by the U.S. Congress. This situation could change if he is not re-elected to a second term in a September 1, 2008 election.

The proposed U.S.-Panama FTA is a comprehensive agreement. Some 88% of U.S. commercial and industrial exports would become duty-free right away, with remaining tariffs phased out over a ten-year period. About 50% of U.S. farms exports to Panama would achieve duty-free status immediately. Tariffs and tariff rate quotas (TRQs) on select farm products are to be phased out by year 17 of the agreement. Panama and the United States agreed to a separate bilateral agreement on SPS issues that would recognize U.S. food safety inspection as equivalent to Panamanian standards, which would expedite entry of U.S. meat and poultry exports. The FTA also consummates understandings on services trade, telecommunications, government procurement, and intellectual property rights (particularly with respect to pharmaceutical products), while supporting trade capacity building.

Chapter 3 - With four successive elected civilian governments, the Central American nation of Panama has made notable political and economic progress since the 1989 U.S. military intervention that ousted the regime of General Manuel Noriega from power. The current President, Martín Torrijos of the Democratic Revolutionary Party (PRD), was elected in May 2004 and inaugurated to a five-year term in September 2004. Torrijos, the son of former populist leader General Omar Torrijos, won a decisive electoral victory with almost 48% of the vote in a four-man race. Torrijos' electoral alliance also won a majority of seats in the unicameral Legislative Assembly.

The most significant challenges facing the Torrijos government have included dealing with the funding deficits of the country's social security fund; developing plans for the expansion of the Panama Canal; and combating unemployment and poverty. In April 2006, the government unveiled its ambitious plans to build a third lane and new set of locks that will double the Canal's capacity. In an October 2006 referendum on the issue, 78% of voters supported the expansion project, which officially began in September 2007. Panama's service-based economy has been booming in recent years, but income distribution remains highly skewed, with large disparities between the rich and poor.

The United States has close relations with Panama, stemming in large part from the extensive linkages developed when the canal was under U.S. control and Panama hosted major U.S. military installations. The current relationship is characterized by extensive counternarcotics cooperation, assistance to help Panama assure the security of the Canal, and negotiations for a bilateral free trade agreement (FTA). The United States is providing an estimated $7.7 million in foreign aid FY2008, and could receive up to almost $4 million in FY2008 supplemental assistance under the Mérida Initiative. For FY2009, the Administration requested $11.6 million in bilateral foreign aid, not including an additional $8.9 million under the Mérida Initiative.

The United States and Panama announced the conclusion of a FTA in December 2006, although U.S. officials stated the agreement was subject to additional discussions on labor. Subsequently, congressional leaders and the Bush Administration announced a bipartisan deal in May 2007, whereby pending FTAs, including that with Panama, would include enforceable key labor and environmental standards. On June 28, 2007, the United States and Panama signed the FTA, which included the enforceable labor and environmental provisions. Panama's Legislative Assembly overwhelmingly approved the agreement in July 2007. The U.S. Congress had been likely to consider implementing legislation in the fall of 2007, but the September 1, 2007 election of Pedro Miguel González to head Panama's legislature for one year delayed consideration. González is wanted in the United States for his alleged role in the murder of a U.S. serviceman in Panama in 1992. His term expires September 1, 2008, and González has said that he will not stand for re-election. This could increase the chance that Congress will consider FTA implementing legislation. For more on the bilateral FTA, see CRS Report RL32540, *The Proposed U.S.-Panama Free Trade Agreement*, by J.F. Hornbeck.

In: Panama: Politics and Economics
Editor: Ricardo Colson

ISBN: 978-1-60692-403-7
© 2009 Nova Science Publishers, Inc.

Chapter 1

U.S.-PANAMA TRADE PROMOTION AGREEMENT: POTENTIAL ECONOMY-WIDE AND SELECTED SECTORAL EFFECTS[*]

U.S. International Trade Commission

ABSTRACT

This report assesses the likely impact of the U.S.-Panama Trade Promotion Agreement (TPA) on the U.S. economy as a whole and on specific industry sectors, including the impact the agreement would have on U.S. gross domestic product (GDP); exports and imports; aggregate employment and employment opportunities; the production, employment, and competitive position of industries likely to be significantly affected by the TPA; and the interests of U.S. consumers.

Panamanian exporters generally face substantially lower tariffs in the U.S. market than do U.S. exporters in the Panamanian market because most U.S. imports from Panama enter free of duty either unconditionally or under trade preference programs. Because of this tariff asymmetry, the primary impacts of the TPA likely would be improved U.S. access to the Panamanian market and an increase in U.S. exports to Panama. Nevertheless, the overall impact of the U.S.-Panama TPA on the U.S. economy would likely be small because of the small size of the Panamanian market relative to total U.S. trade and production.

The partial equilibrium model used by the Commission indicates that full implementation of the market access provisions (elimination of tariffs and tariff-rate quotas (TRQs)) of the TPA would likely cause U.S. exports to Panama of the products selected for analysis in this report to increase by between 9 and 145 percent.

The Commission analyzed the impact of both the immediate and the phased elimination of tariffs and TRQs by the TPA using sector-specific analysis of selected U.S. product sectors. The sectors analyzed were meat (beef, pork, and poultry), grain (corn and rice), frozen potato products (e.g., frozen French fries), certain processed foods, sugar and sugar-containing products, passenger cars and light trucks, and certain machinery. For most of these sectors, the TPA would provide small but positive benefits for U.S. exports.

---

[*] This is edited, reformatted and augmented version of an United States International Trade Commission, Ivestigation No. TA-2104-025, Publication 3948 dated September 2007.

The TPA would likely generate a small increase in U.S. services exports to Panama. Finally, the TPA also could increase trade and investment through trade facilitation, such as the reduction of impediments in customs processing; an improved regulatory environment, such as enhanced investor protections; and increased regulatory transparency. The effects of such measures on bilateral trade and investment flows could become more significant in the medium and long term.

EXECUTIVE SUMMARY

This report finds that the U.S.-Panama TPA may have a small, positive impact on the U.S. economy. The benefits would likely be small due to the small size of Panama's economy relative to that of the United States, Panama's small share of U.S. trade (about 0.1 percent of total U.S. goods trade in 2006), and the duty-free access most Panamanian products already receive in the U.S. market.

About the Agreement

The TPA provides for the eventual elimination of duties and tariff-rate quotas (TRQs) on bilateral trade in all goods except sugar.

- **U.S. merchandise exports to Panama:** Almost 76 percent of industrial goods and textile tariff lines and almost 68 percent of agricultural tariff lines would be free of duty upon implementation of the TPA. Duties on all other industrial and textile tariff lines would be phased out over a 5- to 10-year period. Agricultural tariff lines that would not be duty-free upon implementation of the TPA would be subject to phased out duty elimination over a 5- to 15-year period, or TRQs that would be phased out over a period of up to 20 years.

- **U.S. merchandise imports from Panama:** More than 99 percent of industrial goods and textile tariff lines and 89 percent of agricultural tariff lines would become free of duty upon implementation of the TPA. All duties on industrial and textile tariff lines would be phased out over a 10-year period. Agricultural tariff lines that would not be duty free upon TPA implementation would be phased out over a period of 5 to 15 years or would be subject to TRQs which – with the exception of the TPA on sugar – would be phased out over a period of up to 17 years.

TPA measures on services trade would provide U.S. firms with levels of market access, national treatment, and regulatory transparency that generally exceed those afforded by Panama's commitments under the GATS. In particular, the TPA would extend trade disciplines to several services sectors for which Panama made limited or no sectoral commitments under the GATS, such as legal services and insurance services, as well as to new services yet to be offered commercially.

Summary of Findings on Market Access

The U.S.-Panama TPA is expected to increase U.S. exports to Panama by removing or reducing trade barriers in the Panamanian market. U.S. imports from Panama would not likely grow significantly as a result of trade liberalization under the TPA because most Panamanian products already enter the U.S. market free of duty either unconditionally or under the Caribbean Basin Economic Recovery Act (CBERA), the Generalized System of Preferences (GSP), or other U.S. provisions. Nevertheless, the TPA could create additional incentives for investment in export-oriented industries in Panama, as it would effectively make CBERA and GSP duty-free treatment permanent.

The Commission conducted specific analyses of the impact of the TPA on certain sectors, including meat (beef, pork, and poultry), grain (corn and rice), frozen potato products, certain processed foods, sugar and sugar-containing products, passenger cars and light trucks, and certain machinery (major household appliances, and heating, ventilation, and air conditioning (HVAC) equipment). Sectors were selected for analysis based on a number of criteria including, *inter alia*, the volume of U.S.-Panama trade in a certain sector and the extent of trade liberalization affecting a particular sector under the provisions of the TPA. The analyses indicate that U.S. exports to Panama would likely increase from 9 percent (for turkey and certain equipment) to 145 percent (for rice) as a result of tariff and quota elimination (table ES.1). Further, the TPA is likely to have a minor effect on U.S. imports and production of sugar and sugar-containing products. Any impact on total U.S. trade in the examined sectors is likely to be minimal because of the small size of the Panamanian market and the fact that the United States already supplies a substantial share of Panama's imports in several of these product sectors.

With regard to services, the TPA would extend trade disciplines to several services sectors for which Panama made limited or no sectoral commitments under the GATS, such as legal services and insurance services, as well as to new services yet to be offered commercially. However, the TPA would likely generate only a small increase in U.S. services exports to Panama because of the small size of the Panamanian market. Further, the TPA would not likely have a significant effect on U.S. imports of services from Panama because the U.S. services market is generally open to foreign firms, including those from Panama, and because the Panamanian industry is small.

Summary of Findings on Trade Facilitation and the Regulatory Environment

The trade facilitation, regulatory, and other provisions of the U.S.-Panama TPA are also expected to have a small impact on the U.S. economy and U.S. industries, primarily reflecting Panama's small economy and the generally open U.S. market.

- **Trade facilitation:** These provisions are expected to expand export opportunities for U.S. firms in general by increasing transparency and providing greater accountability and predictability they will be especially beneficial, particularly for goods subject to technical and regulatory standards and requirements. In particular, U.S. agricultural exporters will likely benefit from the U.S.-Panama Agreement Regarding Certain Sanitary and Phytosanitary Measures and Technical Standards Affecting Trade in

Agricultural Products (U.S.-Panama SPS Agreement), under which Panama agrees to recognize the equivalence of the U.S. meat inspection system and the U.S. regulatory system for processed foods.

- **Regulatory-related and other provisions:** These provisions would likely enhance the environment for bilateral trade and investment, particularly over the medium and long term. U.S.-based firms would likely benefit from Panama's commitments with respect to transparency; trade remedies; government procurement, particularly in light of the expansion of the Panama Canal; investment; the protection of intellectual property rights; and dispute settlement. Such benefits may include, *inter alia*, reduced IPR infringement in Panama and increased investment opportunities in Panama's retail sector.

Table ES.1. Selected Products: Estimated Effect of Eliminating Panamanian Duties and Trqs on U.S. Exports and Production[a]

	U.S. exports to Panama (% change)
Grains	60.7
Corn	20.1
Rice	145.4
Passenger vehicles and light trucks	42.9
Passenger vehicles	42.9
Light trucks	26.3
Certain machinery products	13.7
Air pumps, compressors, fans	9.2
Air conditioners/parts	16.4
Refrigerators and heat pumps	11.1
Washing machines	20.4
Processed food	35.7
Food preps, nesoi	35.5
Sauces	25.2
Bread, pastry	39.2
Malt extract	53.1
Soups and broths	33.4
Mixes and doughs	9.8
Meat	62.0
Turkey meat	9.0
Pork	96.0
Chicken	45.3
Beef[b]	74.1
Frozen potato products	23.0

Source: USITC estimates.

[a]Based on 2006 data.

[b]The Commission used 2003 beef production and trade data to model the potential impact of the TPA on U.S. beef exports to Panama. These data were used in lieu of 2006 data because of Panamanian concerns arising toward the end of 2003 over the possibility of bovine spongiform encephalopathy (BSE) in U.S. beef, which resulted in significantly reduced U.S. exports to Panama during 2004–06.

INTRODUCTION

Scope and Approach of the Report

In accordance with section 2104(f) of the Trade Act of 2002 (19 U.S.C.§ 3804 (f)), this report assesses the likely impact of the U.S.-Panama Trade Promotion Agreement (TPA) on the U.S. economy as a whole and on specific industry sectors, including the impact of the TPA on U.S. gross domestic product (GDP); exports and imports; aggregate employment and employment opportunities; the production, employment, and competitive position of industries likely to be significantly affected by the TPA; and the interests of U.S. consumers. The assessment is based on a review of all 22 chapters of the draft text of the U.S.-Panama TPA, as well as its annexes, notes, tariff schedules, and associated side letters. Summaries of TPA provisions are presented in chapters 2–5 and appendix D of this report.

In assessing the likely impact of the TPA, the Commission relied on a combination of quantitative and qualitative data. The Commission quantified the likely impact of the TPA on specific industry sectors where data were sufficient to do so. It was not possible to provide a quantitative assessment of economy-wide effects because the models presently used by the Commission to produce such estimates require information on interactions in Panama's economy, which was not available. Without these data, the Commission was generally limited to providing quantitative assessments of the likely impact of tariff liberalization (provisions related to increased market access) in specific sectors as it affects trade in those sectors. The reduction or elimination of tariff and nontariff barriers will likely increase the competitiveness of U.S. manufacturers, farmers, and service providers in the Panamanian market and make some Panamanian imports available at a lower price to U.S. consumers.

While it was not possible to quantify the impact of the TPA on U.S. GDP, overall trade, aggregate employment, and overall consumer welfare, the Commission was able to conclude that the impact would likely be small based on the quantitative assessments available and additional qualitative assessments of the effects on sectors most directly affected by the TPA, and due to the small size of the Panamanian economy relative to the U.S. economy. The Commission's qualitative assessments rely on information regarding current market conditions, TPA provisions and measures that affect trade in the absence of a TPA, and the views of academics and industry and government representatives regarding the potential impact of the agreement on a particular industry or the economy as a whole. On the basis of its quantitative and qualitative assessments, the Commission concluded that the impact of the TPA on the U.S. economy as a whole and on virtually all U.S. industry sectors would likely be small.

To assess the impact of the market access provisions of the TPA, the Commission employed a partial equilibrium model which simulates the effects of changes to tariffs and tariff-rate quotas (TRQs) on trade between the United States and Panama in specified goods. It uses data on trade between the two countries, as well as trade between them and other countries. The static nature of the model assumes that the TPA is fully implemented immediately, and not phased in over time;[1] therefore, the estimated effects reflect long-term adjustments to a fully implemented TPA. The model assumes that imports and domestic products are imperfect substitutes in every sector except sugar, where products are assumed to be perfect substitutes. See appendix F. The model does not provide estimates of the effects of changes in policy or sectors other than those briefly affected, or on the economy as a whole. Other policy assumptions of the model are discussed in chapter 2 of this report.

The U.S. product sectors analyzed include meat products (beef, pork, and poultry), grain (corn and rice), frozen potato products, certain processed foods (food preparations, sauces, and dough, among others), sugar and sugar-containing products, passenger vehicles and light trucks, and certain machinery (including major household appliances and heating, ventilation, and air conditioning (HVAC) equipment). These sectors were selected for analysis based on a number of criteria, including the importance of the sector or key sector segments in terms of bilateral trade, the volume of Panama's trade flows with the rest of the world, the extent of tariff and nontariff measures affecting U.S.-Panama trade in the absence of a TPA, and the extent of tariff and nontariff liberalization under the TPA.

The Commission also assessed the impact of TPA provisions with respect to trade in services, trade facilitation, (e.g., customs administration, technical barriers to trade, and electronic commerce), and the regulatory environment (e.g., government procurement, investment, competition policy, intellectual property rights, labor, the environment, and dispute settlement). The impact of these provisions was not quantified because of limited data availability; however, as discussed in chapters 3, 4, and 5 of this report, some of these provisions may have a small positive impact on U.S. GDP, exports and imports, employment, production, and U.S. consumers.

Data and other information included in this study were obtained from industry reports, interviews with government and industry contacts, official reports of the trade advisory committees, written submissions received in response to the Commission's *Federal Register* notice of institution of this investigation,[2] and testimony at the public hearing held by the Commission in connection with this investigation.[3] Other sources include, *inter alia*, the U.S. Department of Agriculture, the U.S. Department of Commerce, the U.S. Department of State, the Office of the United States Trade Representative, the World Bank, the World Trade Organization (WTO), and the Global Trade Information Services' Global Trade Atlas Database.

This report is organized as follows: the remainder of chapter 1 provides overviews of the TPA and U.S.-Panama bilateral trade; chapter 2 provides a summary of the TPA market access provisions for goods and presents the Commission's partial equilibrium analyses and assessment of the impact of the TPA in selected goods sectors; chapter 3 covers the impact of provisions regarding market access for services; chapter 4 covers the impact of trade facilitation provisions; chapter 5 covers the impact of provisions related to regulation, including those pertaining to investment; and chapter 6 presents a literature review and summarizes hearing testimony and written submissions to the Commission in this investigation. Table 1.1 identifies the chapters of the TPA and where they are analyzed or summarized in this report.

Overview of the U.S.-Panama TPA

The U.S.-Panama TPA would establish a bilateral free trade area[4] that eliminates tariffs on the vast majority of goods that satisfy the agreement's rules of origin. There are specific provisions in the agreement on customs administration and trade facilitation that would facilitate bilateral trade in goods. The U.S.-Panama TPA also would liberalize cross-border trade in virtually all services, with specific chapters focused on financial services and telecommunication services. It would build upon existing WTO agreements, as well as other agreements and international commitments, by strengthening the rules that govern investment, intellectual property rights, labor, the environment, and government procurement. The agreement establishes a bilateral Free Trade Commission to supervise the implementation of the agreement and to supervise the work of all committees and working groups established under the agreement. In addition, there are numerous provisions throughout the agreement that would promote bilateral consultation and cooperation, procedural and substantive due process, administrative and judicial review, transparency, and the rule of law.[5] Finally, the U.S.-Panama TPA contains a transitional safeguard measure and a mechanism for settling disputes.

Chapter 3 of the U.S.-Panama TPA contains the core obligations regarding bilateral market access for goods.[6] It affirms that each party shall accord national treatment to the goods of the other party, and it provides that each party shall progressively eliminate its customs duties on goods that satisfy the agreement's rules of origin. Under the agreement, customs duties on goods that satisfy the agreement's rules of origin will either be eliminated immediately or be phased out over 5, 10, 15, or 17 years.[7] There is a separate schedule of tariff commitments for each party that provides the specific staging period for each individual product category. In addition, the agreement contains TRQs for certain agricultural goods and a specific safeguard measure for certain agricultural goods. It also contains special rules for textiles and apparel, including a transitional safeguard measure.

Chapter 4 contains the agreement's rules of origin provisions, which are the rules that determine whether a product qualifies for favorable tariff treatment under the agreement. There are several ways for a good to qualify as an originating good.[8] Under the agreement, a good is an originating good if it is wholly obtained or produced entirely in the territory of the parties. The concept of "wholly obtained or produced" is defined to include (1) plants and plant products harvested in the territory of the parties, (2) live animals born and raised in the territory of the parties, (3) goods obtained in the territory of the parties from live animals, (4) minerals and other natural resources extracted from the territory of the parties, and (5) goods produced in the territory of the parties exclusively from goods that are wholly obtained or produced in the territory of the parties.

In addition, a good is an originating good for purposes of the agreement if it is produced entirely in the territory of the parties and each of the "nonoriginating materials" used in the production of the good undergoes an applicable change in tariff classification, or the good otherwise satisfies any applicable regional value content or other requirement in the agreement. Nonoriginating materials are defined as materials that do not meet the rules of origin, typically third-country goods or materials that do not undergo an applicable change in tariff classification. The agreement contains specific rules of origin for each individual product category, including the applicable changes in tariff classification that are necessary for a good to qualify for favorable tariff treatment and whether a regional value content requirement applies. Lastly, a good is an originating good for purposes of the agreement if it is produced entirely in the territory of the parties exclusively from originating materials.

Summaries of the TPA provisions affecting services trade, trade facilitation, and regulatory issues are included in chapters 3, 4, and 5 of this report.

Table 1.1 U.S.-Panama TPA: Location of Summary or Analysis of TPA Chapters in the Commission's Report[a]

TPA chapter	Chapter of Commission's report where analyzed
1. Initial Provisions	Appendix D
2. General Definitions	Appendix D
3. National Treatment and Market Access for Goods	Chapter 1 and 2
4. Rules of Origin Procedures	Chapter 1
5. Customs Administration and Trade Facilitation	Chapter 4
6. Sanitary and Phytosanitary Measures	Chapter 4
7. Technical Barriers to Trade	Chapter 4
8. Trade Remedies	Chapter 5
9. Government Procurement	Chapter 5
10. Investment	Chapter 5
11. Cross-Border Trade in Services	Chapter 3
12. Financial Services	Chapter 3
13. Telecommunications	Chapter 3
14. Electronic Commerce	Chapter 4
15. Intellectual Property Rights	Chapter 5
16. Labor	Chapter 5
17. Environment	Chapter 5
18. Transparency	Chapter 5
19. Administration of the Agreement and Trade Capacity Building	Appendix D
20. Dispute Settlement	Chapter 5
21. Exceptions	Appendix D
22. Final Provisions	Appendix D
Annex 1 Non-Conforming Measures for Services and Investment	Chapters 3 and 5
Annex II Non-Conforming Measures for Services and Investment	Chapters 3 and 5
Annex III Non-Conforming Measures for Financial Services	Chapters 3 and 5

[a] Chapters. 1, 2, 19, 21, and 22 of the U.S.-Panama TPA address primarily administrative and legal matters with respect to the agreement and, hence, are summarized in appendix D but are not analyzed in the report.

U.S.-Panama Trade Overview

In 2006, most U.S. imports from Panama (96 percent, by value) entered the United States free of duty because they qualified for normal trade relations (NTR) status or under the Caribbean Basin Economic Recovery Act (CBERA), the Caribbean Basin Trade Partnership Act (CBPTA), or the U.S. Generalized System of Preferences (GSP). Consequently, it is expected that the main impact of the U.S.-Panama TPA would be to increase U.S. exports as a result of enhanced access to a more open market in Panama. This section presents an overview of U.S.-Panama bilateral merchandise trade in 2006.[9]

U.S. Exports

U.S. merchandise exports to Panama were valued at $2.5 billion in 2006, ranking Panama as the 45th largest market for U.S. exports.[10],[11] Panama accounted for less than 0.5 percent of total U.S. exports of $929.5 billion in 2006. U.S. exports to Panama have increased at compound annual growth rates of 8.0 percent since 1989 and 15.6 percent since 2001 (figure 1.1). Leading U.S. exports to Panama in 2006 are reported in table 1.2 and appendix table E.1. Petroleum oils ranked as the single largest U.S. export to Panama in 2006, with exports valued at $775 million.[12] Other leading U.S. exports to Panama were airplanes and parts for airplanes, medicaments, machinery-related equipment, corn, perfumes and toilet waters, and passenger motor vehicles.

Panamanian tariff rates applied on U.S. exports are summarized in table 1.3. This table shows that 70 percent of Panamanian 8-digit tariff rate lines on U.S. exports currently have base tariff rates exceeding 0 percent, and more than 50 percent have base rates exceeding 5 percent. Table 1.4 shows selected Panamanian nontariff impediments to trade. The sectoral effects of these nontariff impediments to trade are discussed in the industry sections in chapter 4 and 6.

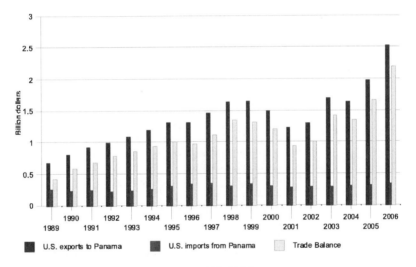

Figure 1.1: U.S. merchandise trade with Panama, 1999-2006

Source: Compiled from official statistics of the U.S. Department of Commerce.

Table 1.2. Leading U.S. Exports to Panama, US$ million, 2006

Mineral fuels	855.5
Machinery and equipment	383.8
Aircraft	166.1
Pharmaceutical products	131.6
Vehicles, other than railway	89.8
Other	896.7
Total	2,523.6

Source: Compiled from official statistics of the U.S. Department of Commerce.

Table 1.3. Applied Panamanian Tariff Rates on U.S. Exports

Tariff base rate (percent)	Number of tariff lines	Percent of total tariff lines
0	2,639	29.6
>0 to 5	1,217	13.6
>5 to 10	1,987	22.3
>10 to 20	2,919	32.7
>20 to 35	73	0.8
>35	88	1.0
Total[a]	8,923	100.0

Source: U.S.-Panama TPA, Panama Tariff Schedule.
Note: Does not include tariff lines where base rate values have been left blank.
[a] Total of 8,923 tariff lines includes 7,494 industrial and textile tariff lines and 1,429 agricultural tariff lines, as described in more detail in chap. 2 of this report. See tables 2.1 and 2.2 for summaries of Panamanian tariff commitments under the TPA.

Table 1.4. Panama: Selected Nontariff Impediments

Topic	Sector or product/service	Selected nontariff issue	Source year	TPA-relevant chapter(s)[a]
Customs procedures	All imports, except pharmaceuticals, foods, and school supplies	Panama applies a 5 percent transfer tax (impuesto a la transferencia de bienes corporales muebles or ITBM) on cost, insurance, and freight (CIF) value and other handling charges.	2006[b]	5
Corruption	All sectors	Anticorruption laws are weak and/or not rigorously applied. The Government of Panama lacks a strong checks and balances system and a well-established professional career work force in public offices.	2006[d]	18
Export-related measures	Raw materials	Raw materials for domestic consumption or processing are assessed a 3 percent import duty and raw materials imported for export production (except rice, dairy, pork, and tomato products) are duty free.	2006[e]	3, 4
Export-related measures	Shrimp farmers, tourism	These export industries are exempt from paying certain types of taxes and import duties.	2006[e]	3, 11
Export-related measures	Multiple products	Export restrictions are imposed on non-pharmaceutical/science-related drugs, staple products as determined by the Panamanian Government, and products excluded by the Panamanian Government for reasons of international agreements or national economic interest.	2006[d]	3

Topic	Sector or product/ service	Selected nontariff issue	Source year	TPA-relevant chapter(s)[a]
Government procurement	All sectors	Lack of transparency in bidding procedures for procurement projects.	2006[c]	9
Import licensing	Manufactured products (non-agriculture)	No import license is required, but the importing entity must be registered with the Panamanian Ministry of Commerce and Industry and importers must hold a commercial or industrial license to operate in Panama.	2006[e]	3
Import licensing	Agricultural products	Licensing process is arbitrary and non-transparent.	2006[e]	3
Import prohibitions	Multiple products	Imports of certain potentially harmful or sensitive products are restricted. These include, *inter alia*, equipment or instruments for manufacturing coins; obscene brochures, books, newspapers, magazines, or postcards containing negative portrayals of the country's culture, civilization or dignity; and plants, seeds, or animals as determined by the Panamanian Ministry of Agriculture.	2006[d]	3
Import quotas	Multiple products	Special import permits are required for all types of firearms, ammunition, fertilizers, and certain foods.	2006[f]	3
Intellectual property rights	Pharmaceutical products	Pharmaceutical patents are initially granted for only 15 years, compared to 20 years for most other products in Panama.	2006[e]	15
Intellectual property rights	Audiovisual services	The legal framework guiding internet use remains incomplete as internet piracy grows in Panama. Panama has the potential to become a regional transshipment point for pirated optical disks.	2006[e]	11, 14, 15
Intellectual property rights	Retailing	Trafficking of counterfeit brand name clothing is a particular problem.	2006[d]	11, 15
Investment-related measures	Tourism	Panamanians are allowed to deduct 50 percent of any amount invested in the tourism sector from their taxable income (Tourism Law of 1994 - Law 8).	2006[e]	10, 11
Investment-related measures	Retailing and media	Foreign ownership is restricted.	2006[c]	10, 11
Investment-related measures	All sectors	Government concessions and contracts are not fully enforced or can be changed abruptly.	2006[e]	10
Investment-related measures	All sectors	Weak judicial system due to poorly trained personnel, large case backlogs, and a lack of independence from political influence.	2006[c]	10, 18

Table 1.4. (Continued)

Topic	Sector or product/ service	Selected nontariff issue	Source year	TPA-relevant chapter(s)[a]
Investment-related measures	All sectors	Labor laws are inflexible, firing practices are highly regulated, and Panama's bankruptcy law is considered antiquated.	2006[f]	10, 18
Investment-related measures	Real estate	Foreign land ownership is prohi-bited within 10 kilometers of the national border or on an island (including beaches or the shores of rivers or lakes).	2006[d]	10
Investment-related measures	Including, but not limited to banking, accounting requirements, formation and functioning of corporations, and taxation	Retention of local legal counsel is highly advisable in these sectors due to the unique features of Panamanian law and practice.	2006[d]	10
Sanitary and phytosanitary measures	Agricultural products	Lack of procedural transparency in the issuance of phytosanitary permits.	2006[f]	6
Services	Medical practitioners, lawyers, and customs brokers	These professions are reserved for Panamanian citizens.	2006[d]	11
Standards, testing, certification and labeling	Poultry, pork, dairy, and beef products	Panamanian health and agriculture officials must certify individual U.S. processing plants as a precondition to importation. However, inspections are often delayed due to budget constraints and lack of personnel.	2006[e]	3, 6

Note: Examples selected based on survey of standard sources regarding nontariff trade impediments. Citations represent the Panamanian environment in the year of publication; no assumptions are made as to whether these represent the current environment.

[a] Including annexes and side letters. *U.S.-Panama Trade Promotion Agreement (TPA),* full text available at http://www.ustr.gov/.

[b] United States Trade Representative (USTR), *2006 National Trade Estimate (NTE) Report on Foreign Trade Barriers,* available at http://www.ustr.gov/; and Economist Intelligence Unit (EIU), "Panama Country Profile 2006," available at http://www.eiu.com.

[c] USTR, *2006 NTE Report*; and U.S. & Foreign Commercial Service (US& FCS) and U.S. Department of State, *Doing Business in Panama: A Country Commercial Guide for U.S. Companies,* 2006, available at http://www.buyusa.gov/panama/en/11.html.

[d] US&FCS and U.S. Department of State, *Doing Business in Panama,* 2006.

[e] USTR, *2006 NTE Report.*

[f] US&FCS and U.S. Department of State, *Doing Business in Panama,* 2006; and EIU, "Panama Country Profile 2006."

U.S. Imports

U.S. merchandise imports from Panama were valued at $337.6 million in 2006, ranking Panama as the 102nd largest U.S. import supplier.[13] Panama accounted for less than 0.1

percent of the total value of U.S. imports in 2006 ($1.8 trillion). U.S. imports from Panama were fairly concentrated in a few product categories, primarily fish and crustaceans, including shrimp, tuna, and frozen fillets of fresh-water fish; cane sugar; gold; coffee; fruit, such as melons and pineapples; fruit and vegetable juice; and glass containers (table 1.5 and appendix table E.2). Fish and crustaceans accounted for more than 30 percent of total U.S. imports from Panama in 2006. Panama supplied more than one-half of total U.S. imports in only two eight-digit HTS categories: certain glass containers (HTS 7010.90.30) and certain single fruit and vegetable juice, other than orange juice (HTS 2202.90.36).

Panama is a designated beneficiary of CBERA, CBPTA,[14] and GSP. These programs afford duty-free entry into the United States for eligible products from designated beneficiaries. Approximately 79 percent of all U.S. duty-free imports from Panama in 2006 entered under NTR, about 10 percent entered under CBERA/CBPTA provisions, and more than 7 percent entered under GSP (appendix table E.3).

Between 2000 (the effective year for CBPTA) and 2006, U.S. imports from Panama have increased at a compound annual growth rate of 2.2 percent, which exceeds the rate of 1.6 percent from 1989 to 2006 (figure 1.1). From 2000 to 2006, all U.S. duty-free imports from Panama increased, but those under CBPTA provisions, particularly apparel articles, increased the most.

Table 1.5. Leading U.S. Imports from Panama, US$ Million, 2006

Fish	101.9
Precious metals and jewelry	35.1
Sugars and sugar confectionery	23.5
Edible fruit and nuts	12.5
Coffee	11.8
Other	152.7
Total	337.6

Source: Compiled from official statistics of the U.S. Department of Commerce.

Based on the U.S. tariff schedule for 2006, summarized in table 1.6, approximately 62 percent of U.S. 8-digit tariff rate lines on imports from Panama have a base rate other than free (excluding any tariff lines eligible for CBERA, CBTPA, or GSP duty-free entry), and almost 11 percent of U.S. tariff rate lines on imports from Panama have base rates exceeding 10 percent.

Trade Balance

The U.S. trade balance with Panama increased to a record surplus of $2.2 billion in 2006. The United States has maintained a trade surplus with Panama since 1989[15] at an average of $1.1 billion (figure 1.1). This trade surplus reflects, in part, higher rates of growth in U.S. merchandise exports to Panama relative to U.S. merchandise imports from Panama, particularly U.S. exports of fuel-related products, which in 2006 accounted for almost 34 percent of total U.S. exports to Panama. This increased value of U.S. exports of petroleum products reflects primarily an increase in unit prices and, to a lesser extent, an increase in the quantity exported in 2006.

Table 1.6. Applied Panamanian Tariff Rates on U.S. Exports

Tariff base rate (percent)	Number of tariff lines	Percent of total tariff lines
0	2,639	29.6
>0 to 5	1,217	13.6
>5 to 10	1,987	22.3
>10 to 20	2,919	32.7
>20 to 35	73	0.8
>35	88	1.0
Total[a]	8,923	100.0

Source: *U.S.-Panama TPA*, Panama Tariff Schedule.

Note: Does not include tariff lines where base rate values have been left blank.

[a] Total of 8,923 tariff lines includes 7,494 industrial and textile tariff lines and 1,429 agricultural tariff lines, as described in more detail in chap. 2 of this report. See tables 2-1 and 2-2 for summaries of Panamanian tariff commitments under the TPA.

GOODS MARKET ACCESS AND SELECTED SECTORAL ANALYSIS AND ASSESSMENT

The main impact of the market access provisions of the U.S.-Panama TPA would likely be in the form of increased U.S. exports resulting from enhanced access to the market in Panama. U.S. imports from Panama are not expected to grow significantly as a result of the TPA, because most Panamanian products already enter the U.S. market free of duty.

This chapter analyses the likely impact of the U.S.-Panama TPA with respect to market access for goods in selected sectors.[16] It begins with a summary of the tariff commitments that would be made by the United States and Panama, followed by a sectoral analysis of the TPA. Using a partial equilibrium model, the Commission estimates the likely impact of the elimination of tariffs and quotas under the agreement on U.S. exports to Panama, as well as the potential effects on total U.S. exports, imports, and production for the following products: meat (beef, pork, and poultry),[17] grain (corn and rice), frozen potato products (e.g., frozen French fries), certain processed foods (food preparations, sauces, and bread and pastry, among others), passenger vehicles and light trucks, and certain machinery (major household appliances and heating, ventilation, and air conditioning (HVAC) equipment).[18] In addition, the Commission used a partial equilibrium model to estimate the likely impact of increased U.S. market access under the agreement for Panamanian raw cane sugar.[19] These sectors were selected for analysis based on a number of criteria, including the importance of the sector or key sector segments in terms of bilateral trade, the volume of Panama's trade flows with the rest of the world, the extent of tariff and nontariff measures affecting U.S.- Panama trade in the absence of a TPA, and the extent of tariff and nontariff liberalization under the TPA.

As discussed in this chapter, the Commission estimates that these sector-specific U.S. exports to Panama would likely increase from 9 percent (for turkey and certain HVAC equipment) to approximately 145 percent (for rice) relative to the base year as a result of tariff and quota elimination under the TPA. Given the limited bilateral trade in these sectors, the impact of the TPA on total U.S. exports and output in these sectors would be small. With respect to U.S. imports, the Commission's partial equilibrium analysis estimates that the quantity of U.S. imports of raw cane sugar from Panama could increase by 23.3 percent as a result of Panama's additional duty-free access to the U.S. market under the TPA, with a small change to the total value of U.S. raw cane sugar imports and U.S. production. The Commission's analysis suggests that the TPA would not significantly increase U.S. imports in any of the other selected sectors.

TPA Tariff Commitments by Tariff Line

Tables 2.1 and 2.2 summarize the U.S. and Panamanian tariff commitments.[20] Of the more than 8,800 U.S. and 7,400 Panamanian industrial and textile tariff lines, more than 99 percent of U.S. tariff lines and almost 76 percent of Panamanian tariff lines are already free of duty or would become so immediately upon entry into force of the TPA. Eighty-nine percent of U.S. agricultural lines and almost 68 percent of Panamanian agricultural lines are already free of duty or would become so immediately upon implementation of the TPA. Because a relatively large share of U.S. tariff lines are already free of duty on an MFN basis, and because U.S. tariff commitments in the TPA would largely make permanent the dutyfree provisions of CBERA and GSP, the primary impact of the TPA likely would be improved U.S. access to the Panamanian market and an increase in U.S. exports to Panama.

Sector-Specific Assessments: Effects on U.S. Imports, Exports, and Production

Analytical Framework

Several recent Commission studies have relied on general equilibrium modeling to show the effects of free trade agreements on the United States in terms of their effects on overall U.S. economic welfare and on trade in particular industry sectors.[21] General equilibrium models can provide a comprehensive assessment of the effects of an agreement involving changes in the policy that directly affect imports and exports in many industry sectors, as well as the secondary indirect effects on other industries, consumers, and governments. A partial equilibrium approach, however, is more appropriate for assessing the U.S.-Panama TPA, because bilateral trade (particularly trade subject to the elimination of import restraints) is concentrated within a few sectors, and because key data on Panama's economic structure, necessary for a general equilibrium analysis, are not available.

Commission staff used a partial equilibrium, perfect substitute model to estimate the economic effects of increased U.S. market access for Panamanian raw cane sugar on total U.S. imports of raw cane sugar,[22] the competing U.S. industry, and U.S. consumers.

Similarly, the effects on the U.S. economy of the elimination of Panamanian duties on various U.S. products (including beef, pork, and poultry; grains, including corn and rice; frozen potato products; certain processed food products; passenger cars and light trucks; and certain machinery, including major household appliances and HVAC equipment) are also estimated.

Table 2.1. U.S.-Panama TPA: Summary of Industrial and Textile Tariff Commitments

Staging	U.S. commitments (8,824 tariff lines)		Panama commitments (7,494 tariff lines)	
	Number of lines	Percent	Number of lines	Percent
Already free of duty (MFN)	3,602 tariff lines included in 77 HS chapters	40.8	2,370 tariff lines included in 55 HS chapters	31.6
Immediate duty-free entry	5,174 tariff lines included in 71 HS chapters	58.6	3,309 tariff lines included in 71 HS chapters	44.2
Subtotal of already free of duty and immediate duty-free entry	8,776 tariff lines	99.5	5,679 tariff lines	75.8
Free without bond	17 tariff lines in HS chapter 98 (e.g., articles for exhibittion, shows; contests, repair or testing; models; order samples)	0.2	None	0.0
5-year linear staging	None	0.0	675 tariff lines in 38 HS chapters	9.0
10-year linear staging	None	0.0	981 tariff lines in 49 HS chapters	13.1
10-year nonlinear staging	30 tariff lines included in HS chapters 16 (certain tuna), 61 (certain baby socks, stockings, and hosiery), and 64 (certain footwear products)	0.3	159 tariff lines in 12 HS chapters	2.1
Total tariff lines	8,824 tariff lines	100.0	7,494 tariff lines	100.0

Sources: *U.S.-Panama Trade Promotion Agreement (TPA)*, U.S. Tariff Schedule (Industrial and Textiles) and Panama Tariff Schedule (Industrial and Textiles).

Note: U.S. and Panama tariff schedules include 8-digit HS tariff numbers. Industrial and textile schedules include fish and seafood. U.S. schedule includes 6 tariff lines included in HS chapter 61 (babies' garments) that have been broken out into 6 subdivisions. The U.S. schedule does not reflect duty-free status available for tariff lines under CBERA or GSP. Zero values indicate less than 0.1 percent. Percent figures may not sum to 100.0 because of rounding.

[a] All industrial and textile tariff lines are free of duty for both parties by year 10 of the agreement.

The model used to estimate changes in U.S. exports of these products to Panama as a result of the immediate elimination of tariffs is a nonlinear, imperfect substitute model.[23] Use of this model provides estimates of the effect on trade volumes of changes in trade policy for a given sector; results for multiple sectors are not additive, unless reported as a group total in the tables (e.g. grains or meat). For example, the effect on trade in corn reflects the elimination of Panamanian trade barriers on corn only, not the secondary effects of the elimination of barriers on other products. The reported effect on grains is a result of eliminating Panamanian barriers to trade in both corn and rice. Furthermore, the reported effects of increased exports of commodities from the United States to Panama are also reported as effects on total U.S. exports and on U.S. production, without allowing for the possibility that U.S. exports to third countries might be diverted to Panama, or that production for U.S. domestic consumption might be diverted to exports.

Table 2.2. U.S.-Panama TPA: Summary of Agricultural Tariff Commitments

Staging	U.S. commitments (1,820 tariff lines)		Panama commitments (1,429 tariff lines)	
	Number of lines	Percent	Number of lines	Percent
Already free of duty (MFN)	389 tariff lines included in 32 HS chapters	21.4	269 tariff lines included in 26 HS chapters	18.8
Immediate duty-free entry	1,230 tariff lines included in 33 HS chapters	67.6	699 tariff lines included in 31 HS chapters	48.9
Subtotal of already free of duty and immediate duty-free entry	1,619 tariff lines	89.0	968 tariff lines	67.7
5-year linear staging	6 tariff lines included in HS chapters 20 (olives) and 51 (processed fine animal hair such as cashmere)	0.3	124 tariff lines included in 14 HS chapters	8.7
8- to 10-year linear and nonlinear staging	9 tariff lines, all 10-year linear, included in HS chapters 07, 18, 22, 23, and 51 (olives, chocolate and cocoa preps, milk-based drinks, milk-based animal feeds, and wool products)	0.5	131 tariff lines included in 12 HS chapters	9.2
11- to 12- year linear and nonlinear staging	None	0.0	39 tariff lines included in 9 HS chapters	2.7
15-year linear and nonlinear staging	80 tariff lines included in 12 HS chapters	4.4	72 tariff lines included in 10 HS chapters	5.0
Special designation[a]	2 tariff lines included in HS chapter 22 (undena-tured and denatured ethyl alcohol suitable for use as a fuel or for producing a mixture of a special fuel and alcohol)	0.1	None	0.0
Tariff-rate quotas	104 tariff lines included in HS chapters 04, 17-19, and 21 covering milk and dairy products, ice cream, and sugar products; inquota items are free of duty; TRQs are	5.7	95 tariff lines included in HS chapters 02, 04, 07, 10-11, 15-16, and 19-22 covering pork and pork products, milk and dairy products, ice cream, fresh or chilled	6.6

Table 2.2. (Continued)

Staging	U.S. commitments (1,820 tariff lines)		Panama commitments (1,429 tariff lines)	
	Number of lines	Percent	Number of lines	Percent
	liberalized over 15-17 years and ended thereafter, except for sugar		onions and potatoes, beans, corn, rice, corn oil, processed tomatoes, and frozen French fries; in quota items are free of duty; TRQs are liberalized over 5-20 years and ended thereafter	
Total tariff lines	1,820	100.0	1,429	100.0

Source: *U.S.-Panama TPA*, U.S. Tariff Schedule (Agriculture) and Panama Tariff Schedule (Agriculture).

Note: U.S. and Panamanian tariff schedules include only 8-digit tariff numbers; however, Panama's tariff schedule includes 6 tariff lines included in HS chapter 02 (beef and poultry) that have been divided into 16 subdivisions to reflect different staging categories and TRQs. Additionally, the U.S. tariff schedule includes 2 tariff lines included in HS chapter 22 (ethyl alcohol) that have been divided into 4 subdivisions to reflect different staging categories or special designation. Table does not include tariff lines where base rate values have been left blank. U.S. schedule does not reflect duty-free status available for tariff lines under CBERA or GSP. Percent figures may not sum to 100.00 because of rounding.

[a] For HTS lines 2207.10.60 and 2207.20.00, the United States shall treat Panama as a "beneficiary country" for purposes of Section 423 of the Tax Reform Act of 1986, as amended, and any successor provisions. See also HTS chapter 99, subchapter I (temporary legislation providing for additional duties), U.S. notes 1–3. These tariff lines have been divided into 4 subdivisions to reflect different staging categories.

Trade data were taken from official statistics of the U.S. Department of Commerce and from Global Trade Information Service's *Global Trade Atlas*.[24] U.S. production data were estimated by USITC industry analysts. Trade, production, and tariff data used are for 2006.

Simulation Results

Almost all U.S. exports to Panama in the goods sectors selected for analysis in this study face high duties, as shown in table 2.3. The most significant U.S. export to Panama, in value terms on a c.i.f. basis, is corn, which faces a duty rate of 40 percent (table 2.4). For the most part, U.S. exports of these products to Panama would increase significantly, although the effects of the TPA on total U.S. exports of goods selected for analysis would likely be small given Panama's small share of U.S. exports to the world of these products (table 2.5).

The only commodity imported by the United States from Panama facing a significant U.S. import barrier is raw cane sugar. The Commission estimates that Panama's additional dutyfree access upon implementation of the TPA would amount to an immediate 23.3 percent increase in the quantity of raw cane sugar imported from Panama, with a small change to the value of total U.S. raw cane sugar imports from the world and U.S. raw cane sugar production.

The likely impact of liberalizing Panamanian import duties is described further in the sector-specific assessments that follow. Key findings from the Commission's sectoral analyses are:

Table 2.3. U.S. Exports (by Value) to Panama by Selected Sector, Share of Total, and Average Duty Rate, Ordered by Value of U.S. Exports to Panama, 2006

Description	Within HS heading(s)	C.i.f. value (1,000 U.S. $)	Share of total (%)	Trade-weighted average Panama duty rate (%)
Grain				
Corn	1005	35,240	22.7	40.0
Rice	1006	9,519	6.1	90.0
Group total		44,759	28.8	50.6
Passenger vehicles/light trucks:				
Passenger vehicles	8703	41,869	25.7	16.5
Light trucks	8704	562	0.3	8.9
Group total		42,431	26.1	16.4
Certain machinery				
Refrigerators and heat pumps	8418	11,525	7.1	5.1
Air conditioners/parts	8415	8,152	5.0	8.8
Air pumps, compressors, fans	8414	7,085	4.4	5.2
Washing machines	8450	4,595	2.8	10.4
Group total		31,357	19.3	6.9
Processed food				
Food preparations, nesoi	2106	15,887	9.8	15.0
Sauces	2103	4,171	2.6	15.0
Mixes and doughs	1901	2,424	1.5	15.0
Bread, pastry	1905	2,272	1.4	15.0
Soups and broths	2104	1,790	1.1	15.0
Malt extract	1901	1,386	0.9	30.0
Group total		27,930	17.2	15.8
Meat				
Turkey	0207, 1602	7,907	4.9	15.0
Pork	0203, 0206, 0210, 1602	3,731	2.3	35.4
Chicken	0207	84	0.1	15.0
Beef	0201, 0202, 0206, 0210, 1602	76	(ª)	25.0
Group total		11,798	7.2	21.5
Frozen potato products	2004	4,568	2.8	20.0
Total		162,843	100.0	24.4

Source: *Global Trade Atlas* and *U.S.-Panama TPA*, Panama Tariff Schedule (Agriculture/Industrial and Textiles).

Note: Data represent Panamanian imports from the United States, including those from Puerto Rico. Figures may not add because of rounding. Sectors are aggregated as follows: corn (HS subheading 1005.90), rice (HS subheading 1006.10), passenger vehicles (HS subheadings 8703.22, 8703.23, 8703.24, 8703.31, 8703.32, 8703.33, and 8703.90), light trucks (HS subheadings 8704.21and 8704.31), refrigerators/heat pumps (HS 8418), air conditioners/parts (HS 8415), air pumps/compressors/fans (HS 8414), washing machines (HS 8450), turkey meat (Panama tariff lines 0207.25.00, 0207.27.11, 0207.27.12, 0207.27.19, 0207.27.21, 0207.27.29, 1602.31.10, and 1602.31.90), pork (HS subheadings 0203.11, 0203.12, 0203.19, 0203.21, 0203.29, 0206.30, 0206.41, 0206.49, 0210.11, 0210.12, 0210.19, 1602.41, 1602.42, and 1602.49), poultry (HS subheadings 0207.13 and 0207.14), food preparations (HS subheading 2106.90), sauces (HS subheading 2103.90), soups/broths (HS subheading 2104.10), bread/pastry (HS subheading 1905.90), malt extract (HS subheading 1901.90), mixes/doughs (HS subheading 1901.20), and frozen potato products (HS subheading 2004.10).

[a] Less than 0.05 percent

Table 2.4. Selected products: Estimated effect of eliminating Panamanian duties and TRQs on U.S. exports and production[a]

	U.S. exports to Panama, by value	U.S. exports to world, by value	U.S. output, by quantity
	Percent change		
Grains	60.7	0.4	0.1
Corn	20.1	0.1	([b])
Rice	145.4	3.7	0.9
Passenger vehicles and light trucks	42.9	([b])	([b])
Passenger vehicles	42.9	0.1	([c])
Light trucks	26.3	([b])	([c])
Certain machinery products	13.7	([b])	([b])
Air pumps, compressors, fans	9.2	([b])	([c])
Air conditioners/parts	16.4	0.1	([c])
Refrigerators and heat pumps	11.1	0.1	([c])
Washing machines	20.4	0.2	([c])
Processed food	35.7	0.2	([b])
Food preps, nesoi	35.5	0.1	([b])
Sauces	25.2	0.2	([b])
Bread, pastry	39.2	0.1	([b])
Malt extract	53.1	0.3	([b])
Soups and broths	33.4	0.2	([b])
Mixes and doughs	9.8	0.1	([b])
Meat	62.0	0.1	([b])
Turkey meat	9.0	0.4	([b])
Pork	96.0	0.2	([b])
Chicken	45.3	([b])	([b])
Beef[d]	74.1	([b])	([b])
Frozen potato products	23.0	0.2	([b])

Source: USITC estimates.

[a] Based on 2006 data.

[b] Less than 0.05 percent.

[c] Not available. Total U.S. production of industry subsectors was not estimated; only total U.S. production of aggregate industry sectors was estimated to model change in U.S. industry sector output.

[d] The Commission used 2003 beef production and trade data to model the potential impact of the TPA on U.S. beef exports to Panama. In 2003, U.S. beef exports to Panama were approximately $1.1 million, accounting for 72 percent of total Panamanian beef imports. These data were used in lieu of 2006 data because of Panamanian concerns arising toward the end of 2003 over the possibility of bovine spongiform encephalopathy (BSE) in U.S. beef, which resulted in significantly reduced U.S. exports to Panama during 2004–06 (in 2006, U.S. beef exports to Panama were $76,000, accounting for less than 5 percent of total Panamanian beef imports).

- **Meat (beef, pork, and poultry):** The TPA likely would result in increased U.S. meat exports to Panama ranging from 9 percent (for turkey) to 96 percent (for pork), although any positive impact on these U.S. industries would likely be small due to the small size of the Panamanian market relative to total U.S. production and exports of beef, pork, chicken, and turkey. Although not explicitly considered by the Commission's model, U.S. exports of mechanically deboned poultry meat (MDM) and chicken leg quarters would likely benefit from the removal of prohibitively high Panamanian tariffs and from the phase out of a TRQ. U.S. meat exports would also benefit from the removal of various nontariff barriers. The TPA would provide opportunities for increased U.S. meat imports from Panama, especially beef, as Panama would gain an exclusive TRQ. However, in the short term, U.S. meat imports from Panama would be limited because Panama is not currently certified to export beef, pork, or poultry to the United States. Regardless, any increase in imports from Panama would not likely to have a significant adverse impact on U.S. meat industries because of the relatively small size of the Panamanian industries.

- **Grain (corn and rice):** The TPA likely would result in increased U.S. grain exports to Panama over the long term by displacing Panamanian production, but with a very small positive impact on the U.S. industry, given the small size of the Panamanian market relative to total U.S. production and exports and the fact that the United States already supplies nearly all Panamanian corn and rice imports. U.S. grain exports to Panama would likely benefit from the immediate duty-free access for specified quantities of corn and rice, which would increase during the TRQ phase-out period while over-quota tariffs are gradually reduced. Because of the lengthy TRQ phase-out period (15 years for corn and 20 years for rice), the full gains from the TPA likely would not be immediately realized.

- **Frozen potato products:** The TPA likely would result in some small, short-term increases in U.S. exports of frozen potato products to Panama, especially since there is currently no potato-processing industry in Panama and there is a demand for such products, particularly from the growing fast-food restaurant trade. Additionally, an expanding TRQ and its eventual removal after 5 years would likely contribute to increased U.S. exports in the long term.

- **Certain processed foods:** The TPA likely would result in significantly higher exports of selected U.S. processed foods to Panama, but would have only a very small positive impact on the U.S. industry. Under the TPA, several processed food products would become duty free immediately, while others would gain increased market access through progressive tariff reductions, eventually leading to unlimited access. Under the U.S.-Panama SPS agreement that was concluded within the context of the TPA negotiations, Panama also will recognize the equivalence of the U.S. regulatory system for processed food products, removing an important nontariff barrier on U.S. exports. These TPA provisions could lead to increases in the value of U.S. exports ranging from 10 to 53 percent over 2006 levels, once the TPA is fully implemented for all of these food products.

- **Sugar and sugar-containing products**: Although Panama is expected to fill its new sugar TRQ, U.S. tariff elimination and quota expansion under the TPA would likely have only a minor effect on U.S. imports and production of sugar and sugar-containing products.

- **Passenger cars and light trucks:** The tariff provisions of the TPA likely would result in increased U.S. exports of passenger cars and light trucks to Panama, although the Commission's model results indicate that there likely would be a small effect on U.S. production and total exports because of the small size of the Panamanian market. About 50 percent of motor vehicle sales in Panama consist of used vehicles. Despite geographic proximity, U.S. automakers do not dominate the Panamanian market because U.S.-built vehicles are reportedly less competitive than Japanese and Korean vehicles in terms of price, fuel efficiency, and service support, among other factors.

- **Certain machinery (major household appliances and HVAC equipment):** The TPA likely would result in increased U.S. exports of certain machinery, although any positive impact on the U.S. industry would likely be minimal because of the small size of the Panamanian market relative to total U.S. exports of these products. As a result of tariff elimination under the TPA, the value of U.S. exports of certain machinery could increase by an estimated 14 percent above the $31.4 million Panama imported from the United States in 2006. Panamanian tariffs on major household appliances, which include refrigerators and washing machines, currently range from 3 percent to 15 percent. U.S. exports of HVAC equipment, which currently incur tariff rates of 3 percent to 10 percent, would likely benefit from the TPA.

Table 2.5. U.S. Exports to Panama and to World, by Value and by Share, and Panama's Imports from World, 2006

Description	Within HS subheading(s)	U.S. exports to Panama (1,000 U.S. $)	Panama imports from world (1,000 U.S. $)	U.S. share of Panama's total imports (%)	Total U.S. exports to world (1,000 U.S. $)	U.S. exports to Panama as a percent of total U.S. exports (%)
Grains						
Corn	1005	35,240	35,329	99.7	7,157,295	0.5
Rice	1006	9,519	9,678	98.4	363,342	2.6
Group total		44,759	45,007	99.4	7,520,637	0.6
Passenger vehicles/light trucks						
Passenger vehicles	8703	41,869	336,426	12.4	31,569,265	0.1
Light trucks	8704	562	21,746	2.6	6,363,126	(a)
Group total		42,431	358,172	11.8	37,932,391	0.1

Certain machinery					
Refrigerators and heat pumps	8418	11,525	35,863	32.1	2,430,899	0.5
Air conditioners/ parts	8415	8,152	19,902	41.0	2,158,809	0.4
Air pumps, compressors, fans	8414	7,085	15,214	46.6	4,702,453	0.2
Washing machines	8450	4,595	12,727	36.1	535,980	0.9
Group total		31,357	83,706	37.5	9,828,141	0.3
Processed food					
Food preparations, nesoi	2106	15,887	44,064	36.1	2,624,136	0.6
Sauces	2103	4,171	9,220	45.2	429,376	1.0
Mixes and doughs	1901	2,424	2,753	88.0	279,574	0.9
Bread, pastry	1905	2,272	9,096	25.0	660,191	0.3
Soups and broths	2104	1,790	7,300	24.5	302,572	0.6
Malt extract	1901	1,386	4,604	30.1	253,559	0.6
Group total		27,930	77,037	36.3	4,549,408	0.6
Meat					
Turkey	0207 and 1602	7,907	8,397	94.2	182,197	4.3
Pork	0203, 0206, 0210, and 1602	3,731	10,207	36.6	2,704,918	0.1
Chicken	0207	84	85	99.4	1,811,563	0.0
Beef[b]	0201, 0202, 0206, 0210, and 1602	76	2,026	3.8	1,656,933	0.0
Group total		11,798	20,715	57.0	6,355,611	0.2
Frozen potato products	2004	4,568	7,164	63.8	499,590	0.9
Total		162,843	591,801	27.5	66,685,778	0.2

Source: Compiled from official statistics of the U.S. Department of Commerce; Global Trade Atlas; and U.S.-Panama TPA, "Panama Tariff Schedule (Agriculture)."

Note: Data represent Panamanian imports from the United States, including those from Puerto Rico. Figures may not add because of rounding. Sectors are aggregated as follows: corn (HS subheading 1005.90), rice (HS subheading 1006.10), passenger vehicles (HS subheadings 8703.22, 8703.23, 8703.24, 8703.31, 8703.32, 8703.33, and 8703.90), light trucks (HS subheadings 8704.21and 8704.31), refrigerators/heat pumps (HS heading 8418), air conditioners/parts (HS heading 8415), air pumps/compressors/fans (HS heading 8414), washing machines (HS heading 8450), turkey meat (Panama tariff lines 0207.25.00, 0207.27.11, 0207.27.12, 0207.27.19, 0207.27.21, 0207.27.29, 1602.31.10, and 1602.31.90), pork (HS subheadings 0203.11, 0203.12, 0203.19, 0203.21, 0203.29, 0206.30, 0206.41, 0206.49, 0210.11, 0210.12, 0210.19, 1602.41, 1602.42, and 1602.49), poultry (HS subheadings 0207.13 and 0207.14), food preparations (HS subheading 2106.90), sauces (HS subheading 2103.90), soups/broths (HS subheading 2104.10), bread/pastry (HS subheading 1905.90), malt extract (HS subheading 1901.90), mixes/doughs (HS subheading 1901.20), and frozen potato products (HS subheading 2004.10).

[a] Less than 0.05 percent.

[b] The Commission used 2003 beef production and trade data to model the potential impact of the TPA on U.S. beef exports to Panama. In 2003, U.S. beef exports to Panama were approximately $1.1 million, accounting for 72 percent of total Panamanian beef imports, but less than 0.05 percent of total U.S. beef exports.

Meat (Beef, Pork, and Poultry)

Assessment

Beef and Pork[25]

The TPA would likely have a small positive impact on the U.S. beef and pork industries. U.S. beef and pork exports to Panama would likely increase, because nontariff measures would be lifted and the high tariffs would be removed. Increased export volumes and values would likely be small relative to total U.S. production and exports of beef and pork, but could be significant relative to current U.S. exports to Panama and the size of Panama's domestic market. Panamanian beef exports to the United States also could increase as a result of the TPA, but the impact would be small because of the relatively small size of the Panamanian industry.

Poultry[26]

The TPA likely would result in increased exports of certain U.S. poultry, although the overall impact on the U.S. poultry industry would likely be small because of the small size of the Panamanian market relative to total U.S. poultry production and exports. The United States currently supplies more than 94 percent of Panamanian turkey imports and almost all Panamanian chicken imports. The immediate removal and gradual reduction of prohibitively high tariff rates on various poultry products, including mechanically deboned poultry meat (MDM) and chicken leg quarters, would likely benefit U.S. poultry exporters. U.S. poultry exports also would likely benefit from the sanitary and phytosanitary (SPS) agreement that was negotiated between the United States and Panama contemporaneously with the TPA.[27] The SPS agreement resolved outstanding SPS issues that have effectively barred U.S. exports of certain chicken meat products, including MDM and chicken leg quarters, to Panama.

Impact on U.S. Exports

Beef and Pork

The Commission's partial equilibrium analysis estimates that U.S. beef exports to Panama could increase by about $838,000 (74.1 percent)[28] and U.S. pork exports could increase by $3,582,000 (96.0 percent) above what Panama imported from the United States in 2006 as a result of trade liberalization under the TPA. Given the small size of the Panamanian market relative to total U.S. production and exports of beef and pork, the tariff elimination under the TPA would likely have little effect on U.S. total production and exports of these products.

U.S. beef and pork exports to Panama are likely to increase as the TPA negotiations resulted in a bilateral agreement that resolved key nontariff barriers that limit trade. Panamanian restrictions related to bovine spongiform encephalopathy (BSE) caused Panamanian imports of U.S. beef to decline from more than $1 million in 2003 to less than

$50,000 in 2004. In the SPS bilateral agreement that was reached on December 20, 2006 and became effective on February 28, 2007, Panama agreed to permit the importation of all beef and beef products accompanied by a USDA FSIS Export Certificate of Wholesomeness. In addition, both beef and pork exports likely will benefit from provisions of this agreement that eliminate other significant SPS restrictions on U.S. exports to Panama, including the recognition by Panama of the equivalence of the U.S. meat inspection system, which eliminates the need for individual plant inspections and duplicative licensing, permitting, or certification requirements for U.S. beef and pork.

Under the TPA, U.S. beef exports would likely be initially stimulated by increased demand for high-quality cuts of U.S. grain-fed beef for the hotel and restaurant sector, as 30 percent duties would be immediately eliminated on beef graded USDA Prime or Choice. Some Panamanians have already developed a preference for high-quality U.S. grain-fed beef.[29] Before the discovery of a case of BSE found in a Canadian-born cow in the state of Washington, the United States was the largest supplier of imported beef in the Panamanian market.[30] Lower prices resulting from the 15-year phase out of the 30 percent duty on other beef should stimulate additional local demand. The phase out of this duty should also make U.S. products more competitive with the beef that Panama is currently importing from Nicaragua, Brazil, and Chile.

Lower domestic prices resulting from increased import competition also would likely result in a decrease in Panama's domestic beef production, which would further increase Panamanian import demand. Protected by 30 percent duties, domestic beef production supplied most of the Panamanian market. During 2002–06, Panama exported nearly 6,300 metric tons (mt) of beef annually, while importing only about 615 mt.[31] Panama has imported less than 2 percent of its domestic beef consumption in recent years. However, removal of 30 percent duties—immediately on USDA Prime and Choice grades and over a 15-year phase-out period for other grades of beef—would likely increase the competitive pressure on Panamanian beef producers.

Upon implementation of the TPA, U.S. pork exports would likely be stimulated by immediate duty-free access for pork variety meats and additional duty-free access for other pork items under various TRQs. U.S. exports to Panama would likely increase over time as TRQ quantities increase and duties of 60 to 80 percent are phased out over 15 years. The immediate duty-free treatment on quantities imported under various TRQs would allow U.S. products to better compete with products currently imported from Denmark and Canada, which currently supply 55 percent of the value of Panamanian pork imports.[32] Lower domestic prices resulting from increased import competition would likely cause a decrease in Panama's domestic pork production.[33] Even with high duty levels, the Panamanian market has relied on imports to meet domestic demand. During 2002-06, Panama imported nearly 7,500 mt of pork annually while Panamanian pork exports were almost nonexistent.

Poultry

The results of the Commission's partial equilibrium analysis indicate that U.S. exports of turkey meat to Panama could increase by over $700,000 (9.0 percent), while U.S. exports of chicken meat other than MDM and chicken leg quarters could increase by $38,000 (45.3 percent) as a result of tariff elimination under the TPA. The impact of the tariff elimination on U.S. poultry products would be positive but small given the small size of the Panamanian market relative to total U.S. production and exports of poultry. The United States supplied more than 94 percent of Panamanian turkey imports and more than 99 percent of Panamanian chicken imports in 2006.

Factors that could not be explicitly considered by the Commission's model also would likely benefit U.S. poultry exports to Panama. For example, U.S. exports of MDM from poultry, which are currently subject to a Panamanian tariff rate of 260 percent, would become immediately duty free under the TPA. Less expensive MDM from poultry can be substituted for other meat in products such as sausage and hotdogs, thereby reducing the cost for such processed meat products. Historically, the United States has not shipped MDM from poultry to Panama because of the prohibitively high tariff rate; however, with implementation of the TPA, potential sales could reach $5–10 million per year.[34]

U.S. poultry producers also would likely benefit from the phased out TRQs. Upon entry into force, the TPA would immediately allow the United States to export to Panama up to 660 mt of chicken leg quarters duty free, which are currently subject to a Panamanian tariff rate of 260 percent. At current import unit values, these exports would be valued at $462,000. The quantity of chicken leg quarters allowed to enter duty free would increase by 10 percent annually, and by 2025, the potential value of U.S. exports of chicken leg quarters to Panama, at current import unit values, would likely increase to $2.1 million (3,330 mt).[35]

Impact on U.S. Imports

Beef and Pork

While the TPA may have an impact on U.S. beef imports from Panama, the agreement likely would not lead to U.S. imports of Panamanian pork products as Panama is a net importer of pork.[36] Upon implementation of the TPA, Panama could shift beef that is currently exported to Mexico, Taiwan, El Salvador, and Jamaica to the higher value U.S. market. U.S. beef imports from Panama could also increase as U.S. grain-fed beef exports to Panama replace consumption of domestically produced beef, making Panamanian grass-fed beef available for export to the United States to supply high U.S. demand for lean beef. However, any increase in beef imports from Panama as a result of the TPA would not likely have an adverse impact on the U.S. cattle and beef industries, as the Panamanian beef industry is very small relative to the U.S. beef industry. Further, Panama does not currently have any processing plants approved for export to the United States; approval of processing plants would be required before Panama can export beef to the United States.[37]

Poultry

The TPA might result over time in increased poultry imports from Panama, but there likely would be no immediate impact on U.S. imports. Although Panama is able to meet domestic demand with domestic production, there is little surplus and Panama currently exports less than 2,000 mt of poultry meat annually. In addition, Panama does not have any establishments that are eligible to export poultry to the United States because it has not been certified as being free of Exotic Newcastle Disease.[38]

Views of Interested Parties

The Agricultural Technical Advisory Committee (ATAC) for Trade in Animals and Animal Products expressed support for the U.S.-Panama TPA.[39] The ATAC stated that it is pleased that Panama's agreement to recognize the equivalence of the U.S. food safety inspection system for beef, pork, and poultry will remove a major nontariff barrier and greatly facilitate U.S. meat trade with Panama. The ATAC stated that it is pleased that Panama has agreed to recognize certain international veterinary standards and will provide access for U.S. beef and poultry that is consistent with international standards. With respect to poultry, the ATAC stated that the reduction in Panamanian tariffs would be positive, but that it had hoped for a larger initial TRQ for chicken leg quarters and a shorter phase-out period.

The National Pork Producers Council (NPPC) stated that the U.S.-Panama TPA would create important new opportunities for U.S. pork producers.[40] The NPPC reported that live hog prices are positively affected by the introduction of expanded export market access and that recent strength in U.S. pork markets can be directly related to increased exports of U.S. pork. The NPPC stated that the TPA would provide U.S. pork products, which compete with exports from Canada and the European Union, with a competitive advantage in the Panamanian market. Citing Dermot Hayes, an economist at Iowa State University, the NPPC said that the TPA would provide a price increase of 20 cents per hog.

The National Chicken Council (NCC) and the U.S. Poultry & Egg Export Council (USAPEEC) both expressed support for the TPA.[41] These organizations stated that the SPS agreement between the United States and Panama removes major obstacles to trade by recognizing the U.S. food safety system as equivalent to the Panamanian system and by recognizing international standards for certain veterinary issues. Both organizations stated that they would welcome the immediate access for all poultry products under the TPA, although they also stated that they would have preferred a larger initial TRQ on chicken leg quarters as well as a shorter phase-out period. The NCC and the USAPEEC stated that they realize that poultry is a sensitive trade issue for Panama, see the immediate inclusion of MDM chicken for duty-free treatment as a positive outcome, and believe that the TPA would represent a significant opportunity for increasing U.S. exports to Panama.

Grain (Corn and Rice)

Assessment

The U.S.-Panama TPA likely would result in significantly higher U.S. grain exports[42] to Panama over the long term by displacing domestic production, but would have a very small positive impact on the U.S. industry as a whole. U.S. grain exports to Panama would benefit from the immediate duty-free access for specified quantities which would increase during the TRQ phase-out period while over-quota tariffs are gradually reduced. The TPA would likely have a small effect on overall U.S. grain production and exports given the small size of the Panamanian market compared to total U.S. production and exports. The TPA would likely have no impact on U.S. imports of grain since Panama's grain production is limited by the country's small land mass, making it a high-cost producer and a net importer of grain.[43]

Impact on U.S. Exports

Based on the Commission's partial equilibrium analysis, U.S. grain exports to Panama could increase by an estimated 60.7 percent above the $44.8 million imported by Panama from the United States in 2006 as a result of increased market access through the annual growth of TRQs and gradual tariff elimination under the TPA. Additionally, Panama would eliminate its domestic production purchase requirement[44] for imports under the TPA, removing an important nontariff barrier.[45] Finally, Panama would prohibit producer groups from administering its TRQs, increasing the likelihood that these TRQs will be filled. Because of the relatively small size of the Panamanian market, the TPA would likely have only a minor effect on total U.S. exports of corn and rough rice, which were $7.5 billion in 2006.

As part of its WTO accession in 1997, Panama removed several nontariff barriers affecting grain imports, including import permits and quotas.[46] The United States has supplied virtually all Panamanian grain imports for the past several years, and thus, the TPA would provide U.S. producers with a small advantage over its Latin American competitors.[47] More than one-half the expected additional U.S. grain exports to Panama would likely consist of corn, with the remainder being wheat and rice.

The United States, a highly competitive exporter, supplied more than 99 percent of Panamanian corn and rice imports in 2006.[48] Panamanian grain imports from the United States, which totaled $44.8 million in 2006, accounted for 0.6 percent of total U.S. grain exports to all countries.[49] Table 2.6 outlines the first full year of market access for all U.S. grain exports to Panama under the TPA. U.S. wheat exports to Panama already receive dutyfree treatment. Up to 298,700 mt of U.S. corn exports to Panama would receive duty-free access under the provisions of a TRQ, and up to 7,950 mt of U.S. rough rice and 4,240 mt of U.S. milled rice would receive duty-free treatment in the first full year of the agreement.[50] The first-year TRQ levels are approximately equal to the level of U.S. yellow corn exports to Panama in 2006, but significantly below the level of U.S. rice exports in 2006.

Corn

Based on the Commission's partial equilibrium analysis, U.S. corn exports could increase by 20.1 percent above the $35 million of U.S. corn imported by Panama in 2006. In the short term, however, growth would be limited by the TRQ on U.S. yellow corn, with an over-quota tariff of 40 percent that would remain in effect through the first five years of the TPA before being phased down. The TRQ on corn would not be completely removed until year 15 of the TPA, as Panama sought sufficient adjustment time for its domestic corn producers to develop alternative crops. Based on U.S. corn exports to Panama during 1996–2006, when annual exports increased by an average of 4.5 percent, U.S. corn exports likely would completely fill the annual within-quota amounts, as this TRQ would be subject to annual increases of only 3 percent until its removal. Increases in U.S. corn exports likely would result from increased corn consumption in Panama stimulated by a lower domestic price (as the tariff is removed) as well as by reduced domestic production. In marketing year 2005/06, Panama imported 93 percent of its corn consumption,[51] and the United States accounted for over 99 percent of Panamanian corn imports. The United States has consistently supplied virtually all

Panamanian corn imports with only minor volumes from Argentina, Chile, and Mexico during 2004–2006.[52]

Table 2.6. U.S. Grain Exports to Panama and U.S. Market Access to Panama

	U.S. exports to Panama		Panamanian market access	
Product	**2002-06 average**	**2006**	**First year TRQ**	**Over-quota tariff**
		(1,000 metric tons)		**(% AVE)**
Wheat	104	100	No quota	Free
Rice[a]	31	44	12[b]	90[c]
Yellow Corn	289	284	299	40[d]

Source: *U.S.-Panama TPA,* Annex 3.3, Panama General Notes, Panama Appendix I, and Tariff Schedule of Panama, app. I; and *Global Trade Atlas.*

[a] Includes both rough and milled rice. Panama's imports of rice from the United States consist almost entirely of rough rice.

[b] In year 1, the TRQ is 7,950 metric tons for rough rice and 4,240 metric tons for milled rice.

[c] For quantities in excess of the TRQ, duties shall remain at base rates during years 1 through 10. In year 11, duties shall be reduced in a 10-year linear reduction, becoming free of duty in year 20. Panama reserves the right to provide reduced duty or duty-free treatment on an additional quantity of rice in excess of the TRQ in order to address a shortfall in supply.

[d] For quantities in excess of the TRQ, duties shall remain at base rates during years 1 through 5. In year 6, duties shall be reduced in a 10-year linear reduction, becoming free of duty in year 15.

Rice

The Commission's partial equilibrium analysis estimates that, upon full implementation of the TPA, U.S. rice exports to Panama would likely increase by 145.4 percent above the $9.5 million level in 2006. Unlike corn, Panama is largely self-sufficient in rice production with imports accounting for an average of 15 percent of total consumption during the 2001/02 through 2005/06 marketing years.[53] The United States has supplied virtually all Panamanian rice imports since Panama established a TRQ for rice as part of its 1997 WTO accession.[54] Similar to corn, Panama has sought to ease the transition to open markets under this TPA through use of TRQs that would not be completely removed until year 20 of the TPA for both rough and milled rice.

In the first year of the TPA, the within-quota TRQ on rough rice would be 7,950 mt, which is well below the annual average of 39,000 mt that Panama imported from the United States during 2004–06. Due to the high over-quota tariff of 90 percent, which would continue through year 10 of the TPA before gradually being phased down to duty free in year 20, U.S. rough rice exports would not likely show any increases above the within-quota TRQ volumes in the near and medium term. However, Panama may provide reduced duty or dutyfree treatment on an additional quantity of rice above the TRQ level to address a shortfall of supply, in which case U.S. rough rice exports could increase.

In the first year of the TPA, the within-quota TRQ on milled rice would be 4,240 mt for U.S. exports, compared to the annual average of 220 mt that Panama imported from the United States during 2004–06. Given that U.S. exports are currently well below the initial within quota TRQ volume and the 6 percent annual growth of the within-quota TRQ, U.S. milled rice exports should increase as they benefit from increasing market access under the TPA. Similar to rough rice, the TRQ for milled rice would be phased out over a 20-year period. Overall, the expected increase in U.S. rice exports would likely stem from increased consumption of U.S. rice in Panama due to lower prices for rice after the elimination of the TRQs and over-quota tariffs under the TPA. As a result, Panamanian farmers would likely shift to alternative crops, leading to an eventual reduction in Panamanian rice production.

Views of Interested Parties

The ATAC for Grains, Feed, and Oilseeds endorsed the TPA, and stated that the agreement would benefit future U.S. feedgrain exports to Panama through the reduction and elimination of tariffs.[55] Additionally, the ATAC stated that the TPA would achieve other long-standing objectives of the U.S. feedgrains industry, as Panama would no longer be able to impose a domestic absorption requirement[56] as a precondition to import; there would be no special safeguard mechanism; and, provisions to ensure the filling of TRQs would be established. However, the ATAC expressed concern about the near-term benefits for the U.S. rice sector because of the TPA's 20-year transition to unlimited access for U.S. rice exports.

The U.S. Grains Council views the TPA as benefitting the U.S. feedgrains industry overall,[57] and stated that the TPA would provide U.S. corn growers improved access to the Panamanian market by increasing the duty-free TRQ and eliminating other nontariff barriers such as absorption requirements. The U.S. Grains Council reported that enhanced access would allow the United States to take advantage of future demand increases from Panama's growing poultry sector.

Frozen Potato Products[58]

Assessment

The U.S.-Panama TPA likely would result in increased U.S. exports of frozen potato products to Panama as a result of the immediate removal of Panama's 20 percent duty on frozen potato products and the phase out of a TRQ. The United States supplied 64 percent of the value of Panamanian imports of frozen potato products in 2006.[59] The overall initial impact of the TPA on U.S. exports would likely be small but positive, as shipments would continue to be limited by a TRQ, but the long term effects of the TPA would likely be somewhat greater. The TPA likely would have no effect on overall U.S. imports because the United States does not currently import frozen potato products from Panama, as nearly all U.S. consumption of frozen potato products is supplied domestically or imported from Canada. Further, although Panama grows fresh potatoes, it does not have a processing industry. Although the U.S. industry is one of the world's largest producers and exporters of fresh and frozen potato products, Panama is a small U.S. export market (in 2006, Panama accounted for 0.9 percent of total U.S. exports of frozen potato products). As such, the TPA likely would have no immediate impact on the U.S. economy as a whole, or on the U.S. frozen potato products industry sector, U.S. employment, and U.S. consumers.

Impact on U.S. Exports

Based on the Commission's partial equilibrium analysis, U.S. exports of frozen potato products could increase by 23.0 percent above the $4.6 million that Panama imported from the United States in 2006. The United States supplied 64 percent of Panamanian imports of frozen potato products in 2006. Panamanian imports of frozen potato products from the United States accounted for about 0.9 percent of total U.S. exports of frozen potato products to all countries. There could be a small positive impact (less than 0.5 percent) on total U.S. exports of frozen potato products as a result of the removal of Panama's 20 percent duty and 5-year phase out of the TRQ, which would enable the U.S. product to be more competitively priced, likely resulting in U.S. exports displacing those of other suppliers to the Panamanian market, including the Netherlands. However, U.S. exports of frozen potato products to Panama would likely have little or no impact on U.S. production and exports of these products because of the small size of the Panamanian market relative to total U.S. production and exports.

Views of Interested Parties

Industry officials reported that the TPA would potentially have a positive impact on the U.S. industry exporting frozen potato products to Panama. U.S. producers are reportedly interested in exporting greater amounts of frozen French fries to Panama in the near future, particularly for institutional sales, pending the immediate removal of the existing 20 percent duty rate and the 5-year staging of the tariff-rate quota.[60]

A former official of the Chamber of Commerce, Industry, and Agriculture of Panama stated that previous efforts by the Ministry of Agriculture to create a nontariff barrier to imported U.S. frozen potato products—in order to address potential competition with Panamanianproduced fresh potatoes—have been addressed and are reportedly no longer in effect.[61] Demand for frozen potato products in Panama is reportedly high.[62] The American Chamber of Commerce and Industry stated that the phase out of the TRQ on frozen potato products would provide U.S. producers with greater access to the Panamanian market, both in the near term as quota levels expand and in year 5 of the TPA, when the quota would be completely removed.[63]

Certain Processed Foods[64]

Assessment

The U.S.-Panama TPA likely would result in increased U.S. exports of processed foods to Panama, but would only have a very small positive impact on total U.S. exports of these products. Under the TPA, several processed food products would become duty free immediately while others would have increased market access through progressive tariff reductions, eventually leading to unrestricted access. Under the U.S.-Panama SPS agreement,[65] which was concluded within the context of the TPA negotiations, Panama also will recognize the equivalency of the U.S. regulatory system for processed food products, removing an important nontariff barrier to U.S. exports.[66] The TPA would likely have a small effect on U.S. processed food exports given the small size of the Panamanian market compared to total U.S. production and exports. The TPA also would likely have very little or no impact on U.S. imports of processed foods since Panama has a very small processed food industry and is a net importer of processed foods.

Impact on U.S. Exports

Based on the Commission's partial equilibrium analysis, U.S. processed foods exports to Panama could increase by 35.7 percent over the $27.9 million in processed foods imported by Panama from the United States in 2006 as a result of the immediate or phased removal of tariffs ranging from 15 percent to 30 percent on these products under the TPA. In the past several years, Panamanian imports of processed foods from the United States have generally fluctuated, decreasing by approximately 5 percent since 2002 (see table 2.7).

However, in addition to tariff liberalization under the TPA, Panama's recognition of the equivalence of the U.S. regulatory system for processed food products also could contribute to increases in U.S. exports ranging from 9.8 percent (mixes and doughs) to 39.2 percent (bread and pastry) over their respective values in 2006 once the TPA is fully implemented for all of these products.

Owing in large part to the longstanding economic ties resulting from the construction and operation of the Panama Canal by the United States, Panamanian consumers have developed a high degree of acceptance for several well-known brands of U.S. processed foods and other household products.[67] Panama's relatively small domestic market has a significant number of consumers with high disposable income who have followed consumption patterns similar to U.S. and European consumers.[68] Also, future growth in the tourism sector is expected to increase demand for imports of processed foods because of the strong brand loyalties of U.S. consumers. Panama had already improved its market access for processed foods by reducing its import tariffs and banning existing market quotas upon its accession to the WTO in November 1997.[69] Upon implementation of the TPA, Panama would immediately eliminate tariffs on mixes and doughs, malt extract, soups and broths, and food preparations. Panama's base tariffs for most of these products are either 10 or 15 percent. Other processed foods such as bread, pastry, and sauces would be subject to longer tariff eliminations, either becoming tariff-free by year 5 or year 10 of the TPA. Unlike some other food products such as pork, chicken, and dairy, market access for all of the processed foods mentioned above would not be restricted by TRQs under the TPA. By year 10, all of these processed foods would have unlimited, duty-free access.[70]

Despite Panama's WTO accession, Panama has continued to maintain substantial nontariff barriers affecting imports of certain agricultural products.[71] The U.S.-Panama Agreement on Sanitary and Phytosanitary (SPS) Measures and Technical Standards, a separate agreement concluded within the context of the TPA negotiations,[72] will remove a significant nontariff barrier on U.S. processed foods exports. Under this agreement, Panama will recognize that U.S. SPS measures and regulatory systems are equivalent to its own measures and standards for meat, poultry, and all other processed foods. Panama also will not require certification of individual shipments or import licensing or permitting as a condition for the import or sale of any processed products.[73]

Table 2.7. Panama's Imports of Selected Processed Foods from the United States

Product	6-digit HTS	2002	2006	2002–06 change	2002–06 % change
		$1,000			
Food preparations, nesoi	2106.90	19,744	15,887	-3,857	-19.5
Sauces	2103.90	2,362	4,171	1,809	76.6
Mixes & doughs	1901.20	1,929	2,424	495	25.7
Bread, pastry	1905.90	1,881	2,272	391	20.8
Soups & broths	2104.10	1,580	1,790	210	13.3
Malt extract	1901.90	2,028	1,386	-642	-31.7
Total		29,524	27,930	-1,594	-5.4

Source: GTIS, *Global Trade Atlas.*
Note: Panama imports from the United States include those from Puerto Rico.

Views of Interested Parties

The ATAC for Trade in Processed Foods expressed support for the TPA as several processed products would become tariff-free upon implementation.[74] The ATAC for Trade in Processed Foods also expressed support for TPA provisions that would streamline import documentation requirements for U.S. processed foods, thereby improving access for U.S. food products. Finally, the ATAC stated that it is pleased that the bilateral agreement on SPS measures—which is consistent with international standards—will enhance access for U.S. processed food products.

The Grocery Manufacturers Association (GMA) and Food Products Association (FPA) stated that they are very supportive of the TPA with regard to processed foods. The GMA and FPA stated that they are especially pleased with the regulatory equivalency implemented under the U.S.-Panama Bilateral Agreement on SPS Measures and Technical Standards. They said that this will improve the ability of U.S. firms to export products into Panama, as it will simplify certification and entry documentation.[75]

The Agricultural Policy Advisory Committee (APAC) for Trade also expressed support for the TPA as tariffs would become duty free immediately upon implementation for many processed foods. APAC noted that the U.S.-Panama Bilateral Agreement on SPS Measures and Technical Standards will address many long-standing concerns by recognizing the equivalence of the U.S. regulatory systems for processed food products and streamlining the import documentation requirements.[76]

Sugar and Sugar-Containing Products[77]

Assessment

The U.S.-Panama TPA provisions concerning sugar and sugar-containing products (SCPs) would likely have a small effect on U.S. producers and users of sugar.[78] Historic production, consumption, and trade patterns suggest that Panama likely would be able to consistently meet the TPA's net-exporter provision.[79] Panama's additional duty-free access to the U.S. market under the TPA would be limited to an initial in-quota TRQ allocation of 7,065 mt, which would increase to 7,675 mt in year 15.[80] The level would increase by 5 mt annually thereafter. These levels are small relative to the size and growth of the U.S. sugar market. U.S. over-quota tariff rates would not be affected by this agreement. The TPA contains a compensation mechanism whereby the United States could limit sugar imports under the agreement in exchange for compensation (the value of which is not specified in the TPA).[81] An overview of U.S. sugar policy is presented in appendix H of this report.

Impact on U.S. Exports

The TPA would not likely have a significant impact on U.S. exports of raw cane and refined sugar because the United States is primarily an importer of these products and generally is a higher cost producer than Panama. Furthermore, although the TPA may result in increased U.S. exports of other sweeteners, such as glucose, high-fructose corn syrup, and SCPs classified in HS chapter 17, it would not likely have an effect on the total exports of such products as Panama is a relatively small market for these products. During 2002–06, U.S. exports of all products classified in HS chapter 17 to Panama accounted for less than 0.5 percent of total U.S. exports of such products, averaging $1.5 million annually to Panama, compared with a total annual average of $763 million.[82]

Impact on U.S. Imports

The TPA itself would not likely have a significant impact on the U.S. domestic sugar market. The results of Commission's partial equilibrium analysis indicate that U.S. import quantities of raw cane sugar from Panama could increase by 23.3 percent above Panama's minimum WTO TRQ, leading to an increase of 0.5 percent in the value of U.S. imports of raw cane sugar from the world as a result of the TPA (table 2.8).[83] As noted, additional duty-free access to the U.S. market for Panamanian sugar and SCPs would be initially limited to 7,065 mt, growing to 7,675 mt in year 15 of the TPA, followed by a perpetual annual increase of 5 mt.[84] These provisions would limit Panamanian sugar exports to the U.S. market because current over-quota duty rates associated with WTO TRQs for sugar and SCPs generally are prohibitive and would not be affected by the TPA.[85] The initial additional in-quota quantity of 7,065 mt represents less than 0.1 percent of the 9.5 million mt of sugar expected to be consumed in the United States during FY2007.[86] Furthermore, assuming U.S. sugar consumption continues to grow at an average annual rate of about 1.0 percent, as it did during 1994–2005, it would be unlikely that the TPA TRQ quantities would ever account for more than 0.5 percent of U.S. domestic sugar consumption, an insignificant share of the total U.S. domestic market for sweeteners.

The Commission's partial equilibrium analysis also measured the consumer surplus, a component of national economic welfare gained from the higher quota for Panamanian raw cane sugar to measure the benefit to U.S. consumers and users of sugar of having access to a larger supply of sugar at a lower price, net of any tariff revenue lost by the U.S. Government. The value of this measure is estimated to be $960,000.[87]

Panama would likely meet the net-exporter provision of the TPA, which would limit Panamanian sugar exports to the United States (beyond those allocated under the U.S. WTO TRQs) to the lesser of the specified TRQ quantity or the amount by which Panama's total exports exceed its total imports, excluding sugar and high-fructose corn syrup trade with the United States.[88] Panama would have easily met the net-exporter provision of the agreement in each of the past 10 years (1997–2006) and is forecast to meet the provision in 2006–07.[89] Panama is a net exporter of sugar, as domestic production exceeded domestic consumption by about 50,000 mt annually since 2001.[90] This amount would enable Panama to fill its entire TPA quota. Panama's FY 2006 WTO TRQ is 37,168 mt (raw value).[91] Panama's cost of production is significantly lower than the typical U.S. market price and the loan forfeiture price administered in the U.S. sugar program.[92] In addition, the U.S. sugar market prices are well above those in the world export market. Recent U.S. raw and refined sugar prices have been well above world prices.[93]

**Table 2.8. Sugar: Estimated Effect of Increased Market Access on
U.S. Imports and Production[a]**

	Raw Sugar
	Percentage change
U.S. imports from Panama (quantity)	23.3
U.S. imports from world (c.i.f. value)	0.5
U.S. production (quantity)	-0.1

Source: USITC estimates.
[a] Based on 2006 data.

Other factors could influence Panama's ability to export sugar in the future. Exogenous factors, mainly weather conditions, affect annual output and technological improvements may increase yields. Also, the potential for substituting high-fructose corn syrup for sugar in soft drinks and for increased imports of SCPs could displace Panamanian sugar in the United States. However, given the relatively small share of Panamanian exports allowed duty-free access to the U.S. market under the TPA provisions, it is unlikely these factors will affect Panamanian exports to the U.S. market.

Views of Interested Parties

U.S. sugar producers state that it is unlikely that the TPA would have a significant negative impact on the U.S. sugar and sweeteners market, given the relatively small increase in market access, the primary product form (raw sugar), the retention of over-quota duties, and a sugar-compensation mechanism, among other provisions.[94] However, U.S. sugar producers state that including sugar in bilateral FTAs does not promote the objectives of the U.S. sugar-producing sector and that U.S. sugar market access should be negotiated in the multilateral WTO context in which foreign subsidies provided to sugar producers and exporters can be addressed.[95]

Representatives of U.S. sugar consumers expressed support for comprehensive product coverage, including sugar, in U.S. regional and bilateral FTAs.[96] Furthermore, they indicate that the U.S. market requires imports; Panamanian sugar exports to the U.S. market are minor; the additional sugar would increase competition in the U.S. market and mitigate recent declines in employment in sugar-using industries; and U.S. consumers would benefit from lower sugar prices.[97] U.S. food manufacturers stated that over-quota sugar tariffs should not be included in the TPA and they oppose the sugar compensation mechanism.[98]

Machinery, Electronics, and Transportation Equipment

The U.S.-Panama TPA likely would result in increased exports of U.S. machinery, electronics, and transportation equipment (machinery and equipment)[99] to Panama, although any positive impact on U.S. industries likely would be minimal because of the small size of the Panamanian market relative to total U.S. machinery and equipment exports. U.S. exports could benefit from the immediate or phased elimination of Panamanian tariffs, which currently range from 5 to 20 percent on U.S. machinery and equipment, as well as from TPA provisions for improved protection of foreign investment and intellection property, greater transparency in government procurement,[100] and enhanced dispute settlement mechanisms.[101]

Machinery and equipment products accounted for 43 percent ($539 million) of total Panamanian imports from the United States in 2006. The United States is the leading import supplier to Panama of nearly all types of machinery and equipment (table 2.9), with the major exception of passenger vehicles and light trucks. Because of the combination of relatively high Panamanian tariffs and the current value of U.S. exports, passenger vehicles and light trucks and certain machinery (major household appliances and HVAC equipment)[102] are the product categories that would likely experience the greatest increase in the value of U.S. exports to Panama as a result of tariff liberalization under the TPA. The prospects for expanded U.S. exports to Panama of passenger vehicles and light trucks and certain machinery are described below.

Table 2.9. Panama's Imports of Selected Machinery and Equipment Product Categories and MFN Tariff Rates in 2006

HS classification/Trade-weighted MFN tariff Product description	Panama's imports from:			
	United States ($1,000)	Rest of the world ($1,000)	Total ($1,000)	U.S. share of total (%)
8471 – 5.0 percent Computer equipment	94,246	22,544	116,790	80.7
8703, 8704 – 15.1 percent Passenger vehicles and trucks	62,582	340,968	403,550	15.5

Passenger vehicles and light trucks[a]	42,431	315,741	358,172	11.8
8525-8529 – 2.7 percent Radio/television/radar broadcast and receiving apparatus and parts	41,940	65,45	1107,391	39.1
8517 – 5.0 percent Telephone/telecommunications equipment	36,047	47,813	83,860	43.0
8414, 8415, 8418, 8450 – 7.8 percent Certain machinery (HVAC, refrigerators, and washing machines)	31,248	52,458	83,706	37.3
8473 – 3.3 percent Parts of computers and other office machines	23,452	8,304	31,756	73.9
8708 – 5.3 percent Certain auto parts	20,462	28,836	49,298	41.5
8429 – 4.3 percent Bulldozers and other self-propelled earth moving machinery	12,763	30,358	43,121	30.0
9018 – 9.0 percent Medical instruments	10,470	7,336	17,806	58.8
Subtotal	333,210	604,068	937,278	35.6
All other	205,321	284,506	489,827	41.9
Total	538,531	888,574	1,427,105	37.7

Sources: Panama's imports statistics from *Global Trade Atlas*; Panama's MFN tariffs are from the Panama Industrial and Textile Tariff Schedule, which is included in the text of the U.S.-Panama TPA.

[a] Passenger vehicles and light trucks, which are subject to this study, are a sub-set of passenger vehicles and trucks. Passenger vehicles include the following HS subheadings: 8703.22, 8703.23, 8703.24, 8703.31, 8703.32, 8703.33, and 8703.90. Light trucks include the following HS subheadings: 8704.21 and 8704.31.

Passenger Cars and Light Trucks[103]

Assessment

The U.S.-Panama TPA likely would result in increased U.S. exports of passenger cars and light trucks to Panama, although any positive impact on U.S. industries likely would be mininal because of the small size of the Panamanian market relative to total U.S. production and exports of passenger cars and light trucks.

Impact on U.S. Exports

The U.S.-Panama TPA is expected to offer increased export opportunities for U.S. passenger car and light truck manufacturers. Based on the Commission's partial equilibrium analysis, U.S. exports of passenger cars and light trucks could increase by 43 percent above the $42.4 million of passenger cars and light trucks that Panama imported from the United States in 2006 as a result of the tariff provisions in the TPA. However, total U.S. exports of passenger cars and light trucks would increase by less than 1 percent, with virtually no effect on U.S. production. The estimated effect on total U.S. exports and U.S. production is supported by the fact that Panama is a relatively small market for passenger vehicles.

Panamanian tariffs on passenger cars and light trucks range from 3 percent to 20 percent; the trade weighted tariff on U.S. exports for the products in this group is about 16 percent. Panama assesses duties on new passenger cars and four wheel drive vehicles based on the vehicle's c.i.f. value, with the tariff rate increasing as the c.i.f. value increases; pickup trucks, ambulances, hearses, prison vans, and all other special purpose vehicles are subject to a flat tariff of 10 percent.[104]

The tariff concessions in the TPA for Panama's 128 8-digit HTS items covered by this product group break down as follows:

Staging	Number of line items
Linear 10-year phase out	40
Linear 5-year phase out	37
Nonlinear 10-year phase out	35
Immediate duty elimination	16

Eight 8-digit HTS numbers account for 71 percent of Panamanian imports of U.S. passenger vehicles; the tariffs on these items range from 15 percent to 20 percent, and the staging also varies—four line items would be immediately duty free, and the tariffs on four items would be phased out over 10 years. The TPA would likely have a more measurable impact on U.S. exports under the line items that immediately become duty free, including nearly all U.S. current and projected exports, which are categorized as passenger vehicles valued at over $12,000 and trucks weighing less than 5 tons.[105]

The Panamanian automotive market is small, and used vehicles account for about 50 percent of motor vehicle sales.[106] U.S. exports of passenger cars and light trucks to Panama accounted for one-tenth of one percent of total U.S. exports of such vehicles in 2006. However, passenger car and light truck sales in Panama have increased considerably in the past 5 years, by a compound annual growth rate of over 16 percent (table 2.10). Substantial increases have occurred in all segments of the passenger car and light truck industry. Overall sales of passenger vehicles and light trucks registered the largest increase (27 percent) in 2006. Panamanian market growth is attributable to heightened consumer confidence, rising incomes, improved financing options, and the poor quality of Panama's public transportation system.[107]

Table 2.10. New Vehicle Sales in Panama, by Type, 2002–06 (Number of Vehicles)

	2002	2003	2004	2005	2006[a]
Passenger vehicles and light trucks:					
Cars	6,226	6,875	9,245	11,292	14,577
SUVs	4,409	5,507	6,072	6,952	8,139
Minivans	254	316	416	577	651
Pickups	2,169	2,389	2,592	3,076	4,398
Subtotal	13,058	15,087	18,325	21,897	27,765

All other	2,006	1,999	2,370	2,819	3,324
Total	15,064	17,086	20,695	24,716	31,089

Source: Republica de Panamá, Contraloría General de la República, Dirección de Estadística y Censo, Principales Indicadores Económicas Mensuales en la República, "Ventas de Automóviles Nuevos" table 4b.

[a] Preliminary.

There is no domestic production of passenger cars and light trucks in Panama. Asian automakers dominate the market for passenger cars and light trucks, and European automakers lead the market for luxury vehicle sales. According to Panamanian import statistics, imports from Japan accounted for the largest share—44 percent—of Panama's passenger vehicle and light truck imports in 2006, Korea accounted for 15 percent, and the United States, 12 percent.[108] The top three sellers are Toyota, Nissan, and Hyundai.[109]

Despite geographic proximity, U.S. automakers do not dominate the Panamanian market for a number of reasons. U.S.-built vehicles are reportedly not suitable to Panamanian market needs; in particular, a Panamanian industry official cites the lack of U.S.-made dieselpowered pickup trucks and SUVs and the limited offerings of small cars, which are preferred by Panamanian consumers. More generally, U.S.-built vehicles are considered to be less competitive than Japanese and Korean vehicles in terms of price, fuel efficiency, styling, dealerships, and service support.[110] Another source confirms that price and fuel efficiency are important to consumers in Panama, and that Japanese models reportedly are popular because of their proven quality, durability, and advanced technology.[111] These market conditions may temper, to some extent, the potential benefits of the TPA.

Views of Interested Parties

At the Commission's hearing, a representative of the Panama Business Council noted that U.S.-built passenger vehicles do not have a noteworthy market presence in Panama, not only because of Panamanian tariffs on imports, but also because of issues relating to the dealership and service infrastructure, availability of spare parts, marketing, image, and price. He said that U.S. companies have not shown substantial interest because Panama is not a large market.[112] These comments were echoed by a representative of the U.S. Chamber of Commerce of Panama, who stated that automakers such as Toyota are market leaders in Panama based on quality, accessibility, and image, and that U.S. automakers need to offer vehicles suited for the Panamanian market.[113] However, in its posthearing brief, the National Association of Manufacturers stated that U.S. motor vehicles and parts would gain significant market access as a result of the TPA.[114]

The Industry Trade Advisory Committee on Automotive Equipment and Capital Goods (ITAC 2) supports the TPA. In its report, the Committee noted that Panama is the largest motor vehicle market in Central America and that the TPA would provide "important safeguards for investment, and also significant new market access opportunities for U.S. manufacturers and automotive equipment."[115] With respect to the automotive provisions, the Committee states that the TPA "provides clear benefits and commercial cost competitive advantages to U.S. auto manufacturers, and is a marked improvement over the agreement reached with the CAFTA countries."[116] The Committee said that Panama's current sliding tariff structure[117] tends to promote the importation of used vehicles by assessing a lower tariff on lower-cost used vehicles and creates customs difficulties, administrative burdens, and delays for U.S. exporters because of the inherent subjectivity of customs valuation. The Committee reports that the TPA tariff concessions would address many of its interests, as they would provide for immediate duty-free treatment for the vehicle classes in which nearly all U.S. current and projected exports are categorized: passenger vehicles valued at over $12,000 and trucks weighing less than five tons. The Committee notes, however, that the 10-year phase out of duties on diesel-powered automobiles and five-year phase out on dieselpowered pickup trucks could be of concern for some U.S. manufacturers. The Committee supports the rule of origin negotiated in the TPA, stating that the menu of methods and percentages, which is the same as that negotiated in the CAFTA agreement, is considered acceptable. The Committee also supports the side letter on used cars.[118]

Several of the Industry Trade Advisory Committees (ITACs) representing machinery and equipment sectors stated their support for the TPA. For example, ITAC 2 stated that the investment chapter of the agreement generally contains the primary protections sought by the committee and highlighted the importance of the investor-state dispute settlement mechanism provided in the agreement. These protections would make companies more confident about investing in or setting up operations in Panama and could lead to increased exports of equipment to support such operations.[119] ITAC 4 stated it is convinced that the agreement would deliver important benefits to consumer goods firms in terms of improved market access, regulatory transparency, and customs procedures and that the agreement would provide for equity and reciprocity within the consumer goods sector.[120] ITAC 8 noted that, owing to the role of the Panamanian government as a key purchaser of information technology and communications products and services, the strong commitments in the government procurement chapter of the agreement would be critically important to ensuring access to the government procurement market in Panama.[121]

Certain Machinery[122]

Assessment

The U.S.-Panama TPA likely would result in increased U.S. exports of certain machinery to Panama as a result of tariff elimination under the agreement. However, because of the small size of the Panamanian market, the increase in total exports of certain machinery likely would be small.

Impact on U.S. Exports

Based on the Commission's partial equilibrium analysis, U.S. exports of certain machinery to Panama could increase by 13.7 percent above the $31.4 million of certain machinery that Panama imported from the United States in 2006 as a result of tariff elimination under the TPA.[123] The TPA would eliminate the duties applied to 91 percent of U.S. exports of certain machinery to Panama immediately upon entry into force. However, because of the small size of the Panamanian market, the increase in total exports of certain machinery likely would be small. Panamanian total imports of certain machinery from the United States were subject to a trade-weighted average tariff rate of about 7 percent in 2006.

In addition to tariff liberalization, U.S. exports of major household appliances may benefit from robust economic conditions in Panama, including a strong residential and office construction sector and increasing demand for higher-end U.S. brand-name major appliances.[124] Panamanian tariffs on major household appliances, such as refrigerators and washing machines, currently range from 3 percent to 15 percent. Presently, all major household appliances are imported into Panama, as there are no local manufacturers.[125] Japan is the leading supplier of major household appliances to Panama, followed by the United States and Korea.[126] U.S. major household appliance brands (e.g., GE, Whirlpool, and Kenmore) dominate the Panamanian market for higher priced products, whereas appliances produced in Japan (Matsushita, Sanyo, and Sharp) and Korea (LG and Samsung) are the leaders in the medium-priced segment of the market. Major appliances from Mexico (Mabe) and Brazil (Brastemp) are strongest in the low- or entry-priced segment of the market. Some U.S. appliance companies may supply lower-priced refrigerators and washing machines to the Panamanian market from their subsidiaries in Mexico and Brazil. It has also been reported[127] that major U.S. appliance producers such as Whirlpool Corp. and GE export to Panamanian customers directly from the United States, whereas Asian firms tend to supply the Panamanian market from large distribution centers in the Colon Free Zone.[128]

U.S. suppliers of HVAC equipment also would likely benefit from elimination of Panamanian tariffs under the TPA. Presently, U.S. exports of HVAC equipment incur tariff rates ranging from 3 percent to 10 percent. There is no production of air-conditioning equipment in Panama. Firms in Japan and Korea are major competitors of leading U.S. firms such as Carrier, Trane Corp. (American Standard Companies), and Lennox International (Lennox) in the Panamanian market. In 2006, Panama's imports of air-conditioning equipment from the United States totaled $15.3 million. Preference for U.S.-brand airconditioning equipment in Panama is strong because of its competitive pricing, quality, and energy efficiency.[129] Panamanian demand for HVAC equipment is expected to be driven by the construction of high-end residential projects, as well as major tourist renovations of former U.S. military housing developments at Ft. Clayton and Ft. Albrook in the Panama Canal Zone.[130]

U.S. exports of additional machinery and equipment also would likely benefit from the elimination of Panama's tariffs under the TPA, although to a lesser extent.[131] Computer equipment and parts accounted for 22 percent ($118 million) of Panama's total imports of machinery and equipment from the United States in 2006. Under the TPA, Panama's trade-weighted average MFN duty rate on such articles—5.0 percent and 3.3 percent, respectively—would become free immediately. However, U.S. exports accounted for over three-quarters of Panama's total imports of computers and parts in 2006, affording limited opportunity to take further market share from competing suppliers following the TPA.

Radio, television, telephone, and other telecommunications equipment accounted for 14 percent ($78 million) of Panama's imports of machinery and equipment from the United States in 2006. With a trade-weighted average MFN tariff of less than 5.0 percent for the combined categories, and because of the small size of the market in Panama, the immediate elimination of Panama's tariffs on such articles likely would lead to a relatively small increase in U.S. exports. Similarly, elimination of the relatively low Panamanian tariffs on bulldozers and similar earth moving equipment and auto parts—averaging 4.3 percent and 5.3

percent, respectively—likely would lead to a small increase in U.S. exports of these products.[132]

Upon entry into force of the TPA, Panama's current trade-weighted average MFN duty rate of 9.0 percent on imports of medical instruments would be eliminated immediately for more than 99 percent of U.S. exports in this category. The United States supplied 59 percent of Panama's imports of medical instruments in 2006, but the U.S. share of Panama's import market would not likely increase appreciably following the elimination of tariffs on U.S. imports under the TPA because the Government of Panama often waives tariffs on medical supplies to lower public and health care costs. In Panama, the Ministry of Health System and the Social Security System are the primary end users and procurers of medical equipment.[133]

Greater volumes of trade in Panamanian ports may lead to increased U.S. exports of materials handling equipment (used to load and offload ships), safety and security equipment, and construction equipment. The $5.5-billion expansion of the Panama Canal likely will increase Panama's demand for certain machinery, including construction and earth moving equipment, which will benefit U.S. suppliers.[134] The U.S.-Panama TPA would reinforce commercial linkages for U.S. companies supplying goods and services associated with the canal expansion.[135] U.S. producers of safety and security equipment have seen a sharp rise in sales of x-ray machines and radiation detectors used to inspect cargo at U.S. and foreign ports as port directors attempt to comply with U.S. Homeland Security guidelines for port and maritime security.[136] Increased trade volumes in Panama in conjunction with the U.S.-Panama TPA could create further demand in Panama for such cargo inspection equipment.

Views of Interested Parties

Representatives of several U.S. machinery and equipment industries have registered their support for the TPA through trade and industry associations and ITACs. These representatives stated that the agreement would improve market access for U.S. industrial goods in Panama. Caterpillar, the U.S. Chamber of Commerce, the Association of American Chambers of Commerce in Latin America, and the Latin America Trade Coalition said that the TPA would give U.S.-made mining and construction equipment a tariff advantage over equipment from competing suppliers, which would be particularly important during the $5.5-billion expansion of the Panama Canal.[137] U.S. exports of other types of manufactured goods identified as likely to increase due to tariff advantages that would accrue from the TPA include sophisticated machinery and TV and sound equipment.[138] The American Chamber of Commerce and Industry of Panama and the Panama Pro-TPA Trade Coalition said that U.S. exports of consumer and industrial goods would benefit from the elimination of Panama's 7.0-percent trade-weighted average rate of duty on imports from the United States.[139] The National Association of Manufacturers identified the TPA's "zero for zero" immediate duty-free access for construction equipment and medical and scientific equipment as a favorable achievement.[140]

The Committee on Consumer Goods (ITAC 4) said that the TPA would deliver important benefits to consumer goods firms in terms of improved market access, regulatory transparency, and customs procedures and that the agreement would provide for equity and reciprocity within the consumer goods sector. The committee noted that under the TPA, over 88 percent of U.S. exports of consumer and industrial products to Panama would be duty free immediately upon entry into force of the agreement. The committee said that the administration should make use of the TPA provision for acceleration of the staged tariff reductions for the remaining articles.[141]

The Committee for Information and Communications Technologies, Services, and Electronic Commerce (ITAC 8) said that, owing to the role of the Panamanian Government as a key purchaser of information technology and communications products and services, the strong commitments in the Government Procurement Chapter of the Agreement are critically important to ensuring access to the government procurement market in Panama.[142]

IMPACT OF MARKET ACCESS PROVISIONS FOR SERVICES

This chapter assesses the potential effect of the U.S.-Panama TPA on the services sector and services trade. The analysis first focuses on cross-border trade in services generally and then discusses financial, telecommunication, professional, and retail services specifically. These sectors were selected for analysis because they account for a relatively large share of U.S.-Panama services trade, because they are the subject of a discrete chapter in the U.S.-Panama TPA, and/or because they are subject to relatively significant trade liberalization under the TPA. Each TPA chapter discussion includes an assessment, a summary of TPA provisions, and the views of interested parties.

Summary of Assessments

The U.S.-Panama TPA would provide U.S. services firms with levels of market access, national treatment, and regulatory transparency that generally exceed those afforded by Panama's commitments under the General Agreement on Trade in Services (GATS).

- **Small Potential Effect:** The TPA would likely generate only a small increase in U.S. services exports to Panama because of the small size of the Panamanian market. The TPA would not likely have a large effect on U.S. imports of services from Panama because the U.S. services market is generally open to foreign firms, including those from Panama, and because the Panamanian industry is small. U.S. firms' sales of financial and retail services would likely grow with the enlargement of the canal.[143] However, the opportunities created by the ongoing canal enlargement project were not factored into the Commission's assessment of the potential impact of the TPA, as this project is not contingent upon TPA provisions.

- **Benefit of "Negative List" Approach:** Improved access for U.S. services firms in Panama would be enhanced by the negative list approach in the agreement. This approach would extend trade disciplines found in the services chapters of the TPA to services for which Panama made limited or no sectoral commitments under GATS, such as legal services and insurance services, as well as to new services yet to be offered commercially.

- **Financial Services:** The financial services provisions of the U.S.-Panama TPA would likely lead to increased penetration of the Panamanian market by U.S. firms. However, new U.S. cross-border exports of financial services and new U.S. investment in the Panamanian financial services market by U.S. firms would likely be limited. Significant new imports of financial services from Panama would be unlikely.

- **Telecommunication Services:** The TPA would likely have minimal impact on both U.S. cross-border imports and exports of telecommunication services, including fixed-line services, largely due to already high levels of price competition for voice telephone services between the United States and Panama. The small size of Panama's telecommunication services market as well as high levels of competition in many product markets would likely act as a deterrent to entry by U.S. firms. Additionally, TPA exclusions for mobile services might limit the ability of U.S. firms to enter Panama's high-growth mobile services market. The TPA would likely have a minimal impact on the sales of subsidiaries of Panamanian telecommunication firms in the United States, largely due to the relatively high existing level of openness in the U.S. telecommunication services market.

- **Professional Services:** The professional services provisions of the TPA would likely contribute to increased market access and national treatment for U.S. professional services practitioners engaged in cross-border trade, especially in such services historically reserved for Panamanian nationals. Certain professional services would likely benefit from a process whereby agreements on mutual recognition could be accomplished over time in professions interested in such mutual recognition such as engineering.

- **Retail Services:** Retail services provisions of the U.S.-Panama TPA would likely improve conditions of market access and national treatment. However, U.S. investment in Panama would likely represent a small portion of total U.S. outbound investment in retail services.

TPA Chapter 11 - Cross-Border Trade in Services

Assessment

The trade in services provisions of the U.S.-Panama TPA would broadly provide U.S. firms levels of market access, national treatment, and regulatory transparency that exceed those afforded by Panama's commitments under the GATS,[144] the first legally enforceable multilateral trade agreement on services.[145] However, the effect of TPA disciplines on overall bilateral services trade would likely be minimal because Panama's services sector is small relative to the size of the U.S. services sector (box 3.1 and table 3.1).[146]

Improvement in U.S. firms' access to the Panamanian market under the TPA would be attributable in large part to the use of a negative list approach in the agreement. Under this approach, all trade disciplines included in TPA chapter 11 would automatically cover virtually all services industries[147] and industry segments except for those specifically exempted in side letters, additional TPA chapters, and annexes I through III on nonconforming measures (table 3.2).[148] Use of the negative list approach would extend the trade disciplines found in the services chapters of the TPA to many services for which Panama made no (or limited) commitments under the GATS, including those yet to be offered commercially.[149] For instance, Panama elected to make no GATS commitments in restaurant services and limited GATS commitments in accounting and insurance services, but did not exempt these services from TPA disciplines. Consequently, U.S. providers of such services would be entitled to unrestricted market access, nondiscriminatory regulatory treatment, and improved transparency in Panama under the terms of the TPA, whereas they may not under the GATS.

Summary of Provisions

Chapter 11 of the TPA[150] covers services other than financial services (covered in chapter 12 of the TPA) and air transport services. The TPA would guarantee national and MFN treatment for providers of the covered services. Local presence would not be required, and regulation of services and qualification requirements could not be unduly burdensome. Chapter 11 contains transparency requirements that supplement those set out in TPA chapter 18 on transparency. The parties would be permitted but not required to recognize education, experience, licenses, or certifications obtained in particular nonparty countries.

The United States and Panama would be obligated to permit unfettered transfers and payments relating to the cross-border supply of services and would be required to allow such transactions to occur in a freely usable currency at the prevailing exchange rate on the date of transfer, subject to explicit exceptions. The benefits of this chapter could be denied under limited circumstances if the service supplier is controlled by persons of a nonparty. Chapter 11 includes language specific to express delivery services, affirming that they are subject to the agreement (article 11.3). Additionally, chapter 11 defines the scope of coverage of express delivery services, confirms the desire to maintain market access for both parties that is no less favorable than that in effect when the TPA was signed, delineates the relationship between covered services and each party's postal monopoly, places limits on state subsidies, and ensures the independent regulation of state postal services (article 11.13).

BOX 3.1 PROFILE OF SERVICES INDUSTRIES IN PANAMA AND THE UNITED STATES

The services sector in Panama accounted for 76 percent of the country's GDP and 67 percent of employment in 2005. Panama posted a services surplus that year, with exports and imports of $3.1 billion and $1.7 billion, respectively. Services accounted for 28 percent ($1.4 billion) of Panama's overall exports in 2005, with transportation services predominating.

The U.S. services sector accounted for 83 percent of U.S. private-sector GDP and 85 percent of private-sector employment in 2005. The United States posted the world's largest services surplus, measuring $62.2 billion in 2005, with exports of $377 billion and imports of $315 billion. Services accounted for 29 percent of U.S. exports in 2005, with business, professional, and technical services predominating.

Sources: International Monetary Fund (IMF), *Balance of Payments Statistics Yearbook 2006*; World Bank, *World Development Indicators Online*.

Table 3.1. Cross-Border Trade in Services with All Trading Partners by the United States and Panama, 2005 (Million U.S. Dollars)

Service industry	United States		Panama	
	Exports	Imports	Exports	Imports
Total services	376,790	314,580	3,144	1,729
Passenger transport	20,930	26,070	328	117
Freight transport	17,340	44,160	12	780
Other transport	24,910	17,950	1,436	45
Travel and tourism	102,010	73,560	780	271
Other services[a]	211,600	152,840	589	517

Source: IMF, *Balance of Payments Statistics Yearbook, 2006,* Part 1: Country Tables, vol. 56, 2006, 748-54 and 1017-1022.

Note: Columns may not sum to totals due to rounding.

[a] Included in "other services" are communications; construction; insurance; financial; computer and information; royalties and license fees; other business; personal, cultural, and recreational; and other government.

No provisions in chapter 11 of the agreement would restrict Panama's exclusive right to appoint the Panama Canal Authority (PCA) as the entity responsible for the use, administration, functioning, conservation, maintenance, modernization and related activities of the Panama Canal (annex 10-F of the agreement). The agreement does, however, contain binding commitments that would provide for non-discriminatory access at or above designated thresholds for the procurement of canal-bound goods and services (annex 9.1 of the agreement).

Table 3.2. U.S.-Panama TPA: Services Sectors Subject to Nonconforming Measures Related to Cross-Border Trade

Panama		United States	
Current Measures	Potential measures	Current Measures	Potential measures
Activities related to fishing	Activities related to the Panama Canal	Air transportation	Communications
Aircraft maintenance and repair services	Construction	Business services	Issues related to minorities
Banking	Fisheries and services incidental to fishing	Insurance	Social services
Contractual positions within Panama Canal authority	Issues related to minority and ethnic groups	Professional services - patent attorneys, patent agents, and	Transportation

-all services		others that practice before the Patent and Trademark Office	
Crude petroleum, hydrocarbons and natural gas – exploit-tation, refining, transportation, storage, marketing, or export.	Public supply of potable water Social services	Transportation services - customs brokers	
Education services			
Electric power distribution and transmission			
Games of luck and chance			
Hotel and restaurant services			
Insurance and insurance-related services			
Maritime transport			
Ports and airports			
Private security agencies			
Professional services			
Retail sales			
Road transport services - passenger and freight			
Panama		**United States**	
Specialty air services			
Telecommunication services			
Travel agencies			
Transmission of radio and television programs			

Source: *U.S.-Panama TPA*, annexes I through III, full text available at http://www.ustr.gov.

Notes: Nonconforming measures are found in annexes I through III of the TPA. Annex I contains reservations for cross-border services, excluding financial services, to preserve existing measures that are inconsistent with the disciplines concerning nondiscrimination, performance requirements, and senior personnel. Annex II contains reservations for cross-border services, excluding financial services, to ensure that a party maintains flexibility to impose measures in the future that may be inconsistent with the disciplines of the TPA. Annex III contains both existing and future nonconforming measures related to financial services, including insurance.

Views of Interested Parties

Overall, U.S. industry representatives have indicated that they are generally satisfied with the TPA provisions on services and regulatory transparency. U.S. industry sources state that the TPA would provide a favorable environment for cross-border services trade, opening many previously closed Panamanian sectors to U.S. services suppliers and investors. In particular, U.S. industry sources said that they are encouraged by the strategic implications of this agreement given Panama's position as a logistics and transportation hub.[151] However, representatives of the U.S. architectural, engineering, and construction industries stated that they are concerned with language in the procurement chapter of the agreement that would allow for possible changes in the Panama Canal Authority's (PCA's) current procurement practices (annex 9.1, section D). Such changes could harm the competitive position of U.S. suppliers of these services for Panama Canal expansion projects.[152]

TPA Chapter 12 - Financial Services

Assessment

The financial services provisions of the U.S.-Panama TPA would likely lead to increased penetration of the Panamanian market by U.S. firms. However, the Panamanian economy is small compared with the U.S. economy, so new cross-border exports of financial services and new investment in the Panamanian financial services market by U.S. firms would likely be limited. Significant new imports of financial services from Panama would be unlikely.

Key provisions of the TPA would enable U.S. financial services firms to provide insurance and asset management services on a cross-border bases and establish branches or subsidiaries on Panamanian soil. Another important new provision would permit U.S. portfolio managers to provide services to both mutual funds and pension funds in Panama.

Financial Services – Except Insurance

The TPA would likely generate only a small increase in U.S. exports of banking, securities, and asset management services to Panama. The anticipated absolute effect is small due to the size of the Panamanian market and the historically small export volume to this region, which is estimated to have accounted for not more than 2.0 percent ($511 million) of total U.S. exports of financial services in 2005.[153]

The market for U.S. financial services is already fairly open, and the Panamanian industry is relatively small. As a result, the TPA would not likely have a significant effect on U.S. imports of financial services from Panama. Total U.S. imports of banking and securities services registered $12.3 billion in 2005, and sales of financial services by U.S. affiliates of foreign firms totaled $23.8 billion in 2004 (latest available).[154] Although precise figures on U.S. imports of financial services from Panama do not exist, available data indicate that cross-border imports did not exceed $147 million in 2005,[155] or less than 2 percent of total U.S. banking and securities services imports. Moreover, such U.S. imports, if any, are most likely concentrated in the provision of trade financing to U.S. clients importing goods from

Panama and do not directly compete with most U.S.-based banks. Any future growth in this industry segment would likely be a result of demand for trade finance services generated by increased trade in goods between the United States and Panama, rather than a direct result of financial sector liberalization.

Insurance

The TPA would likely generate only a small increase in U.S.-Panama bilateral trade in insurance services, with little or no change in overall U.S. insurance imports and exports. The insurance market in Panama is small compared with that in the United States and, therefore, the potential for cross-border U.S. exports or sales by foreign affiliates of U.S. firms in this sector likely is limited. With respect to the potential for increased U.S. imports from Panama, the U.S. insurance market is already open to foreign firms, so market access gains for Panamanian firms would likely be marginal. In 2005, U.S. cross-border imports of insurance services from the world were $28.5 billion, and insurance sales by U.S. affiliates of foreign firms totaled $81.3 billion in 2004 (latest available).[156] Precise figures on U.S. cross-border imports of insurance services from Panama are not available, but existing data indicate that such imports did not exceed $13 million in 2005,[157] or less than 0.1 percent of total U.S. imports of insurance services. Similar to other financial services, any future growth in this industry segment would likely result from demand for insurance generated by increased trade in goods between the United States and Panama, rather than as a direct result of insurance sector liberalization, as Panamanian insurance companies do not hold the capital base to compete directly with U.S. insurers.

Summary of Provisions

Though certain provisions of chapter 11 would apply to the U.S. and Panamanian financial services markets, these markets would in most part be governed by chapter 12 provisions.[158] Chapter 12 of the TPA would generally require each party to allow cross-border trade in financial services, accord national treatment and MFN treatment to investors of the other party, and provide market access for financial institutions without limitations on the number of financial institutions, value of transactions, number of service operations, or number of persons employed.

As in previous bilateral U.S. FTAs, cross-border trade would be limited to certain segments of the financial services industry, as outlined in annex 12.5.1. For insurance, TPA coverage of cross-border trade in insurance is limited to marine, aviation, and transit (MAT) insurance; reinsurance and retrocession;[159] and insurance intermediation services such as brokerage and agency services. However, for Panama, the commitment on MAT insurance would not apply to commercial aviation until two years after entry into force of the agreement. For banking and securities, TPA coverage of cross-border trade is limited to the provision and transfer of financial information and financial data processing, advisory, and other auxiliary financial services as defined in the text of the chapter. Cross-border intermediation services (i.e., deposit taking and lending) would be prohibited.

Each party would be required to permit a financial institution of the other party to provide new financial services similar to those that it permits its own domestic institutions to provide, without additional legislative action. The chapter would not require either party to furnish or allow access to information related to individual customers or confidential information, the disclosure of which would impede law enforcement, be contrary to the public interest, or prejudice legitimate commercial concerns.

Under chapter 12, a party could not require financial institutions of the other party to hire individuals of a particular nationality as senior managers or other essential personnel and could not require more than a simple majority of the board of directors to be nationals or residents of the party. The parties would agree that transparent regulations and policies are important, commit to publishing in advance all regulations of general application, and agree to maintain or establish mechanisms to respond to inquiries from interested persons. Where a party requires membership in a self-regulatory organization, the chapter provides that such organizations would be subject to the national treatment and MFN obligations of this chapter. The two parties would recognize the importance of maintaining and developing expedited procedures for offering insurance services.

The TPA would establish a financial services committee to implement the provisions of chapter 12. Chapter 12 also would provide for consultations and dispute resolution, and includes cross references to the provisions covering dispute settlement procedures. Under the TPA, parties could retain specific financial services measures that do not conform to the TPA by including the measures in annex III of the agreement.

Views of Interested Parties

Many aspects of the TPA were lauded by financial services industry representatives, notably the granting of full rights to establish subsidiaries or branches in Panama, inclusion of transparency requirements, and use of the negative list format, which follows the model of previous bilateral U.S. free trade agreements. However, the ITAC 10 report said that the agreement falls short of industry expectations, as it would not include national treatment provisions for investment by financial services firms and would not allow for investor-state arbitration regarding the prudential carve-out.[160]

A representative of the banking sector said that the industry supports the agreement and felt that despite the small size of the Panamanian market, significant opportunities for the provision of trade financing would result from the TPA.[161] Asset management firms would also benefit from the agreement because it would allow them to provide portfolio management services to mutual funds and pension funds in Panama.[162] The agreement would also allow for the cross-border provision of portfolio management services, which has been an important issue for the industry in recent FTA negotiations.

ITAC 10 supports the agreement's inclusion of MFN and national treatment provisions across the insurance sector.[163] ITAC 10 also expressed support for provisions that would allow U.S. insurers to supply MAT insurance, reinsurance, retrocession, intermediation, and services auxiliary to insurance to Panamanian residents on a cross-border basis. However, ITAC 10 was disappointed that the cross-border provision of intermediation services would be allowed only for MAT and reinsurance, thereby preventing U.S. firms from supplying other services to established life and nonlife insurers in the Panamanian market. In addition, the ITAC 10 report noted that U.S. firms would be required to wait two years after entry into force of the TPA before they would be allowed to provide the aviation component of MAT insurance.[164]

TPA Chapter 13 – Telecommunications

Assessment

The TPA would likely have minimal impact on U.S. cross-border exports of telecommunication services,[165] largely due to already high levels of price competition for voice telephone services between the United States and Panama. The TPA also would be unlikely to affect the sales of subsidiaries of U.S. telecommunication companies in Panama, because of the small, competitive nature of Panama's telecommunication services market; TPA exclusions and licensing issues; and regulatory enforcement in Panama. Although the TPA's telecommunication provisions represent a substantial improvement upon Panama's WTO accession commitments,[166] the small size of its telecommunication services market and high levels of competition in many market segments would likely to entry by U.S. firms (see box 3.2).[167] In addition, TPA exclusions for mobile services[168] could limit the ability of U.S. firms to enter Panama's high-growth mobile services market. In wire-line services, the impact of the TPA would also likely be minimal, due to the reported reluctance of Cable & Wireless Panama, Panama's incumbent wire-line carrier, to negotiate and/or implement interconnection agreements with new entrant carriers.[169]

The telecommunication provisions of the U.S.-Panama TPA would likely have minimal impact on U.S. cross-border imports of telecommunication services, largely due to already high levels of price competition for voice telephone services between the United States and Panama. Overall, the price of a telephone call from Panama to the United States reportedly dropped from $1.50 per minute[170] in December 2002 to less than $0.10 per minute in 2007, largely due to high levels of competition in the provision of international voice services.[171] The TPA would likely have minimal impact on the sales of subsidiaries of Panamanian telecommunication firms in the United States, largely due to the relatively high existing level of openness in the U.S. telecommunication services market. As a result, several multinational firms maintaining important operations in Panama currently offer telecommunication services in the United States. For example, Telefónica S.A., the Spanish parent of Telefónica Móviles Panamá, operates in the United States through Telefónica Contenidos, Telefónica Empresas, and Terra Networks.[172] Similarly, Cable & Wireless plc, which owns 49 percent of Cable & Wireless Panama, offers international voice and data services to corporate and government customers in the United States.[173]

Summary of Provisions

Though the provisions of chapter 11 apply to telecommunication services, regulatory principles and obligations agreed to in chapter 13 are most important in assessing the trade implications of the TPA.[174] The provisions of chapter 13 would require each party to ensure that enterprises of the other party have access to and use of any public telecommunication service offered in its territory and/or across its borders on reasonable and nondiscriminatory terms and conditions. Specifically, the chapter would obligate suppliers of public telecommunications services to provide network interconnection,[175] services resale, number portability, and dialing parity to telecommunication service providers of the other party on reasonable and nondiscriminatory terms and conditions.[176] In addition, major suppliers of one party would be required to offer telecommunication services to suppliers of the other party on terms and conditions no less favorable than those accorded to their own subsidiaries, affiliates, and nonaffiliated service suppliers, particularly regarding the availability, provisioning, rates, and quality of such services. Major suppliers would also face additional obligations related to competitive safeguards, services resale, network unbundling, interconnection, leased circuits, co-location, and access to rights-of-way and submarine cable systems.[177]

Chapter 13 would commit the Governments of the United States and Panama to ensure the independence of their respective telecommunications regulatory bodies and bestow such entities with the authority to enforce compliance with TPA obligations. The parties to the agreement would also be required to maintain transparent and nondiscriminatory procedures related to licensing, allocation and use of scarce resources, and dispute resolution. An annex to chapter 13 establishes exemptions in the United States for the provision of telecommunication services in rural areas.[178] Similarly, annex I to the TPA establishes exemptions to national treatment,[179] market access,[180] and local presence[181] provisions in the TPA.

Views of Interested Parties

Members of ITAC 8 expressed support for the commitments detailed in the telecommunications chapter, noting the strong "WTO-plus" nature of many of the commitments.[182] In particular, the ITAC 8 report noted provisions in chapter 13 which would be particularly important to ensuring market access for U.S. telecommunication services providers, specifically provisions that create an independent regulatory body in Panama, ensure the enforcement authority of the regulator, guarantee recourse to regulatory bodies, and clarify dispute resolution procedures.

BOX 3.2 COMPETITIVE CONDITIONS IN THE PANAMANIAN TELECOMMUNICATION SERVICES MARKET

Fixed-Line Services

In order to promote competition, the Government of Panama supports the issuance of an unlimited number of wireline licenses free-of-charge. As of June, there were more than approximately 130 wire-line licenses issued, although only 17 firms had commenced operations. Cable & Wireless Panama (CWP), the incumbent wire-line carrier, maintained an exclusive right to offer wire-line services until the end of 2002. Following the liberalization of the wireline market in 2003, new entrant firms, including TeleCarrier, Galaxy Communications, Advanced Communications Network, and Optynex Telecom, began to offer services. Competition in facilities-based services is reportedly stifled by CWP's reluctance to lease elements of the local network infrastructure to new entrant competitors. By contrast, increased competition in long distance and international voice services has resulted in large price declines, particularly on international routes. Despite an aborted attempt by Panama's telecommunications regulator to block Voice-over-Internet-Protocol (VoIP) traffic, a growing number of companies and Internet cafés now offer such services. CWP and Cable Onda, Panama's cable television provider, also offer voice services using VoIP technologies.

Mobile Services

Mobile service licenses, which are granted via public tender, are strictly rationed. Currently, only two companies, CWP and Telefónica Móviles, are licensed to offer mobile services in Panama, although these two concessions expire at the end of 2007. Fierce competition between CWP and Telefónica Móviles has left each company with approximately 50 percent of the mobile services market. In May 2007, Panama's regulatory authority announced plans to auction two additional 30-year mobile licenses in October 2007. The issuance of these licenses, which are expected to net at least $60 million, are intended to increase mobile penetration to 70 percent, up from 60 percent in 2007. As of August 2007, 12 firms reportedly expressed interest in bidding for Panama's mobile licenses. Contenders include Panamanian firms like Cable Onda, Advanced Communications, and Galaxy Communications as well as international mobile services firms that specialize in developing countries, including América Móvil (Mexico), Digicel (Jamaica), and Millicom International (Luxembourg).[1]

High-speed Internet Services

Low-levels of both wire-line and personal computer penetration have hindered the development of high-speed Internet access services in Panama, with the bulk of users accessing the Internet at public locations such as schools, libraries, and Internet cafés. High-speed Internet services are largely offered over wire-line infrastructure using ADSL technology, although access via cable modem, wireless, and satellite technologies is also available. Leading providers of high-speed Internet services include CWP, Telecarrier, Optynex, and Cable Onda. High tariffs for highspeed Internet access have fallen significantly due to increasing competition.

Sources: Budde, *Panama-Telecoms Market Overview & Statistics*, April 2007; Primetrica, Inc., "Panama," *GlobalComms Database*, TeleGeography, June 2007; "Twelve Companies Interested In Mobile Licences," *CommsUpdate*, August 23, 2007.

[1] Competion in Panama's mobile services market has impacted the pricing of such services. For example, the price of a 3-minute, peak-time local call fell from $1.44 in 2003 to $0.54 in 2005, a decline of approximately 63 percent. International Telecommunications Union, *World Telecommunications/ICT Indicators 2006*, 2006.

Professional Services[183]

Assessment

The professional services provisions of the TPA would likely contribute to increased market access and national treatment for U.S. professional services practitioners engaged in crossborder trade, especially in such services historically reserved for Panamanian nationals. Moreover, certain professional services would likely benefit from TPA provisions that would establish a process whereby agreements on mutual recognition could be accomplished over time in interested professions such as engineering. Additionally, as noted earlier, the TPA negative list approach would extend trade disciplines to certain professional services for which Panama made limited or no commitments under the GATS, including many accounting, architectural, and engineering services.[184] Nevertheless, the TPA would likely have a minimal effect on bilateral services trade in the near term, because Panama's professional services market[185] offers only limited opportunities that are heavily dependent on significant expansion of Panama's infrastructure services, such as transportation. Certain U.S. professional services firms providing legal or engineering services and major worldwide networks of accounting firms already participate in the Panamanian market through means such as joint ventures and associations with licensed Panamanian firms,[186] and Panamanian law firms reportedly participate in the U.S. market.[187]

Summary of Provisions

Annex 11.9 to chapter 11 of the TPA would commit each party to encourage relevant bodies to develop mutually acceptable standards and criteria[188] for licensing and certification of professional service suppliers and to make recommendations on mutual recognition to the parties to the TPA.[189] The parties would be obligated to review such recommendations on mutual recognition within a reasonable time to determine consistency with the TPA. Upon a favorable review, each party would commit to encourage its respective competent authorities to implement the recommendation within a mutually agreed time. The annex would also commit each party, upon agreement, to encourage relevant bodies in its territory to develop procedures for the temporary licensing of the other party's professional service suppliers. The annex would further require parties to review implementation of the provisions of the annex at least once every three years.

Panama specified nonconforming measures (NCMs) that would apply to services provided by foreign lawyers, accountants, architects, and engineers, and others in numerous occupations identified by Panama as professional services. The most prevalent NCMs—Panamanian nationality requirements—would apply to those professionals in Panama who are certified to practice Panamanian law,[190] provide official certifications or attestations as licensed Authorized Public Accountants, or are authorized to practice in additional designated occupations. For example, the NCM that applies to lawyers states that foreign nationals are neither permitted to practice Panamanian law nor make representations before tribunals, courts, and authorities in Panama. Instead, they would be permitted to provide advice solely on international law and home country (i.e., non-Panamanian) law.[191] For accountants, Panama would allow a U.S. national who is licensed to practice accounting in the United

States to apply for a license to practice in Panama, contingent on reciprocity and subject to the same requirements as Panamanian nationals. Additionally, the TPA would allow Panama to require that foreign nationals obtain a special permit to practice accounting, and to require that a foreign accounting firm operate only in association with a local accounting enterprise. A third NCM allows that the relevant authority in Panama would be permitted to certify foreign nationals as engineers and architects eligible to practice in Panama, only if they are married to a Panamanian or have a child who is a Panamanian national, or are licensed in a jurisdiction that grants Panamanian nationals reciprocity in applying for a license under the same conditions. The measure also states that the relevant authority would be permitted to authorize an enterprise to contract with a foreign architect and engineer for up to 12 months if no Panamanian is qualified, although the enterprise would be required to hire a Panamanian national to replace the foreign national when the contract ends. Panama also included a potential measure that would adopt or maintain residency, registration, or other local presence requirements, or require a financial guarantee, prior to the cross-border provision of construction services.

Views of Interested Parties

U.S. industry sources stated that under the TPA, Panama would provide new access for U.S. nationals to supply professional services previously reserved for Panamanian nationals.[192] Industry sources responded favorably to the provision for temporary licensing of recognized expert professionals, noting the provision's potential value especially to U.S. individual practitioners and small firms.[193] An industry source further stated that the TPA would simplify the continuation of interaction and cross-training between U.S. and Panamanian architectural, engineering, legal, and medical service firms.[194]

Industry sources noted satisfaction with the cross-border trade provisions on accounting services, observing the high importance of ensuring market access to U.S. accountants and small accounting firms.[195] The sources further observed that large international accounting networks operate satisfactorily in Panama under contractual or other arrangements with local firms, which would be preserved or could be expanded under the TPA. U.S. sources noted that, in addition to allowing U.S. CPAs to apply for a license to practice accounting in Panama contingent on reciprocity in U.S. states,[196] the TPA would provide an opportunity for U.S. accountants through the provision that a special permit would be granted conditionally to foreign accountants to provide non-attest accounting services in Panama.[197]

Regarding the TPA-s the coverage of architectural and engineering services, U.S. industry sources accepted the general provisions that would apply to the development of professional standards and criteria, temporary licensing and review, and the absence of exceptions for national treatment, most-favored-nation treatment, and market access.[198] The same sources also accepted Panama's current nonconforming measure on the practice of architecture and engineering, because the sole criterion for the restriction would be reciprocity, which in most cases was not deemed an issue for U.S. state licensing boards. The sources advocated establishment of a working group on professional services to deal with procedures to develop temporary licensing, with priority given to engineers, and encouraged the early conclusion of an agreement on temporary licensing of engineers and architects.

Nevertheless, the sources noted that Panama's local presence requirement for an enterprise (not the practitioner), while not deemed onerous, is not included in other agreements recently negotiated by the United States. The sources further stated concerns over government procurement, whereby a potential erosion in the current position for U.S. suppliers of services could result if the Panama Canal Authority were to change its procurement practices on contract awards below the thresholds set out in the TPA.

U.S. industry sources stated that the TPA would afford limited opportunities to U.S. lawyers to provide legal advice in Panama solely concerning U.S. and international law.

Retail Sales

Assessment

Retail services provisions of the U.S.-Panama TPA would likely improve conditions of market access and national treatment by legalizing foreign investment in Panama's retail services market.[199] However, due to the small, competitive nature of Panama's retail services market (box 3.3), U.S. investment in Panama would likely represent a small portion of total U.S. outbound investment in retail services.

Summary of Provisions

Provisions liberalizing nationality restrictions on ownership in the Panamanian retail services market are found in annex I of the TPA and also in a side letter to the agreement. The provisions stipulate that nationality restrictions would not apply either to foreign-owned retailers selling products exclusively of their own brand or to foreign-owned retailers engaged primarily in the sale of services.[200] TPA provisions further stipulate that by 2011, nationality restrictions would not apply to foreign-owned retailers investing more than $3 million in retail establishments that sell both goods and services.[201]

Views of Interested Parties

Although U.S. retail industry representatives generally expressed support for the TPA market access provisions, as importers they expressed dissatisfaction with the current system of U.S. TPAs and FTAs generally.[202] U.S. retailers expressed their belief that costs associated with understanding the TPA's rules of origin, tariff schedules, and other provisions would outweigh potential benefits.[203] Industry representatives expressed varied opinions regarding the $3 million minimum investment requirement; some indicated this nontariff measure would be insignificant, while one representative cited it as a significant barrier.

BOX 3.3 COMPETITIVE CONDITIONS IN PANAMA'S RETAIL SERVICES MARKET

Panama's retail services market, valued at $5.0 billion in 2006, experienced an average annual growth rate of 5 percent from 2003 through 2006, just trailing that of the global market at 6 percent during the same period.[1] However, Panama accounts for a fraction of the $12.1 trillion global market.[2]

Panama's domestic retail market is relatively competitive, modern, and developed compared to other Central American retailers.[3] The three largest retailers account for approximately 14 percent of Panama's retail market, while the market shares of other competitors each account for less than 1 percent.[4] The two largest retailers, supermarket chains Super 99 and Rey Holdings, each have over 30 stores and annual sales of approximately $300 million.[5] The third largest is U.S.-owned PriceSmart, which despite the current prohibition on foreign ownership, operates 4 warehouse club stores with annual sales of approximately $80 million.[6] Given PriceSmart's presence, it is unclear how rigorously the prohibition of foreign ownership in the Panamanian retail sector is enforced.[7]

[1] Planet Retail, *Grocery Retailing in Panama*, 7, and EIU, *World Consumer Goods and Retail Forecast: End to Easy Money.*
[2] EIU, World Consumer Goods and Retail Forecast: *End to Easy Money.*
[3] Industry representative, telephone interview by Commission staff, May 23, 2007; CentralAmerica.com, "Panama City;" and Planet Retail, *Grocery Retailing in Panama*, 4.
[4] Planet Retail, *Grocery Retailing in Panama*, 7, 10.
[5] Ibid, 14.
[6] Ibid, 10.
[7] Sosa, hearing transcript, 88-89.

IMPACT OF TRADE FACILITATION PROVISIONS

This chapter assesses the likely impact of provisions in the U.S.-Panama Trade Promotion Agreement (TPA) related to trade facilitation. These provisions are covered in TPA chapters addressing customs administration and trade facilitation, sanitary and phytosanitary (SPS) measures, technical barriers to trade (TBT), and electronic commerce.

Summary of Assessments

The U.S.-Panama TPA provisions on trade facilitation are designed to expedite the movement of goods and the provision of services between the United States and Panama through specific improvements in customs administration, SPS measures, TBTs, and electronic commerce.

- **Customs Administration and Trade Facilitation:** The customs administration and trade facilitation provisions of the U.S.-Panama TPA would likely have a small beneficial impact on U.S. industries that export to and invest in Panama. U.S. industry would likely benefit from reduced transaction costs, because the TPA commitments to transparent and efficient procedures, greater accountability and predictability, improved customs efficiency, reciprocity and fairness, and expedited goods clearance would likely reduce paperwork and speed goods delivery. Full implementation of provisions on express shipments and advanced rulings would build on commitments to streamline goods processing and documentation and provide binding advanced rulings. Moreover, TPA provisions on customs administration and trade facilitation would likely enhance Panama's investment climate, a positive outcome for U.S. industry.

- **Sanitary and Phytosanitary Measures (SPS):** The SPS provisions negotiated within the framework of the U.S.-Panama TPA will likely have a positive impact on U.S. agricultural producers and exporters by resolving certain SPS issues affecting agricultural trade, particularly those regarding food safety inspection procedures for U.S. meat, poultry, and derived products, and regulatory requirements and documentation for processed products. These SPS provisions, many of which are contained in a separate agreement that was concluded within the context of the TPA negotiations, will likely provide expedited and improved market access for U.S. agricultural exports to Panama and reduce costs to U.S. exporters by reducing regulatory delays. The TPA agreement would establish a bilateral Standing Committee to address relevant SPS issues, which likely would allow the United States and Panama to address future bilateral SPS concerns in a more efficient and timely manner.

- **Technical Barriers to Trade (TBT):** TBT provisions of the U.S.-Panama TPA would likely benefit U.S. companies by reinforcing transparency obligations in rulemaking, increasing opportunities for direct participation on a nondiscri-minatory basis in Panama's standards development activities, establishing informal mechanisms for rapid resolution of disputes, and reinforcing WTO TBT obligations. However, the overall impact on U.S. industries or the U.S. economy based on implementation of the TPA would likely be small as the United States and Panama already generally meet the principal TBT obligations of the agreement. U.S. product sectors identified as potentially benefiting from the TPA provisions include transportation equipment, IT equipment, electrical equipment and appliances, construction materials and equipment, food products, and energy services and equipment.

- **Electronic Commerce (e-commerce):** Provisions within the U.S.-Panama TPA relating to e-commerce, such as provisions that provide for nondiscriminatory treatment of digital products transmitted electronically, would likely improve trade in electronic services between the United States and Panama. Business and industry sectors that would most likely benefit from the TPA include U.S. exporters of information technology (IT) products that facilitate e-commerce, as Panama imports most of such goods and services from the United States.

TPA Chapter 5—Customs Administration and Trade Facilitation

Assessment

The customs administration and trade facilitation provisions of the U.S.-Panama TPA likely would have a small beneficial impact on U.S. industries that export to and invest in Panama.[204] U.S. industry would likely benefit from reduced transaction costs with the implementation of the customs administration and trade facilitation provisions of the TPA,[205] as several recent studies suggest that both developed and developing countries can derive benefit from trade facilitation measures as either the exporting or the importing country.[206] The commitments to transparent and efficient procedures,[207] greater accountability and predictability, improved customs efficiency, reciprocity and fairness, and expedited goods clearance would likely reduce paperwork and speed goods delivery.[208] Although certain provisions, such as those for express shipments and advanced rulings, would be deferred as in other recently negotiated FTAs, their full implementation would build on commitments to streamline goods processing and documentation and provide binding advanced rulings.

Moreover, chapter 5 provisions likely would enhance Panama's investment climate,[209] a positive outcome for U.S. industry. A working group[210] for customs administration and trade facilitation issues would be established with a focus on the implementation of the provisions in this chapter.[211]

Summary of Provisions

Chapter 5 of the U.S.-Panama TPA is largely identical to provisions in recent FTAs concluded with Peru, Colombia, and CAFTA-DR countries.[212] The chapter would support many of the GATT goals in the areas of fees and formalities (article VIII of the GATT) and publication and administration of trade regulations (article X of the GATT) (table 4.1). The TPA would likely facilitate the goods clearance process[213] through greater use of information technology, establish procedures for resolving disputes, and improve risk management and cooperation among parties. The parties would commit to providing immediate cooperation in the areas of information exchange, technical advice and assistance for trade facilitation, and enforcement of customs rules and regulations.[214] Additionally, chapter 5 would call for the immediate implementation of articles that provide for simplified release procedures, advanced publication of Panamanian customs regulations, confidential information guidelines, review and appeal of customs matters, and penalties for customs violations. Unlike the CAFTA-DR and U.S.-Peru TPA, however, chapter 5 does not include a formal commitment to explore other means of cooperation.

The express shipments section, deferred for one year,[215] includes two liberalization measures also found in the U.S.-Peru TPA and the U.S.-Colombia TPA. Such shipments would not be limited by a maximum weight or customs value, and express shipments valued at $100[216] or less would not be assessed duties or taxes and would not require any formal entry documents, except when expressly identified by each party's laws and regulations. Like the previously noted TPAs, this agreement would require each party to adopt separate customs administration measures for express shipments. These measures would facilitate express shipment processing by allowing electronic submission of documents, prearrival processing of information, and submission of a single manifest covering all goods in an express shipment, and would minimize release documentation, where possible. Chapter 5 would require release of express shipments within 6 hours of the submission of the necessary documents, which is comparable to the release times negotiated in both the U.S.-Peru TPA and the U.S.-Colombia TPA.

Table 4.1. Selected WTO GATT Articles and U.S.-Panama TPA Commitments Related to Customs Administration

WTO, GATT Articles	U.S.-Panama TPA
Article VIII—Fees and Formalities	**Article 5.2—Release of Goods**
1. (c) *Minimize* the incidence and *complexity* of import/export formalities.	1. Shall adopt or maintain *simplified customs procedures* for the efficient release of goods (immediate).
Article X—Publication and Administration of Trade Regulations	**Article 5.1—Publication**
1. (in part) *Laws, regulations, etc. shall be published promptly* and in such a manner as to enable government and traders to become acquainted with them; trade policy agreements in force shall be published.	1. *Internet publication of laws, regulations, and administrative procedures* (2-year deferment).
2. *No measures* may be enforced to change import duties or charges or other customs administrative practices *before official publication*	2. Designate or maintain customs inquiry points and provide procedural information for inquiries via Internet (2-year deferment)..
	3. *Advance publication of regulations* gover-ning proposed customs matters and comm.-ent period (immediate).
WTO, GATT Articles	**U.S.-Panama TPA**
Article X—Publication and Administra-tion of Trade Regulations	**Article 5.5—Cooperation**
2. No measures may be enforced to change import duties or charges or other customs administrative practices *before official publication.*	1. *Advance notice* of significant modifica-tions of administrative policy likely to sub-stantially affect Agreement's operation (immediate).
Article X—Publication and Adminis-tration of Trade Regulations	**Article 5.6—Confidentiality**
1. (in part) *Prevents disclosure of confidential information.*	1. Designated *confidential information* shall be maintained as such and *will not be disclo-sed without prior permission* (immediate).
	2. Parties may decline to provide such information if confidentiality has not been maintained (immediate).
	3. Adopt or maintain procedures to protect unauthorized disclosure (immediate).
Article X—Publication and Administra-tion of Trade Regulations	**Article 5.8—Review and Appeal**
3.(b) Maintain and establish *independent tribunals to review* and correct customs administrative actions.	Importers will have access to *independent administrative review* and judicial review of determinations (immediate).

Sources: *U.S.-Panama TPA*; and WTO, "Trade Facilitation," available at
http://www.wto.org/English/tratop_e/tradfa_e/tradfa_e.htm.

An additional section in chapter 5 addresses commitments specific to the Panama Free Zone Monitoring Program. This section outlines Panama's responsibility to continue monitoring the trade, processing, and manipulation of goods in Panamanian free zones and provides procedures and measures to address U.S. concerns about the illegal transshipment of goods. Commitments would include measures for requesting and making available relevant records; conducting verification visits to a free zone; limiting data retention, collection, and reporting by shippers or exporters; and providing guarantees of confidentiality to information provided by Panama.

Staggered implementation schedules comparable to those incorporated in the U.S. FTAs with Colombia and Peru and CAFTA-DR would defer the entry into force of certain provisions. Internet access to Panamanian customs information and designation of point(s) of contact, and the requirement that importers be able to obtain binding advance rulings, would not apply to Panama until two years after the date of entry into force of the TPA. The United States already has a system in place that allows requests for advance rulings. Commitments pertaining to customs automation and the use of risk maintenance systems would be subject to a three-year deferral.

Views of Interested Parties

The Industry Trade Advisory Committee on Customs Matters and Trade Facilitation (ITAC 14) stated that the U.S.-Panama TPA would substantially meet the committee's objectives, in particular its goal for consistency with customs chapters in other agreements,[217] and would provide equity and reciprocity in the area of customs administration.[218] The committee noted that the agreement would include the adoption of many current best practices in international customs administration, such as 48-hour release of goods and advanced publication of rules and regulations. Moreover, according to the committee, the commitments to trade facilitation and capacity building, and the formation of a capacity building committee, are viewed as provisions that would lead to the simplification and harmonization of customs procedures, improved transparency and predictability of the customs process, and efficiency and fairness for express delivery service suppliers.[219]

However, the committee noted that since the customs administration chapter was concluded more than 2 years ago, its provisions would not meet the current industry standard which sets a $200 de minimis level for determining whether shipments are assessed duties or taxes and require formal entry documents. Moreover, although the TPA provides for express shipments clearance in 6 hours, the express shipment industry would prefer a clearance standard of one hour.[220]

The Advisory Committee for Trade Policy and Negotiations (ACTPN) said that chapter provisions regarding customs administration should "greatly improve customs administration in Panama." ACTPN highlighted in particular commitments on information sharing and the specificity of the TPA commitments on customs procedures.[221] The Industry Trade Advisory Committee on Services and Finance Industries (ITAC 10) said that it believes that the agreement includes important provisions that would facilitate customs clearance of express delivery shipments.[222]

TPA Chapter 6—Sanitary and Phytosanitary Measures

Assessment

The sanitary and phytosanitary (SPS) provisions negotiated within the context of the U.S.-Panama TPA likely would have a positive impact on U.S. agricultural producers and exporters. These provisions have provided the United States and Panama an opportunity to resolve certain SPS issues affecting agricultural trade, particularly those regarding food safety inspection procedures for U.S. meat, poultry, and derived products and regulatory requirements and documentation for processed products.[223] Under the United States-Panama Agreement Regarding Certain Sanitary and Phytosanitary Measures and Technical Standards Affecting Trade in Agricultural Products (U.S.-Panama SPS Agreement),[224] a separate bilateral agreement negotiated within the framework of the TPA, Panama agreed to recognize the equivalence of the U.S. meat inspection system for meat, poultry, and their derived products and the equivalency of the U.S. food regulatory system for processed products, including dairy products. Under the U.S.-Panama SPS Agreement, Panama also recognized that measures that the United States has implemented in regard to bovine spongiform encephalopathy (BSE) for beef and avian influenza and Newcastle disease for poultry are in accordance with international standards and agreed to import U.S. beef and beef products and poultry and poultry products from all 50 U.S. states. In addition, the U.S.-Panama SPS Agreement contains language whereby Panama will streamline the documentation requirements for U.S. agricultural exports to that country. These SPS provisions will provide expedited and improved market access for U.S. agricultural exports to Panama and likely will reduce costs to U.S. exporters by reducing regulatory delays. The establishment of a bilateral Standing Committee[225] to address relevant SPS issues—as provided under the TPA—would allow the United States and Panama to address future bilateral SPS concerns in a more efficient and timely manner.

Summary of Provisions

This chapter covers the protection of human, animal, or plant life or health in the parties' territories, insofar as they directly or indirectly affect trade between the parties, and the enhancement of the WTO Agreement on the Application of Sanitary and Phytosanitary Measures (WTO SPS Agreement).[226] The United States and Panama would agree to establish a Standing Committee on Sanitary and Phytosanitary Matters to coordinate administration of the chapter (article 6.3). The Standing Committee would provide a forum to help each party implement the U.S.-Panama SPS Agreement, enhance mutual understanding of each government's SPS measures, resolve future bilateral SPS matters, coordinate technical assistance programs, and consult on issues and positions in the WTO, various Codex Committees,[227] and other fora. The chapter specifies that any SPS issue that requires formal dispute resolution would be resolved through the formal process established under the WTO SPS Agreement.

Under the United States-Panama SPS Agreement, Panama agreed by February 28, 2007, (1) to recognize the U.S. food safety inspection system for meat, poultry, and their derived products as equivalent to its own and not require approval of individual U.S. establishments by Panamanian authorities;[228] (2) to recognize that the U.S. food safety regulatory system for all processed products, including dairy products, is equivalent to Panama's regulatory system for those products and not require approval of individual U.S. establishments by Panamanian authorities, or certification of individual shipments; (3) to eliminate product registration requirements for products accompanied by an export certificate issued by a U.S. authority and issue such registration within one working day of receiving basic product information for other agricultural products subject to such registration; (4) to recognize that the United States has taken measures with regard to BSE consistent with the World Organization for Animal Health (OIE) and permit importation of all beef and beef products[229] from the United States and all pet food containing animal origin ingredients;[230] (5) to recognize that the United States has taken measures to meet the guidelines set by the OIE on avian influenza and Newcastle disease and permit imports of U.S. poultry and poultry products from all U.S. states; (6) to recognize the U.S. grading system for U.S. beef cuts and allow imports from the United States to be labeled using U.S. nomenclature; and (7) to notify U.S. authorities within 24 hours when a Panamanian authority detains a U.S. shipment due to a suspected SPS concern.

Under the United States-Panama Agreement on Cooperation in Agricultural Trade, a separate bilateral agreement negotiated within the framework of the TPA, the United States and Panama agreed to undertake technical and scientific research to enhance bilateral trade in poultry and pork products, and horticultural products. Such technical and scientific research also would assist Panama in achieving designation of "Mediterranean Fruit Fly Free Areas."

Views of Interested Parties

Several groups indicate that the SPS provisions negotiated as part of the U.S.-Panama TPA would have a favorable effect on the U.S. agriculture sector. With regard to SPS measures, the Agricultural Policy Advisory Committee (APAC) noted that by requiring Panama to bring its SPS regulations into conformity with international standards, the U.S.-Panama SPS Agreement will allow U.S. exports of beef and chicken to resume after being blocked for several years.[231] The Animal and Animal Products Agricultural Trade Advisory Committee (ATAC) noted that Panama's recognition of the U.S. food safety inspection system for meat and poultry will remove a significant nontariff barrier and said that it would greatly facilitate meat and poultry exports to Panama.[232] In addition, the Animal and Animal Products ATAC stated that it supports the SPS provisions whereby Panama will provide access for all U.S. beef and beef products and poultry and poultry products consistent with international standards.[233] The ATAC for Trade in Processed Foods stated that the SPS provisions will streamline import documentation requirements and thus will significantly expedite access for U.S. food exports.[234] This ATAC also said that the U.S.-Panama SPS Agreement is farreaching in nature as it provides access for U.S. beef and poultry and their derived products, including pet foods, consistent with international standards.[235] The National Pork Producers Council (NPPC) in its submission to the Commission, stated that the U.S.-Panama TPA process has resolved significant sanitary and technical issues through Panama's recognition of the U.S. meat inspection system. According to the NPPC, the SPS provisions ensure that U.S. pork producers will benefit from the Panama TPA without being blocked by unnecessary SPS barriers.[236]

TPA Chapter 7– Technical Barriers to Trade

Assessment

The TBT provisions of the U.S.-Panama TPA likely would benefit U.S. firms investing in and exporting to Panama. However, the overall impact on U.S. industries or the U.S. economy based on U.S. implementation of the TPA would likely be small because, in general, the United States and Panama already meet the principal TBT obligations of the agreement. Among other things, and much like the provisions included in the U.S.-Colombia TPA, U.S.-Panama TBT provisions would benefit U.S. companies by reinforcing transparency obligations in rulemaking, increasing opportunities for direct participation on a nondiscriminatory basis in Panama's standards development activities, establishing informal mechanisms for rapid resolution of disputes, and reinforcing WTO TBT obligations. U.S. product sectors identified as potentially benefitting from these provisions include transportation equipment, IT equipment, electrical equipment and appliances, construction materials and equipment, food products, and energy services and equipment.[237]

Summary of Provisions

Chapter 7 of the U.S.-Panama TPA would require both parties to intensify efforts to improve transparency, enhance bilateral cooperation on standards-related issues,[238] increase mutual acceptance of each other's regulations and procedures, and reduce or eliminate unnecessary technical trade barriers.[239] As such, the chapter would largely affirm and improve on the implementation of the WTO TBT agreement rather than substantively expanding it.[240] To improve transparency, each party would agree to allow persons from the other party to participate in the development of its standards, technical regulations, and conformity assessment procedures. Further, each party would agree to transmit proposals for new technical regulations and conformity assessment procedures electronically to the other party at the same time that they are transmitted to the WTO pursuant to the TBT agreement; to allow the other party at least 60 days to review and comment on such proposals; and to publish or otherwise make available to the public its responses to significant comments no later than the date it publishes the final technical regulation or conformity assessment procedure. The chapter would encourage each party to consider a broad range of alternatives for accepting the results of the other party's conformity assessment procedures and technical regulations, and to provide an explanation when this is not possible. Finally, the chapter would establish a Committee on Technical Barriers to Trade, comprising representatives of each party, to monitor the implementation and administration of the chapter and address any issues arising from the other party's standards, technical regulations, or conformity assessment procedures.

Views of Interested Parties

U.S. industry representatives have suggested that there is little evidence of certification, testing, labeling, or other standards-related practices or issues that currently serve as unreasonable or unnecessary technical barriers to trade in Panama.[241] U.S. industry and government officials indicated that Panama's application of its technical regulations and conformity assessment procedures for nonagricultural goods conform with WTO guidelines.[242] Panama reportedly has a transparent standards development process[243] and permits the participation of the United States and other foreign countries[244] and individuals in its standards development activities.[245] Although importers still must register certain products with the Ministry of Commerce and Industry before marketing them in Panama, in general, that country has eliminated formerly time-consuming and expensive product registration procedures for most products.[246] Remaining procedures reportedly are easy to understand and are applied evenly to domestic and imported products.[247] Labeling and testing requirements for imports are limited primarily to food products.[248] Products that comply with U.S. labeling and marking requirements are generally accepted for sale in Panama.[249]

The Industry Trade Advisory Committee on Standards and Technical Barriers to Trade (ITAC 16), representing a wide range of U.S. industries, expressed the view that the TBT chapter of the TPA would adequately address the standards and technical trade barrier issues advanced at the beginning of the negotiations.[250] In general, U.S. industry representatives said that the TBT provisions of the TPA would be conducive to increased trade and investment with Panama, as they would foster greater transparency and bilateral coordination.[251] These representatives also asserted that the TPA transparency obligations would enhance U.S. companies' opportunities to participate in Panama's standards development activities and to have their views taken into account on proposals for new Panamanian rules on technical regulations and conformity assessment.[252] However, some industry representatives indicated that they would have preferred a three-year implementation period for transparency obligations, rather than the five-year implementation period included in the TPA, to serve as a benchmark for future agreements.[253]

TPA Chapter 14 - Electronic Commerce

Assessment

Provisions in the U.S.-Panama TPA relating to electronic commerce (e-commerce) likely would improve trade in electronic products between the two countries. For example, TPA provisions that provide for nondiscriminatory treatment of digital products transmitted electronically could promote e-commerce trade by limiting the transaction costs associated with electronically traded goods and services. Business and industry sectors that would most likely benefit from the TPA's e-commerce provisions include U.S. exporters of IT products that facilitate e-commerce—notably software, personal computers, and networking equipment—as Panama imports most of such goods and services from the United States. However, market conditions in Panama relating to intellectual property rights (IPR) and piracy concerns could limit opportunities for cross-border e-commerce trade and investment. Further, a low level of personal computer ownership and limited Internet access could limit the growth of e-commerce in Panama's consumer markets. Consequently, Panama's business-to-business e-commerce market likely will offer U.S. companies the greatest opportunities for export sales in the near future.

Summary of Provisions

The parties would commit to nondiscriminatory treatment of digital products transmitted electronically, agree not to impose customs duties, fees, or other charges on such products, and agree to cooperate in numerous technical, policy, and legislative areas related to e-commerce.[254] Provisions also recognize the importance of avoiding economic, regulatory, and technical barriers to e-commerce and the applicability of WTO rules to e-commerce. Additional provisions stipulate that the customs value of an imported carrier medium that includes a digital product would be determined by the cost of the medium alone, without regard to the value of the digital products stored on the carrier medium.[255] Moreover, a party would not be able to accord less favorable treatment to certain digital products than it accords to other like products because they were created, stored, transmitted, published, or first made commercially available outside its territory or because of the nationality of the author, performer, producer, developer, or distributor of such digital products. Provisions emphasize cooperation between the parties to promote the development of e-commerce. Such cooperation could entail either encouraging the private sector to establish a system of self-regulation or sharing of information on laws, regulations, and other practices and procedures that promote such activity. The agreement also would set forth procedures for resolving disputes regarding trademarks used in Internet domain names.[256]

Views of Interested Parties

U.S. industry representatives indicated that they support the establishment of guarantees of nondiscrimination, instituting a binding prohibition on customs duties on products delivered electronically, and creating a favorable environment for the development of global e-commerce as would be provided under the U.S.-Panama TPA. Further, industry representatives said that fostering e-commerce opportunities and capabilities would eventually lower the transaction costs and opportunity costs of trading with Panama, thereby increasing the ability of small businesses in the United States to participate in the Panamanian market.[257] Industry representatives generally supported measures that would promote the most liberal treatment of e-commerce possible, as well as a moratorium on taxes, duties, and other fees pertaining to e-commerce, the Internet, or electronic transmissions of software or other digital products.[258] Industry representatives also said that they support the measures Panama has proposed or initiated as part of the TPA that would likely simplify and encourage the use of e-commerce, such as increased protection of intellectual property rights, which leads to a stronger legal infrastructure for e-commerce and improved market conditions for the distribution and transmission of materials over the Internet.[259] Other practices that industry representatives considered particularly useful to promoting the growth of the domestic Panamanian e-commerce market include fostering consumer confidence in e-commerce and providing greater data privacy protection.[260]

IMPACT OF REGULATORY AND OTHER PROVISIONS

This chapter assesses the likely impact of the provisions in the U.S.-Panama Trade Promotion Agreement (TPA) that are included in the eight TPA chapters covering trade remedies, government procurement, investment, intellectual property rights, labor, environment, transparency and dispute settlement. Each TPA chapter discussion includes an assessment, summary of TPA provisions, and views of interested parties.

Summary of Assessments

Although the impact is difficult to quantify, certain TPA regulatory-related provisions would likely improve the regulatory climate for bilateral trade and investment, particularly with regard to government procurement, investment, intellectual property rights, and transparency.

- **Trade Remedies:** The trade remedy provisions in the U.S.-Panama TPA are similar to provisions in other TPAs that the United States has implemented with other parties and would not likely have a notable impact on U.S. industries or the U.S. economy.

- **Government Procurement:** U.S. goods and services providers would likely benefit from provisions on government procurement in the U.S.-Panama TPA, primarily as a result of improvements in regulatory transparency and market access. The agreement would provide significant opportunities for U.S. exporters to participate in the planned $5.25 billion expansion of the Panama Canal.

- **Investment:** Investment provisions of the U.S.-Panama TPA would likely contribute to a more secure and stable investment environment for U.S. investors in Panama. The TPA incorporates important investor protections, particularly the investor-state dispute settlement mechanism. Although these were included in Panama's existing bilateral investment treaty (BIT) with the United States, the TPA would extend coverage to a significant number of industry sectors which were excluded from the BIT. One particular area of new opportunity for U.S. investors is in Panama's retail sector, where investment would be permitted beginning in 2010, provided that the initial investment is valued at a minimum of $3 million.

- **Intellectual Property Rights:** The intellectual property rights (IPR) provisions of the U.S.-Panama TPA likely would benefit U.S.-based industries that rely on IPR protection and enforcement, although the impact likely would not be substantial given Panama's market size. The standards in the TPA, if fully implemented and enforced, may reduce IPR infringement in Panama. Full implementation and enforcement of the IPR chapter, and particularly the digital technology protection provisions, likely would benefit the U.S. motion picture, sound recording, business software, entertainment software, and book publishing industries. U.S. industries that may benefit from patent and confidential data protections include pharmaceuticals and agricultural chemicals. A broad range of U.S. industries may benefit from the strengthened trademark and enforcement provisions of the TPA.

- **Labor and Environment:** The labor and environment provisions contained in the proposed U.S.-Panama TPA text would likely have little impact on the U.S. or Panamanian labor markets or on U.S.-Panama trade because of the chapters' focus on the enforcement of existing regulations.

- **Transparency:** Transparency-related provisions of the TPA create the potential to foster U.S.-Panama trade and investment, as such provisions offer some significant improvements over the policies and practices that they are intended to replace. The TPA contains provisions that would provide the public with improved access and information in the settlement of trade dispute cases, improved transparency in customs operations, and more open and public processes for customs rulings and administration.

TPA Chapter 8 - Trade Remedies

Assessment

The trade remedy provisions in the U.S.-Panama TPA are similar to provisions in TPAs that the United States has implemented with other parties and would not likely have a notable impact on U.S. industries or the U.S. economy. Each party would retain all rights and obligations of article XIX of GATT 1994, the WTO Agreement on Safeguards, and the WTO agreements on antidumping and countervailing measures and would gain no additional rights or obligations under the TPA.

Summary of Provisions

Section A of Chapter 8 of the TPA contains a bilateral safeguard provision similar to the bilateral safeguard provisions included in other U.S. free trade agreements. It would allow a party to increase a rate of duty or suspend further reductions in the duty rate if its designated competent authority finds, as a result of the reduction or elimination of a duty under the agreement, that imports of a particular good from the other party are in such increased quantities as to be a substantial cause of serious injury, or the threat of serious injury, to the domestic industry producing a like or directly competitive good. No duty could be increased to an amount that exceeds the lesser of the current MFN rate of duty or the rate in effect immediately before entry into force of the agreement. The duration of any measure could not exceed 4 years. Measures could be applied only during the transition period of the agreement and only once against a particular good. A party applying such measure would be obligated to provide mutually agreed trade liberalizing compensation to the other party; if the parties are unable to agree on compensation, the other party could suspend the application of substantially equivalent concessions. Section A states that the parties would retain their rights and obligations under article XIX of the GATT 1994 and the WTO Safeguards Agreement.

However, section A states that a party applying a (global) safeguard measure under the WTO Safeguards Agreement could exclude imports of a particular good from the other party if such imports are not a substantial cause of serious injury or threat thereof.

Section B of Chapter 8 of the TPA addresses antidumping and countervailing duties. It states that the United States would continue to treat Panama as a "beneficiary country" for purposes of 19 U.S.C. 1677(7)(G)(ii)(III) and 1677(7)(H) and any successor provisions (i.e., Panama, as a country designated as a beneficiary country under the CBERA, would continue to be exempt from the cumulation provisions of the U.S. antidumping and countervailing duty laws). Section B states that, with the exception of this provision, no provision in the agreement could be construed as imposing any rights or obligations on the parties with respect to antidumping or countervailing duty measures.

Views of Interested Parties

Few of the trade advisory committee reports addressed the trade remedy chapter of the TPA. The Labor Advisory Committee (LAC) said that the safeguard provisions in the U.S.-Panama TPA "offer no more protection than the limited safeguard mechanism in NAFTA," and are unacceptable. The LAC stated that the "safeguard provisions invite producers to circumvent the intended beneficiaries of the trade agreement and fail to adequately protect workers from the import surges that may result."[261] The Industry Trade Advisory Committee on Distribution Services (ITAC 5) stated in its report that it would favor the exemption of U.S. bilateral trade agreement partner countries from the antidumping law. The committee stated that, since a trade agreement precludes the ability of a country to maintain a sanctuary market, the major argument underpinning the application of antidumping remedies ceases to exist.[262]

The Industry Trade Advisory Committee on Steel (ITAC 12) stated that the safeguard provisions mirror those in other U.S. FTAs – including those with Singapore, Chile, Australia, Central America and the Dominican Republic, Bahrain, Oman, Peru, and Colombia – and the committee did not cite any objections to these provisions.[263]

TPA Chapter 9 - Government Procurement

Assessment

U.S. goods and services providers would likely benefit from provisions on government procurement in the U.S.-Panama TPA, primarily as a result of improvements in regulatory transparency and market access (box 5.1). The agreement would provide opportunities for U.S. exporters to participate in the planned $5.25 billion expansion of the Panama Canal. This expansion is due to begin in 2008 and is expected to be completed in 2014.[264]

BOX 5.1 GOVERNMENT PROCUREMENT LAW IN PANAMA

In 1995, the Government of Panama passed Law 56 regulating government procurement. The law is managed by the Ministry of Economy and Finance and provides for a transparent bidding process for government contacts but allows for exceptions, such as for procurements relating to national defense.[1]

Issued in 1996, Executive decree number 18 regulates Act 56 and executive decree number 19 regulates the "Transparency Principle."[2]

In 2006, Panama's government passed Law 22. This Law streamlines and modernizes Panama's contracting system by establishing an internet-based procurement system and requiring publication of all proposed government purchases. The Law also created an administrative court to handle all public contracting disputes, the rulings of which are subject to review by the Panamanian Supreme Court.[3]

[1] USTR, *National Trade Estimate Report on Foreign Trade Barriers*, 2006, 503.
[2] *National Legislation, Regulations and Procedures Regarding Government Procurement in the Americas, Free Trade Area of the Americas Working Group on Government Procurement*, found at http://www.wto.org, retrieved May 21, 2007.
[3] USTR, *National Trade Estimate Report on Foreign Trade Barriers*, 2007, 452-53.

Panama is an observer but not a signatory to the WTO Government Procurement Agreement[265]. The TPA seeks to establish clear procedures, ensure greater predictability in the government procurement process, and provide U.S. suppliers with nondiscriminatory rights to bid contracts to supply goods and services to numerous Panamanian central and subcentral (equivalent to U.S. State level) government entities.[266] The text of the government procurement chapter generally mirrors the government procurement chapters of the U.S.–Colombia and U.S.-Peru TPAs[267]; however, the annex contains unique provisions, such as those that address the Panama Canal Authority.

The Panamanian government is generally viewed as handling bids in a transparent manner, although occasionally U.S. companies have indicated that certain procedures have not been followed.[268]

However, considering the small size of Panama's economy and market relative to the United States,[269] any economic effects resulting from increased access to the Panamanian market for government purchases of goods and services, including purchases associated with the canal expansion project, would likely be minimal.[270]

Summary of Provisions

Chapter 9 of the U.S.–Panama TPA would apply to covered government procurement of goods and services by any contractual means where the value concerned exceeds thresholds set out in an annex to the chapter. The thresholds would be adjusted every two years, with the first adjustment taking place on January 1, 2008, according to a formula set out in the annex. The chapter includes definitions, general principles such as national treatment and nondiscrimination, criteria on the rules of origin used in the normal course of trade, and restrictions on the use of offsets. The chapter's provisions would set forth advanced notice requirements for intended procurements, time frames for the tendering process, documentation requirements, rules on the declaration of technical specifications, conditions for participation, criteria for awarding contracts, requirements concerning the publication of information on selected tenders, and a mechanism for the review of supplier challenges. The chapter would set forth procedures and conditions pertaining to selective tendering and limited tendering. TPA Chapter 9 would further provide for the establishment or designation of at least one impartial administrative or judicial authority to receive and review supplier challenges.

The annex to chapter 9 of the TPA lists covered entities, covered purchases, and service exclusions and establishes the threshold amounts for purchases of goods and services by covered entities. The annex further divides covered entities into four categories: the central government, the subcentral government, other government entities, and the Panama Canal Authority. Each category has separate threshold procurement values and specific provisions (table 5.1). These threshold values are identical to those established in the U.S.-Colombia and U.S.-Peru TPAs with the exception of the value of goods and services purchases by the central government. In the U.S.-Colombia TPA the threshold value for such purchases was lower ($64,786) than the threshold value that would be established by the U.S.-Panama TPA.

In general, most goods and services would be covered by the agreement; however, both the United States and Panama would exclude certain purchases and service sectors. For example, at the central government level, Panama would exclude certain procurements of the Ministries of Agriculture, Education, Government and Justice, the President, Health, and the Public and procurements for the issuance of currency, coinage, tax, or postage stamps. The U.S. exclusions would include certain procurements by the Departments of Agriculture, Commerce, Defense, Energy, Homeland Security, Transportation, and the General Services Administration. Subcentral provisions would apply to all of Panama's nine provinces (analogous to U.S. states) and its three provincial-level indigenous regions. With regard to the United States, subcentral provisions would apply only to the states of Arkansas, Colorado, Florida, Illinois, Mississippi, New York, Texas, and Utah, as well as to Puerto Rico.[271]

Table 5.1. Proposed Procurement Value Thresholds, U.S. Dollars

Level of government	Goods and services	Construction services
Central	193,000	7,407,000
Subcentral	526,000	7,407,000
Other entities:		
List A	250,000	7,407,000
List B	593,000	7,407,000
Panama Canal Authority	593,000	12,000,000[a]

[a] The Panama Canal Authority procurement value threshold for construction services will be $12,000,000 for 12 years after entry into force of the Agreement, and then will be set at $10,300,000. Draft Annex 9.1, Section D(b).

The TPA includes special provisions for government procurement by the independently operated Panama Canal Authority.[272] The Panama Canal Authority(Authority) would be permitted to allow set-asides for the procurement of goods, services, and construction services for Panamanian nationals or suppliers owned and controlled by Panamanian nationals during the first 12 years of the agreement. These set-asides could only be applied when the Authority's total procurement for the year exceeds $200 million and the total value of such goods and services set-asides could not exceed 10 percent of the total value of the authority's procurement contracts for goods and services. In addition, Panama could maintain the canal authority dispute settlement system under the provisions of the TPA.[273]

Section H of the annex includes a micro, small, and medium enterprise reservation for Panama, which would exempt businesses that have 100 or fewer employees and total annual sales of no more than $2,500,000. The section further provides that the government procurement chapter would not apply to set-asides on behalf of small or minority businesses in the United States. The U.S. reservation has no dollar limitation.

As a result of a bipartisan agreement between USTR and the U.S. Congress, the government procurement provisions of the U.S.-Panama TPA were modified to include language that strengthens labor standards in government procurement. A statement was added to article 9.7, "Technical Specifications," that the agreement would not preclude a procuring entity from preparing, adopting, or applying technical specifications to require a supplier to comply with generally applicable laws regarding fundamental principles and rights at work and acceptable conditions of work with respect to minimum wages, hours of work, and occupational safety and health. Congress also proposed additional language on environmental standards although it was not added to the final agreement. However, the draft language of article 9.7 pertaining to the conservation of natural resources was retained in the final text.

Views of Interested Parties

In their reports on the draft text of the U.S.–Panama TPA, the trade advisory committees indicated general support for the government procurement chapter, but noted that certain, and in some cases strong, reservations remain. At the Commission's hearing on this investigation, witnesses speaking on behalf of Panamanian and U.S. business groups indicated that they support the TPA's treatment of government procurement.

Interested parties that indicated that they wholly support the agreement include the Advisory Committee for Trade Policy and Negotiation (ACTPN), the American Chamber of Commerce of Panama (AMCHAM), the Chamber of Commerce of Panama, the Industry Trade Advisory Committee for Information and Communication Technologies, Services, and Electronic Commerce (ITAC 8), and the Industry Trade Advisory Committee for Steel (ITAC 12).

ACTPN stated that the agreement's government procurement provisions would lead to increased U.S. access to the Panamanian market, particularly the sizable purchases of the Panama Canal Authority. The ACTPN stated that it supports the TPA's broad coverage of Panamanian government purchasing agencies,[274] and a representative of AMCHAM stated that the agreement enhances government transparency and accountability. Both ACTPN and the AMCHAM representative expressed support for provisions which criminalize bribery in government procurement.[275] A representative for the Chamber of Commerce, Industry and Agriculture of Panama expressed support for, and promotion of, the TPA's actions and regulations aimed at transparency and government procurement.[276] ITAC 8 expressed support for the TPA as a whole and the government procurement provisions that relate to digital products in particular.[277] Finally, ITAC 12 stated that the government procurement provisions in the TPA mirror language in previously negotiated FTAs reviewed by the committee and, therefore, appear acceptable.[278]

Trade advisory groups that expressed qualified support for the agreement included the Intergovernmental Policy Advisory Committee (IGPAC), the Industry Trade Advisory Committee on Services and Finance Industries (ITAC 10), the Labor Advisory Committee for Trade Negotiations and Trade Policy (LAC), and the Industry Trade Advisory Committee on Non-Ferrous Metals and Building Materials (ITAC 9).

IGPAC said that it generally supports the objectives of the agreement but expressed concern that the "reciprocity policy,"[279] whereby reciprocal market access would be granted at the subcentral level to businesses located in states that agree to the procurement provisions of the TPA, could compromise the possible benefits to states.[280] In its report, IGPAC also expressed concern about the public's increasingly negative perception of trade liberalization and stated that the public should be educated by federal agencies on the benefits to U.S. firms of such liberalization.[281] The IGPAC report reiterated the comments and feedback concerning the reciprocity agreement that the committee provided to the USTR in 2004, and asked that further negotiations take those comments into account. IGPAC also noted that certain of the TPA's government procurement provisions differ from such provisions in other FTAs and the WTO government procurement agreement, which could cause confusion and difficulties in implementation.

ITAC 10 also provided mixed support for the government procurement chapter of the TPA. ITAC 10 said that the binding procurement thresholds for the Panama Canal Authority are too high.[282] Under current practice, the Panama Canal Authority awards contracts to U.S. suppliers for canal procurements below the binding thresholds in the agreement, and ITAC 10 indicated that it would like this practice to continue.[283] ITAC 10 urged the USTR to encourage the Government of Panama to exercise its option and undertake procurements in the canal zone at levels below the agreement's bound thresholds.[284] Finally, the members of ITAC 10 that represent architectural, engineering, and construction firms expressed concern that the language contained in annex 9.1 section D of the agreement could result "in a significant deterioration in the position that U.S. suppliers of goods and services currently enjoy (under the U.S. Army Corps of Engineers rules), if the Panama Canal Authority changes its current procurement practice of awarding contracts to U.S. architectural and engineering firms below the thresholds set out in the Agreement."[285] In view of the relatively high threshold levels of $593,000 for goods and services and $12 million for construction services,[286] these ITAC 10 members express concern that U.S. suppliers could lose opportunities to compete for smaller value projects under the agreement's terms.[287]

The report submitted by ITAC 9 listed several concerns regarding the TPA. First, the report stated that most small-and medium-sized contracts for the Panama Canal Zone expansion project currently are being reserved for Panamanian contractors and suppliers. The ITAC 9 report characterized this reservation as a trade barrier and called for its removal.[288] Second, the report expressed concern that the threshold amounts for procurement contracts would impose sharp limits on U.S. access to such contracts. Third, the report expressed significant reservations with respect to the strength of TPA language that would preclude the Panama Canal Authority from dividing large contracts into smaller contracts in order to exclude U.S. participation.[289] The report submitted by the LAC stated that the TPA's proposed government procurement rules would restrict the United States' ability to address public policy aims through federal procurement policies.[290]

BOX 5.2 FOREIGN INVESTMENT IN PANAMA

The United States is the world's largest destination for FDI, with 2005 inbound direct investment stock of $1.6 trillion, representing 16 percent of total worldwide inbound investment stock. Inbound FDI accounts for 13 percent of the U.S. GDP. Panama, with a much smaller economy, registered $9.9 billion in inbound direct investment stock in 2005, equal to 64.8 percent of Panama's GDP.[1]

United States and Panama: Investment Data, 2005

	Panama	United States
Inbound investment stock (*million dollars*)	9,873	1,625,749
Inbound stock as percentage of GDP (*percent*)	64.8	13.0
Outbound investment stock (*million dollars*)	12,891	2,051,284
Outbound stock as percentage of GDP	84.6	16.4
Investment inflows (*million dollars*)	677	99,443
Bilateral outbound investment stock (*million dollars*)	11,470	5,162

Sources: Data on total investment stock and investment inflows: UNCTAD, *World Investment Report 2006.* Data on U.S. bilateral investment: USDOC, BEA, Survey of Current Business, September 2006.

Note: Bilateral outbound investment stock reflects U.S. Government statistics for U.S. outbound direct investment position in Panama on a historical-cost basis, and U.S. inbound direct investment position from Panama on a historical-cost basis.

Panama is generally open to foreign investment. Companies must secure a commercial license from the Ministry of Commerce and Industry to do business with Panama, but there is no indication that this is a burdensome process. There are no regulations prohibiting the acquisition of Panamanian companies by foreign firms. The United States is the largest source of FDI in Panama, followed by the United Kingdom and Mexico. Transport, tourism, and utilities are the sectors with the highest levels of foreign investment.[2] As of 2007, there were at least 96 U.S.-based companies operating in Panama, including globally recognized brands from a variety of industries. The largest in terms of global annual revenue were Citigroup, AIG, and Bank of America; the largest by global employment were Manpower, McDonalds, and Citigroup.[3] Other prominent U.S.-owned firms included mining firm Minnesota Mining, agriculture firm Chiquita Brands

International, consulting firms Deloitte Touche, Booz Allen Hamilton, and Ernst & Young, and hotel companies Starwood and Marriott International.[4]

[1] UNCTAD, *World Investment Report 2006,* annex tables B.2 and B.3.

[2] EIU, "Country Commerce Panama – Main report: November 17, 2006," http://www.eiu.com, accessed May 1, 2007.

[3] Annual revenue and employment data are not available specifically for the Panamanian operations of these firms.

[4] Uniworld, "American Firms Operating in Foreign Countries," http://www.uniworldbpcom, accessed May 1, 2007.

At the Commission's hearing, witnesses for business and industry groups expressed general support for the government procurement provisions of the proposed agreement, but said that the impact of such provisions would likely be small. The U.S. Chamber of Commerce noted that the size of Panamanian government procurement has decreased as Panama has steadily privatized industries. According to the Chamber, the TPA would not likely affect transparency in Panamanian government purchasing because such purchases are already transparent.[291] A representative of the U.S. Panama Business Council said that while the canal expansion will create opportunities for U.S. businesses,[292] the expansion will be complete by 2014 and U.S. businesses need to position themselves to benefit from government procurement well beyond that date.[293]

TPA Chapter 10 – Investment

Assessment

The investment provisions of the U.S.-Panama TPA would likely contribute to a more secure and stable investment environment for U.S. investors in Panama (box 5.2). The TPA incorporates important investor protections, particularly the investor-state dispute settlement mechanism. Although these were included in Panama's existing bilateral investment treaty (BIT) with the United States, the new TPA would extend coverage to a significant number of industry sectors which were excluded from the BIT.[294] The BIT has been suspended in favor of the new TPA; however, the provisions of the BIT which include coverage of investment agreements concluded prior to the implementation of the TPA[295] have been retained. One particular area of new opportunity for U.S. investors is in the Panamanian retail sector, where investment would be permitted beginning in 2010, provided that the initial investment is valued at a minimum of $3 million.

Summary of Provisions

The two principal objectives of the TPA investment chapter are to create a welcoming environment for investors from each party by outlining the rights of investors and the rules that govern new cross-border investment and to provide a clear outline of the investor-state dispute settlement process.[296] Section A of the chapter outlines the rules governing new investments and sets forth the types of investments to which these rules apply.[297] Specifically, the TPA would require each party to give national and MFN treatment to investors and covered investments of the other party. The treatment of investors under the TPA would be required to comply with customary international law. Other provisions include:

- Expropriation could occur only for a public purpose; it would need to be nondiscriminatory and accompanied by payment of prompt, adequate, and effective compensation in accordance with due process of law.

- All financial transfers relating to covered investments, including, but not limited to, contributions to capital, payment of interest, and payments under contracts, could cover the full value of the investment and could be made freely and without delay.
- Neither party would be permitted to impose performance requirements as a condition of investment.[298]
- Neither party could require that senior management or boards of directors be of any particular nationality.

The benefits of this chapter could only be denied in limited, delineated instances, as outlined in the TPA annexes. This section of the chapter also deals with nonconforming measures, as well as special formalities and information requirements.

Section B of this chapter provides for consultation and the negotiation of disputes and provides detailed information and procedures on the investor-state dispute settlement process, including submission of claims to arbitration, selection of arbitrators, conduct of the arbitration, transparency of the arbitral proceedings, governing law, and awards of monetary damages (not including punitive damages) or restitution. Under the terms of the provisions of section B, each party would consent to claims being submitted according to the process outlined in the TPA. The awards made by any arbitration tribunal would have binding force only between the disputants and with regard to the particular case. Section C of the chapter contains definitions of terms and relevant conventions for use in the resolution of investment disputes. An annex defines "customary international law" for purposes of the chapter, while another deals with expropriation (direct and indirect) in some detail. To be considered expropriation, a party's action or series of actions would need to interfere "with a tangible or intangible property right or property interest in an investment." Other annexes deal with the service of documents in such matters and the possible establishment of an appellate body.

Annex 10-C would require a U.S. investor to choose to pursue an investment claim either in the Panamanian court system or under the TPA investor-state dispute settlement process. Annex 10-F would safeguard the right of the Government of Panama to appoint the members of the Panama Canal Authority, which has the exclusive responsibility for the administration of the Panama Canal and related activities. In addition, disputes related to the Panama Canal could not be submitted to investor-state arbitration without first being submitted to the Panama Canal Authority for a period of not less than three months. After the three-month period, U.S. investors would not be required to wait for a ruling by the Panama Canal Authority before submitting the dispute to the investor-state process.

Nonconforming Measures Related to Investment

Provisions for the treatment of existing or future measures that are inconsistent with the agreement's investment disciplines are included in annexes I, II, and III of the TPA. Annex I lists exemptions for existing laws or regulations, maintained at the central or regional government level, that violate the provisions of the agreement. Nonconforming measures at the local government level would be exempted without requiring any notation in an annex. Annex II lists reservations to ensure that a party maintains flexibility to impose future measures that may be inconsistent with TPA disciplines. The actual content of the reservations in annexes I and II varies widely. Some reservations are horizontal in nature, meaning that they address general policy provisions that affect all investment, whereas others would only apply to specific industry segments. Annex III lists nonconforming measures specific to financial services that would apply to both existing and potential laws and regulations.

Panama has not listed any investment-related horizontal reservations under annex I. There are two horizontal reservations listed by Panama under annex II. The first measure would accord differential treatment to countries that have signed international agreements with Panama prior to the entry into force of the U.S.-Panama TPA, specifically including agreements involving aviation, fisheries, or maritime matters. The second would permit Panama to restrict the transfer of a state interest in a state-owned company to Panamanian nationals. However, this restriction would apply only to the initial privatization of a stateowned company, as outlined in a side letter attached to the TPA. An exception would apply to public utilities, which would be covered by a sector-specific non-conforming measure in Panama's annex I.

Horizontal reservations listed by the United States under annex I address the programs of the Overseas Private Investment Corporation and the registration of public offerings of securities, as well as existing nonconforming measures at the state level. Under annex II, the only horizontal reservation listed by the United States that would apply to investment mirrors the reservation taken by Panama, which would accord differential treatment to countries under international agreements that were signed prior to the U.S.-Panama TPA.

The specific sectors for which investment-related reservations are listed in annexes I and II are presented in table 5.2.[299] The inclusion of a sector in an annex does not necessarily exempt the entire sector from coverage under the investment disciplines of the TPA. The exception related to the retail sector is of particular note. Under Panama's annex I, ownership of a retail business would primarily be restricted to Panamanian nationals, with the exception of singlebrand retail firms[300] and service firms that only sell products associated with the sale of services. However, according to a side letter attached to the TPA, U.S.-owned retail firms would be permitted to invest in Panama, provided that they have a minimum investment of $3 million, beginning no later than December 31, 2010. This provision would involve a change to Panama's constitution.[301]

Table 5.2. U.S.-Panama TPA: Industry Sectors Subject to Nonconforming Measures Related to Investment

Panama		United States	
Current measures (Annex I)	Potential measures (Annex II)	Current measures (Annex I)	Potential measures (Annex II)
Retail sales	Social services	Communications: Radio	Minority affairs
Real estate	Native populations and minorities	Atomic energy	Satellite broadcasting
Public utilities	Activities related to the Panama Canal	Mining	Cable television
Public water supply	Fisheries	Transportation services: Air transportation	Social services
Audiovisual services (radio and TV broadcasting)		Customs brokerage	Transportation services: Maritime transportation

Table 5.2 – (Continued)

Telecommunication services		Banking and other financial services	Insurance
Mining		Insurance	
Nonmetallic mineral exploration			
Fishing			
Private security agencies			
Road transport, passenger and freight services			
Air transport			
Publishing			
Legal services			

Source: U.S.-Panama TPA, Annex I, and Annex II, available at
  http://www.ustr.gov/Trade_Agreements/Bilateral/Panama_FTA/Draft_Text/Section_Index.html.
Note: Nonconforming measures are found in annexes I through III of the TPA. Annex I contains
  reservations for cross-border services, excluding financial services, to preserve existing measures
  that are inconsistent with the disciplines concerning nondiscrimination, performance requirements,
  and senior personnel. Annex II contains reservations for cross-border services, excluding financial
  services, to ensure that a party maintains flexibility to impose measures in the future that may be
  inconsistent with the disciplines of the TPA. For information on the nonconforming measures
  related to financial services, see table 3-2.

Views of Interested Parties

ITAC reports expressed satisfaction with the investment provisions of the U.S.-Panama
TPA, and particularly cited the agreement's broad definition of investment, ban on
performance requirements, and inclusion of the investor-state dispute settlement process as
safeguarding the rights of U.S. investors in Panama.[302] According to the American Chamber
of Commerce & Industry of Panama, U.S. industry representatives active in Panama have
been fully supportive of the TPA and cited Panama's willingness to sign the agreement as
helping to create a positive investment climate for U.S. investors.[303] The Chamber further
stated that the investor protections and government procurement provisions of the TPA would
give U.S. firms an advantage over their non-Panamanian competitors in bidding for contracts
related to the expansion of the Panama Canal, expected to begin in 2008.[304]

Reports by ITAC 2 (Automotive Equipment and Technical Goods) and ITAC 10
(Services and Financial Industries) said that the so-called "fork in the road provision" (annex
10-C)[305] could be confusing for investors and increase the complexity of investment
arbitrations, partly due to the fact that most other recent FTAs and BITs do not have such a
provision. This could cause investors to unwittingly give up their access to the investor-state
dispute settlement process. As a remedy, ITAC 10 called on the U.S. government to ensure
that investors in Panama are well informed of their options regarding dispute settlement.[306] By
contrast, while a report by the Intergovernmental Advisory Committee (IGPAC) was
generally unsupportive of the TPA's investor-state dispute settlement provisions, it
considered the "fork-in-the-road" language of annex 10-C to be an improvement over the

investment provisions of previous free trade agreements, as that language would eliminate the option of investor-state arbitration once a dispute has already been addressed by U.S. courts.[307]

The ITAC 10 report said that the investment provisions of the TPA would be particularly important for the provision of services, which often requires a local presence, and that the agreement would help provide a secure and predictable legal framework for U.S. services investors in Panama.[308] The American Chamber of Commerce in Panama stated that, in particular, firms in the construction, telecommunications, and transportation industries would likely increase investment in Panama.[309] Reports submitted by ITAC 2, ITAC 8 (Technology and Electronic Commerce), and ITAC 10 noted the importance of retaining investor protections for investment agreements already in place under the existing U.S.-Panama BIT.[310]

The ITAC 4 (Consumer Goods) report stated that Panama's commitment to lift most restrictions on investment in retail trade would likely have a beneficial effect on access to Panama's consumer goods market.[311] By contrast, the ITAC 5 (Distribution Services) report noted that under a side letter to the TPA, Panama would still maintain a significant initial minimum investment requirement for U.S. retailers to open stores in the country, which could make it difficult for smaller retailers to access the Panamanian market. It stated that smaller companies currently account for much of the U.S. investment in retail operations in Central America."[312]

While the ITAC reports expressed strong support for the investor-state dispute settlement process, the IGPAC report generally did not support the TPA investment provisions, particularly those regarding investor-state dispute settlement. The IGPAC cited three specific concerns with the TPA investment chapter. First, the committee said that the definition of investment is overly broad, indicating that it is more broad than the definition included in the NAFTA agreement and includes licenses and permits as covered investments. Second, the committee expressed concern that the language in article 10.5 (Minimum Standard of Treatment) could be interpreted to mean that state court actions would be subject to review by international investment tribunals. Third, the committee expressed concern that the due process standards outlined in article 10.5 are based on international standards that are not as clear as U.S. constitutional norms regarding substantive due process.[313]

Regarding the investor-state dispute settlement process, a report by the Center for International Environmental Law (CIEL) stated that legal challenges brought by foreign investors against U.S. state and local regulations have overly burdened state and local governments and caused confusion regarding the scope of states' regulatory authority. The report expressed concern that sophisticated investors would use these provisions in the United States to subvert state and local regulatory efforts, a concern shared by a minority of the Trade Policy and Environment (TEPAC) committee.[314]

The TEPAC report expressed additional concerns about the investor-state dispute settlement process. First, the report asserted that the definition of investment in section C of chapter 10 is overly broad, noting that coverage of both tangible and intangible assets could permit a broad array of investor-state claims, which could have unintended environmental consequences. Second, it asserted that the provision for an appellate body to review awards rendered by investment arbitration tribunals is overly vague and would be improved by additional transparency provisions and the ability of outside groups to submit amicus briefs to the arbitration panels.[315] Further, a minority of committee members expressed the belief that investor-state rules would permit investors to challenge environmental regulations in arbitration tribunals rather than in domestic courts in both the United States and in Panama. These committee members stated that the threat of such action could be enough to deter some governments from adopting environmental standards likely to be challenged.[316] These committee members also called for the inclusion of a general environmental exception to the investment chapter, possibly similar to the carve-out from the expropriation provisions for tax laws in article 21.3 of the TPA.[317]

TPA Chapter 15—Intellectual Property Rights

Assessment

The intellectual property rights (IPR) provisions of the U.S.-Panama Trade Promotion Agreement (TPA) likely would benefit U.S.-based industries that rely on IPR protection and enforcement, although the effect would not likely be substantial given the relatively small size of the Panamanian market. The standards in the TPA, if fully implemented and enforced, may reduce IPR infringement in Panama (box 5.3) and thus increase opportunities for U.S. intellectual property-dependent industries to generate revenue. Full implementation and enforcement of the IPR chapter, and particularly the digital technology protection provisions, likely would benefit the U.S. motion picture, sound recording, business software, entertainment software, and book publishing industries. U.S. industries that could benefit from patent and confidential data protections include pharmaceuticals and agricultural chemicals. A broad range of U.S. industries could benefit from the strengthened trademark and enforcement provisions of the TPA. Implementation by the United States of its TPA obligations would have little effect on the U.S. economy, because the United States already meets or exceeds the high standards of IPR protection contained in the TPA.

BOX 5.3 RECENT CONDITIONS OF IPR PROTECTION IN PANAMA

Panama is not included on any of the USTR Special 301 lists that identify countries with particularly problematic IPR laws or enforcement practices.

IPR policy and practice in Panama is coordinated by an Inter-institutional Commission on Intellectual Property consisting of six government agencies and led by the Ministry of Commerce and Industry. The creation of a National Intellectual Property Prosecutor's Office, with a permanent budget and staff, has strengthened and centralized the protection and enforcement of IPR. Specialized IPR departments in the Colon Free Zone, the Customhouse General Offices, and the Judicial Technical Police, as well as special intellectual property courts, also aid protection and enforcement. The International Intellectual Property Alliance (IIPA), a coalition of trade associations representing the U.S. copyright-based industries, reports that the Panamanian police and prosecutors work cooperatively with U.S. industry to enforce the IPR laws. A summary of Panama's legal framework and recent conditions of IPR protection and enforcement appears below.

Copyrights and Trademarks

Panama's Law on Copyright and Related Rights was passed in 1994 based on a World Intellectual Property Organization (WIPO) model law. It modernized copyright protection in Panama by, among other things, protecting computer software and making copyright infringement a felony. Panama was one of the first countries to join the two WIPO Internet Treaties, the WIPO Copyright Treaty (WCT), and the WIPO Performances and Phonogram Treaty (WPPT), which clarify how IPR apply in the digital environment. To date, however, Panama has not promulgated the regulations required to implement the WIPO Internet Treaties.

The Business Software Alliance (BSA) has calculated the rate of software piracy in Panama based on a comparison of PC shipments and records of the amount of software that was legally paid for. BSA estimates that Panama had a piracy rate of 74 percent in 2006 with corresponding industry losses of $18 million. IIPA estimated a relatively low motion picture piracy rate of 15 percent in 2003 (the latest year for which it has provided data) and corresponding trade losses of $2 million. In 2006, the music industry estimated that the level of music piracy in Panama exceeded 50 percent of the total market. U.S. industry also is concerned that Panama is becoming a trans-shipment point for pirated goods from around the world. In response to this concern, in 2005, Panamanian Customs signed a cooperation agreement with the recording industry association, IFPI-Latin America, focused on the collection of statistical data and information, training of border personnel and the creation of a specialized IP unit in Customs.

Trademark protection in Panama lasts for 10 years from the date granted and is renewable indefinitely. The law also grants authority to government agencies to conduct investigations and seize materials suspected of being counterfeit. The Trademark Registration Office has been modernized and includes a searchable computerized database as well as online registration.

Patents

The Industrial Property Law generally provides for 20 years of patent protection from the date of filing, although pharmaceutical patents are granted for 15 years only but renewable for an additional 10 years if the patent owner licenses a national company to work the patent. The following types of inventions are unpatentable: scientific theories and principles, economic and business methods, computer programs that refer to designated computer uses, therapeutic, diagnostic and surgical methods, and inventions contrary to health, public safety or good morals.

Foreign patenting is particularly active in Panama. During the period from 2001-05, approximately 91 percent of patent applications were filed by foreign inventors and 9 percent by domestic applicants. U.S. applicants were predominant, filing 52 percent of all applications.

Sources: USTR, "Panama," *NTE Report*, IIPA, "Panama," *2007 Special 301: Historical Summary*, IIPA, "IIPA Panama FTA Letter to USITC," BSA and IDC, *Fourth Annual BSA and IDC Global Software Piracy Study*, EIU, "Costa Rica, Nicaragua, Panama," *Country Commerce 2006*, and MICI, "Solicitudes Presentadas Segun Pais del Titular Entre el 2001 y 2005."

Summary of Provisions

Chapter 15 of the TPA would establish enhanced standards for the protection of intellectual property, including greater protection for copyrights, trademarks, patents, and confidential test data and more rigorous enforcement provisions. The enhanced standards address the negotiating objectives that Congress set for trade agreements in the Trade Promotion Act of 2002. These objectives include providing strong protection for emerging technologies, ensuring that IPR provisions reflect standards similar to those found in U.S. law, and ensuring strong civil, administrative, and criminal IPR enforcement.[318] Among U.S. FTAs, the IPR chapter of the U.S.-Panama TPA is most similar to that of the CAFTA-DR, which was negotiated during the same time frame as this chapter.[319]

General Provisions

The general provisions of the IPR chapter (article 15.1) would require accession to key intellectual property treaties and contain national treatment, nondiscrimination, and other obligations governing all of chapter 15. In particular, Panama would be obligated to ratify or accede to the Patent Cooperation Treaty by the date the TPA enters into force, to the International Convention for the Protection of New Varieties of Plants (UPOV Convention) by January 2010, and to the Trademark Law Treaty by January 2011.

Trademarks, Geographical Indications, and Domain Names

The trademark section of the TPA (article 15.2) would broaden the scope of trademarks to be protected, strengthen existing protections, and provide for increased automation of trademark services. The TPA would require protection for diverse types of marks including collective, certification, and sound marks. It would also enhance protections for well-known trademarks, provide for the automation of trademark services with online databases and electronic means of communication with trademark officials, and eliminate the requirement that trademark licenses be recorded. With regard to geographical indications, article 15.3 sets forth procedures for the protection of geographical indications and would prohibit recognition of a geographical indication that is confusingly similar to a prior trademark. In the area of internet domain names, article 15.4 would require the establishment of Uniform Domain Name Dispute Resolution Procedures.

Copyrights and Related Rights and Protection of Certain Satellite Signals

The copyright and related rights sections (articles 15.5–15.7) contain detailed provisions that would require implementation of the obligations of the WIPO Internet Treaties in a manner that is consistent with the U.S. Digital Millennium Copyright Act. Under article 15.5, Panama would also agree to extend its term of copyright protection from life of the author plus 50 years to life of the author plus 70 years for most copyrighted works. Article 15.5 would also require the two governments to issue decrees mandating the use of legal software in government agencies. Article 15.8 includes provisions similar to those in the NAFTA that protect against the theft of encrypted satellite signals and the manufacture of, and trafficking in, tools to steal those signals.

Patents and Measures Related to Certain Regulated Products

These sections of the TPA (articles 15.9 and 15.10) contain amendments to the final text that were made pursuant to a bipartisan trade agreement between certain Democratic Members of Congress and the U.S. Trade Representative and agreed by Panama.[320] These sections contain new language on three issues: the extension of patent terms in cases of unreasonable delay ("patent extension"); the protection of data submitted to regulators to obtain marketing approval ("data exclusivity"); and measures to prevent the marketing approval of the generic version of a drug while a patent for the original is still in force ("patent linkage"). The TPA also contains a new provision (article 15.12) affirming the parties' commitment to the Doha Declaration on the TRIPS Agreement and Public Health (the Doha Declaration) and clarifying that the TPA would not prevent them from taking measures to protect public health by promoting universal access to medicines. This issue was previously addressed in a side letter to the TPA.

The patent extension provision of the TPA (article 15.9.6) would require best efforts to process patent and marketing approval applications expeditiously. The TPA would require that the patent term be adjusted to compensate for unreasonable delays for nonpharmaceutical patents. For pharmaceutical products, patent extension would be permitted but not required. Patent term extension would also be permitted but not required to compensate for an unreasonable delay in the marketing approval process for the first commercial marketing of a pharmaceutical product.

The data exclusivity provisions of the TPA (articles 15.10.1–15.10.2) provide that undisclosed safety and efficacy data submitted for the purpose of product approval would be protected against third party use without the submitter's consent for a period of 10 years for agricultural chemicals and 5 years for pharmaceuticals. If Panama relies on U.S. approval of a pharmaceutical, and grants its approval within 6 months of the filing of the application in Panama, then the period of data protection would be concurrent with that provided in the United States. Notwithstanding these data exclusivity provisions, the parties could take measures to protect public health in accordance with the Doha Declaration and its implementation.

The TPA would further require procedures and remedies for the expeditious adjudication of disputes concerning pharmaceutical patents, a transparent system to provide notice to a patent holder that another person is seeking to market an approved pharmaceutical product during the patent term, and sufficient time and opportunity to challenge the marketing of allegedly infringing products (article 15.10.3). If a party chooses to implement patent linkage in its marketing approval process, it also would be obligated to provide an expeditious procedure to challenge the validity of the identified patent and effective rewards for a successful challenge (article 15.10.4).

Enforcement

The enforcement section of the TPA, article 15.11, contains detailed measures intended to promote full and effective IPR enforcement. It contains general obligations, including presumptions in copyright cases; civil and administrative procedure and remedies provisions; provisional measures that would require *ex parte* relief to be available in civil cases; special requirements related to border measures; criminal procedures and remedies; and limitations on the liability of internet service providers. Finally, a side letter on traditional knowledge and folklore commits the governments to consult when these issues arise at WIPO.

Views of Interested Parties

The Industry Trade Advisory Committee on Intellectual Property Rights (ITAC 15) expressed support for the IPR chapter of the TPA as currently drafted, stating that it meets the negotiating objectives of the Trade Act of 2002 and of U.S. intellectual property-based industries.[321] ITAC 15 said that it supports the TPA because it "takes into account the significant legal and technological developments that have occurred since the TRIPS and NAFTA agreements entered into force" and mirrors or improves upon provisions contained in previous agreements.[322]

Similarly, the International Intellectual Property Alliance (IIPA), which represents members of the U.S. copyright-based industry, expressed support for the TPA because it "offers a tool for encouraging compliance with other evolving international trends in copyright standards (such as fully implementing WIPO Treaties obligations and extending copyright terms of protection beyond the minimum levels guaranteed by TRIPS) as well as outlining specific enforcement provisions."[323] IIPA noted that copyright-based industries are among the fastest growing and most productive U.S. sectors and that effective IPR protection and enforcement can operate to reduce the piracy that causes substantial trade losses to these industries. The IIPA also stated that full implementation of the IPR chapter would assist in attracting new foreign investment to Panama and new trade in valuable digital and other intellectual property-based products, particularly in the area of e-commerce.[324]

The Advisory Committee for Trade Policy and Negotiations (ACTPN) also endorsed the IPR chapter. In particular, the ACTPN expressed support for the IPR enforcement mechanisms and penalty provisions, including the criminalization of end-user piracy and counterfeiting, the requirement that authorities be permitted to seize not only counterfeit goods but also the equipment used to produce them, the removal of recording requirements for trademarks, and Panama's agreement to accede to the Trademark Law Treaty.[325] The Industry Trade Advisory Committee for Information and Communications Technologies, Services, and Electronic Commerce (ITAC 8) also expressed support for the IPR chapter.[326]

The Industry Trade Advisory Committee for Chemicals, Pharmaceutical, Health/Science Products and Services (ITAC 3) includes members representing both brand name and generic pharmaceuticals. ITAC 3 members have expressed different opinions on the provisions relating to patent term extension, data exclusivity, and linkage. A majority of ITAC 3 members have indicated that they support the initial TPA provisions on these issues. By contrast, the Generic Pharmaceutical Association (GPHA) asserted that the provisions went further than U.S. law in imposing barriers to market access for generic drugs.[327] GPHA indicated that it supports the final TPA provisions as suggested in the bipartisan trade agreement, because they are consistent with U.S. law and provide a better balance between fostering drug innovation and ensuring access to affordable medicines.[328] Pharmaceutical Research and Manufacturers of America (PhRMA) has not expressed a position on the final text of the TPA.

Certain Trade and Environment Policy Advisory Committee (TEPAC) members also expressed opposition to those provisions of the IPR chapter that they believe are not consistent with the Doha Declaration. In particular, they cited data exclusivity provisions believed to unduly extend patent terms and limit the availability of generic drugs. Moreover, they expressed the concern that the TPA, and other free trade agreements, could limit the ability of Congress to address the affordability of medicines for U.S. consumers through new legislation.[329]

Similarly, in June 2005 the Minority Staff of the U.S. House of Representatives Committee on Government Reform expressed concern that U.S. free trade agreements, including the U.S.-Panama TPA, would restrict the ability of developing nations to acquire lifesaving medicines at affordable prices. The report noted that the data exclusivity, patent extension, and linkage provisions are particularly problematic.[330]

TPA Chapter 16—Labor[331]

Assessment

The labor provisions contained in the proposed U.S.-Panama TPA text likely would have minimal impact on the U.S. or Panamanian labor markets or on U.S.-Panama trade because of the chapter's focus on the enforcement of existing labor regulations and the *ILO Declaration on Fundamental Principles and Rights at Work and Its Follow-up* (1998) (ILO Declaration), which the United States and Panama are already committed to observe as members of the International Labour Organization (ILO). The principal labor provisions of the agreement would require the parties to effectively enforce their own existing labor laws (box 5.4) and to maintain the labor rights specified in the ILO Declaration in their regulations and statutes. Parties could challenge the failure to fulfill these obligations under certain circumstances through consultations or the dispute settlement procedures established in chapter 20 of the TPA.

Industry and labor groups have expressed differing views regarding the adequacy and potential value of the initial draft TPA labor provisions, which focused solely on the enforcement of existing labor regulations. Although such groups have not yet provided their views on the final text of the agreement, they generally indicated that they support the type of enforceable provisions that have been incorporated into the labor chapter of the U.S.- Panama TPA, but for differing reasons.[332]

Box 5.4 Labor Market Conditions in Panama

Panama maintains relatively stringent workers' rights protections, having established and enforced legislation on labor issues such as the right to organize and bargain collectively, minimum employment age, and child labor. However, certain groups indicate that some problems persist with regard to the observance of workers' rights and working conditions in Panama.

As compared with the United States, Panama's labor market is small and is characterized by relatively high unemployment. Specifically, the Panamanian labor market comprised 1.4 million workers and posted an unemployment rate of 9.6 percent in

2005.[1] In that same year, the U.S. labor market comprised 149.3 million workers and registered an unemployment rate of 5.1 percent.[2] The service sector is the principal employer in both countries, having accounted for 65 percent and 76 percent of total employment in Panama and the United States, respectively, in 2002.[3] Comparable data on hourly labor costs are not available. However, in March 2006, new minimum wage levels were established in Panama, ranging from $0.89 per hour to $1.68 per hour, depending on business size, industry, and geographic location.[4] U.S. federal legislation has established a minimum wage of $5.15 per hour, although several states maintain higher minimum wage levels.[5]

Panama has undertaken significant international obligations on labor standards, having ratified the eight fundamental International Labour Organization (ILO) conventions on workers' rights.[6] Panama's labor laws reportedly are strong compared to those maintained by other Central American countries,[7] and one source indicates that business representatives view the country's particularly pro-labor legislation as a potential deterrent to operating in Panama.[8] Panamanian law permits the establishment of unions in the private sector, allows organization and collective bargaining by certain public-sector employees and all private-sector employees, bans compulsory labor, places limits on the employment of children,[9] sets minimum wage levels which reportedly compare favorably to those in other Latin American countries,[10] and establishes standards regarding worker health and safety, the length of the work week, and overtime.[11] There are indications that many of these worker rights are observed in practice, as the government has inspected more than 500 workplaces to monitor observance of child labor laws, private-sector employees have actively engaged in organization and collective bargaining, and there have been no reported incidents of forced labor.[12] Workers seeking to pursue a complaint against an employer reportedly have access to free legal counsel provided by Panama's Labor Ministry.[13] Further, the Congressional Research Service (CRS) reports that the Panamanian unemployment rate has decreased in recent years and that the current government has indicated its intention to boost job creation.[14]

Despite its relatively strong labor regulations, some sources report remaining problems with the observance of workers' rights and working conditions in Panama. For example, Panama's minimum wage reportedly is not sufficient to cover the needs of a working family, and despite recent decreases, the Panamanian unemployment rate remains high, particularly among women.[15] The U.S. State Department reports that retailers frequently sidestep regulations regarding worker dismissals by hiring employees on a short-term basis, that problems remain with the enforcement of occupational safety and health regulations, and that the employment of child laborers continues to occur, particularly in rural regions and the informal sector.[16] The Labor Advisory Committee suggests that there are several weaknesses in the provisions and enforcement of Panamanian labor law, such as limitations on employee rights in the canal zone and the public sector and inadequate enforcement of anti-trafficking regulations, among others.[17] Further, a significant share of Panama's workers are employed in the informal sector, and are not protected by Panamanian labor legislation.[18]

---

[1] Economist Intelligence Unit, "Country Commerce: Costa Rica, Nicaragua, Panama," 120.
[2] Economist Intelligence Unit, "Country Commerce: United States of America," 68.
[3] World Bank, *World Development Indicators*.

[4] Economist Intelligence Unit, "Country Commerce: Costa Rica, Nicaragua, Panama," 121.

[5] Washington state maintained the highest minimum wage as of April 2007, at $7.93 per hour, while Illinois has established the highest future standard, with a minimum wage that is scheduled to reach $8.25 per hour on July 1, 2010. U.S. Department of Labor (DOL), "Compliance Assistance - Fair Labor Standards Act (FLSA)," and "Minimum Wage Laws in the United States."

[6] Panama's ratification of the ILO's eight core conventions took place over a period of time, with the earliest ratifications having occurred on June 3, 1958 and the most recent ratifications having occurred on October 31, 2000. ILO, "Ratifications of the Fundamental Human Rights Conventions by Country."

[7] Congressional Research Service (CRS), "Panama: Political and Economic Conditions and U.S. Relations," 12; and Raul del Valle, Former President, Chamber of Commerce, Industry, and Agriculture of Panama, Testimony before the U.S. International Trade Commission, May 16, 2007, Hearing Transcript, 9.

[8] Economist Intelligence Unit, "Country Commerce: Costa Rica, Nicaragua, Panama," 120.

[9] U.S. Department of State, "Panama," Country Reports on Human Rights Practices, March 6, 2007, found at *http://www.state.gov/drl/rls/hrrpt/2006/78900.htm*, retrieved March 19, 2007.

[10] Raul del Valle, Hearing Transcript, 9; and Juan B. Sosa, President, U.S. Panama Business Council, Testimony before the U.S. International Trade Commission, May 16, 2007, Hearing Transcript, 82-83.

[11] U.S. Department of State, "Panama."

[12] U.S. Department of State, "Panama;" and Raul del Valle, Hearing Transcript, 60.

[13] David Hunt, Executive Director, American Chamber of Commerce of Panama, Testimony before the U.S. International Trade Commission, May 16, 2007, Hearing Transcript, 61.

[14] Congressional Research Service (CRS), Panama: Political and Economic Conditions and U.S. Relations, 6.

[15] Department of State, "Panama;" and, Grupo de Análisis Socio-laboral, "Characteristics of the Panamanian Labor Market," Global Policy Network country report, march 17, 2006, found at http://www.gpn.org/data/panama/panamaanalysis- en.pdf, retrieved March 19, 2007.

[16] Department of State, "Panama;" and Labor Advisory Committtee for Trade Negotiations and Trade Policy (LAC), "The U.S.-Panama Free Trade Agreement," April 25, 2007, 13, 14, found at http://www.ustr.gov/assets/Trade_Agreements/Bilateral/Panama_FTA/Reports/asset_upload_file69 6_11235.pdf, retrieved May 9, 2007.

[17] LAC, "The U.S.-Panama Free Trade Agreement," 8-14.

[18] Raul del Valle, Hearing Transcript, 45-46; and Department of State, "Panama."

Summary of Provisions

As with the labor chapters of previous FTAs, chapter 16 of the U.S.-Panama TPA would commit each party to effectively enforce its respective labor laws while providing for the reasonable exercise of discretion regarding such enforcement. In addition, the parties would reaffirm their obligations as members of the ILO. However, chapter 16 of the U.S.-Panama TPA would also commit the parties to maintain the rights specified in the ILO Declaration in their regulations and statutes. Further, whereas the labor provisions in many previous FTAs were subject to a separate dispute settlement mechanism, the provisions in Chapter 16 of the U.S.-Panama TPA would be subject to the same dispute settlement procedures as the agreement's other obligations.

Each party would agree to provide domestic tribunal proceedings, allowing persons with a recognized interest under its law in a particular matter to seek enforcement of its labor laws. Such proceedings would be required to be fair, equitable, and transparent and adhere to due process of the law. Each party would agree to ensure independent review of tribunal actions, provide legal remedies to ensure enforcement, and promote public awareness of its labor laws. The TPA defines labor laws as statutes or regulations that directly relate to internationally recognized labor rights, including the right of association, the right to organize and bargain collectively, a ban on forced or compulsory labor, the protection of children and other young laborers, a ban on discrimination in occupation or employment, and standards on conditions of work, including minimum wages, hours of work, and occupational health and safety.

The TPA would establish a Labor Affairs Council that would oversee the implementation of chapter 16 provisions, may prepare public reports on the implementation of the chapter, develop guidelines for the consideration of input from persons of a party, endeavor to resolve matters related to cooperative labor consultations, and act on the TPA's labor-related objectives. Each party would be required to designate an office within its labor ministry to serve as a contact with the other party and the public. The TPA would allow each party to establish national labor advisory committees or consult existing committees, which could include representatives of business and labor and members of the public. The TPA would also creates a Labor Cooperation and Capacity-Building Mechanism to further advance common commitments on labor matters, including the ILO Declaration of Fundamental Principles and Rights at Work and Its Follow-up and ILO Convention No. 182 Concerning the Prohibition and Immediate Action for the Elimination of the Worst Forms of Child Labor, and to enhance opportunities to improve labor standards.

A party could request consultations with the other party on matters under this chapter with a view toward finding a mutually acceptable resolution. Failing to find a mutually acceptable resolution, a party would be able to call upon the Labor Affairs Council to consider the matter. If a matter is not resolved within 60 days of a request for cooperative labor consultations, the complaining party could ask for consultations or a meeting of the Commission under the TPA's dispute settlement provisions (contained in chapter 20), following which the party could seek to settle the dispute under the other provisions included in chapter 20 of the agreement. Provisions regarding the establishment of a roster of individuals to hear labor disputes, including required qualifications for roster members, are included in chapter 16.

Views of Interested Parties

Because the final text of the U.S.-Panama TPA was only recently published, the views expressed in U.S. advisory group reports are largely based on the initial draft text of the TPA, in which the only enforceable labor provision was the obligation to enforce existing labor regulations. Based on this initial draft text, the advisory groups reported differing views on the potential effect of the proposed TPA labor provisions and on whether the TPA meets established negotiating objectives.[333] The Advisory Committee for Trade Policy and Negotiations (ACTPN) stated that the TPA fulfilled U.S. negotiating objectives on labor issues and supports the agreement's cooperative approach to these issues. ACTPN stated that such cooperative efforts can be particularly helpful where resources to enforce labor regulations are limited.[334] However, one industry representative suggested that the agreement's capacity building measures could have a limited effect on the Panamanian labor market, as the Panamanian Government effectively enforces its labor legislation.[335] By contrast, the Labor Advisory Committee for Trade Negotiations and Trade Policy (LAC) report stated that the agreement did not fulfill U.S. negotiating objectives, advance U.S. economic interests, or protect the rights of U.S. or Panamanian workers. The LAC report contended that weaknesses exist in the rights regime of Panamanian workers (see box 5-4), and noted that the agreement would not obligate parties to adhere to international worker rights standards, would not preclude the weakening or elimination of labor regulations, and would not protect workers from the possible trade effects of provisions regarding safeguards and rules of origin.[336]

In general, the provisions that have been included in the final text of the labor chapter of the U.S.-Panama TPA have received a favorable response from industry groups and non-governmental organizations. Early support remained tentative due to a lack of specific information regarding how the new provisions would be incorporated into the agreement, and reasons for this support differed among various groups and organizations. The AFL-CIO indicated that the proposed provisions likely would improve upon the original labor text of the U.S.-Panama TPA, but also indicated that several issues, such as outsourcing, continued to be inadequately addressed.[337] Both the U.S. Chamber of Commerce and the National Association of Manufacturers expressed support, as initial descriptions of the new provisions suggested that they would not require the parties to alter domestic labor laws in accordance with ILO conventions.[338] The Business Roundtable did not specifically refer to the TPA's proposed labor chapter provisions, but made a general statement indicating that, as a whole, the revised trade policy outlined in the bipartisan trade agreement would benefit U.S. workers.[339]

TPA Chapter 17 - Environment[340]

Assessment

The environmental provisions of the U.S.-Panama TPA likely would have little effect on the U.S. economy or on U.S.-Panama trade because of the chapter's focus on the enforcement of existing regulations. The U.S. trade negotiating objectives for the TPA regarding environmental matters were similar to those for CAFTA-DR,[341] although the environmental provisions in the TPA now reflect the recent agreement between the Bush Administration and the U.S. Congress to incorporate several environmental changes in the FTAs.

Summary of Provisions

Chapter 17 of the TPA would commit each party to strive to ensure that its environmental protection laws provide for high levels of protection and to strive to improve those laws, to provide appropriate and effective remedies and sanctions for violations of environmental protection laws, to not fail to effectively enforce its laws, to provide opportunities for public participation in environmental protection, and to promote public awareness of its environmental laws. The parties would agree that trade or investment would not be encouraged by weakening or reducing domestic environmental laws, although there is a provision for a waiver or a derogation that is not inconsistent with a party's obligations under a covered agreement. The parties also would agree to ensure that domestic judicial, quasijudicial, or administrative proceedings would be available to sanction or remedy violations of environmental laws. Such proceedings would be required to be fair, open, and equitable; comply with due process of law; and provide access to persons with recognizable legal interests. The parties would agree to establish an Environmental Affairs Council that would meet to consider the implementation of the provisions contained in chapter 17 as well as the separate Environmental Cooperation Agreement (ECA) (annex 17.10) and to strive to resolve any controversies that may arise regarding these environmental provisions. The parties would agree to pursue cooperative environmental activities and provide for environmental consultations. The parties would also commit to work in multilateral forums to enhance the mutual supportiveness of multilateral environmental and trade agreements.

The TPA would incorporate a specific list of multilateral environmental agreements to which the United States and Panama have obligations, including the Convention on International Trade in Endangered Species (CITES), the Montreal Protocol on Ozone Depleting Substances, the Convention on Marine Pollution, the Inter-American Tropical Tuna Convention (IATTC), the Ramsar Convention on Wetlands, the International Whaling Convention (IWC), and the Convention on Conservation of Antarctic Marine Living Resources (CCAMLR) (annex 17.2). Further, all FTA environmental obligations would be enforced on the same basis as the commercial provisions of the agreements and would be subject to the same remedies, procedures, and sanctions.[342] In previous FTAs, as well as in the current text of the U.S.-Panama TPA, environmental dispute settlement procedures have focused on the use of fines, as opposed to trade sanctions, and were limited to the obligation to effectively enforce environmental laws.[343]

Views of Interested Parties

The views expressed in this section are based on the draft text of the TPA and for the most part these views address provisions that were either included in both the draft and final texts of the TPA, or that were suggested by the bipartisan trade agreement and ultimately included in the final text .

The Advisory Committee for Trade Policy and Negotiations (ACTPN) report stated that the environmental provisions of the U.S.-Panama TPA meet congressional environmental objectives. The ACTPN said that it endorses the environmental provisions of the TPA and believes they provide effective ways of contributing to environmental improvement.[344] The ACTPN also indicated that it supports the establishment of the Environmental Cooperation Commission created under the ECA, which is intended to strengthen the ability to implement and enforce environmental laws, increase public participation, and promote clean technologies.

The Trade and Environment Policy Advisory Committee (TEPAC) reported that the majority of its members believe that the U.S.-Panama TPA meets the U.S. environmental negotiating objectives[345] and support the provisions on public participation and the ECA, which are similar to those incorporated in CAFTA. However, TEPAC reported that the majority also believes that without a competent and well-funded Secretariat, the objectives of these provisions would not be met. In addition, the majority also expressed the belief that the dispute resolution procedures are sufficient to meet U.S. environmental negotiating objectives and that the monetary penalties in the TPA (up to $15 million per year for noncompliance with rulings confirming violations of enforcement requirements) are adequate.[346] The majority noted they were disappointed with the absence of an article on biological diversity despite its inclusion in other FTAs.[347] On the other hand, TEPAC said that a minority of its members believes that dedicated funding for the ECA would mean that funding for other priorities such as trade capacity-building would not be available.[348] The minority's differing views highlighted concerns that the TPA did not include a provision to ensure that timber and timber products were legally sourced.[349]

Other trade advisory committees also commented on the environmental provisions of the TPA. The Industry Trade Advisory Committee on Non-Ferious Metals and Building Materials (ITAC 9) said that it supported the use of side agreements as opposed to the inclusion of environmental provisions in the text of the TPA. ITAC 9 also expressed concern about environmental provisions that seem to approve the use of measures to achieve environmental goals in the context of multilateral environmental agreements (MEAs), noting that there is no assurance that these trade measures are the least disruptive means necessary to meet the goals of the MEAs.[350] The Industry Trade Advisory Committee for Forest Products (ITAC 7) said that it believes the U.S.-Panama TPA and the ECA "serve as an opportunity to demonstrate our respective countries' commitment to improving global forestry practices and taking steps to eliminate illegal logging and the use of illegally obtained timber in the manufacturing of forest products."[351] The Industry Trade Advisory Committee for Chemicals, Pharmaceuticals, Health/Science Products and Services (ITAC 3) stated its belief that approaching environmental issues through bilateral free trade agreements is inadvisable. The industry members of ITAC 3 also indicated that it is misguided to include environmental provisions in future trade agreements in such a way as to lead to trade sanctions.[352]

TPA Chapter 18 – Transparency

Assessment

Several provisions of the U.S.-Panama TPA regarding transparency would likely offer significant improvements over the policies and practices that they are intended to replace.[353] For example, provisions are included to improve public access and information in trade dispute cases. Such dispute settlement mechanisms would provide for open public hearings, public access to documents, and the opportunity for third parties to submit views. The agreement also contains provisions that would improve transparency in customs operations by expediting express delivery shipments and requiring more open and public processes for customs rulings and administration. Panama would commit to publish laws and regulations relating to customs procedures on the internet and to allow interested parties an opportunity to comment on the proposals to the extent possible.[354] Consequently, the transparency-related provisions of the TPA could foster increased U.S.-Panama trade and investment.

Summary of Provisions

Chapter 18 of the U.S.-Panama TPA is virtually identical to the corresponding section of the U.S.-Colombia TPA and the U.S.-Peru TPA. The Panama TPA would continue the U.S. effort to obtain bilateral commitments to transparency disciplines that are applicable to domestic regulation, including provisions that enhance and ensure communication and disclosure between parties. As in earlier TPAs, the U.S.- Panama agreement would require each party to make publicly available all laws, regulations, and procedures regarding any matter covered by the agreement. Further, each party would be obligated to establish or maintain procedures to provide review and appeal capabilities to any entities that would be affected by actions, rulings, measures, or procedures under the TPA. The agreement would require transparency and efficiency in many specific areas, such as customs procedures. Applicable provisions also cover protection for U.S. trademarks, procedures for government procurement contracts, as well as the administration and enforcement of environmental laws. The U.S.-Panama TPA contains a prior notice and comment period for all new laws and regulations. Chapter 18 also includes anticorruption provisions that seek to improve trade environments by establishing penalty procedures for bribery and corruption.

Views of Interested Parties

The Industry Trade Advisory Committee for Services and Finance Industries (ITAC 10) stated that the agreement's commitments would improve the business climate in Panama, help stimulate new investment, improve the operation of financial and other markets, and reduce corruption. Further, ITAC 10 said that greater transparency in domestic regulation would enhance the quality of the regulatory environment, thereby creating new market opportunities for U.S. services providers.[355] For example, ITAC 10 noted that the agreement's chapters on transparency and investment would improve or maintain the environment within which energy services providers conduct their work in Panama. ITAC 10 also said that the TPA also seeks improved transparency in the investor-state mechanism, as sought by the Trade Act of 2002, and would provide for the consideration of a bilateral appellate mechanism after three years.[356] ACTPN reports that commitments relating to regulatory transparency would help promote a more open framework for cross-border trade and investment between the United States and Panama.[357] At times, transacting business in Panama involves cumbersome and complex procedures and regulations that may cause delays, increase costs, and leave foreign firms at a competitive disadvantage. Consequently, the Industry Trade Advisory Committee for Information and Communications Technologies, Services and Electronic Commerce (ITAC 8) said that it encourages an overall effort to ensure that product testing, licensing and certification requirements, customs procedures, and certificate of origin mandates are fair, transparent, and streamlined.[358]

TPA Chapter 20 - Dispute Settlement

Assessment

Chapter 20 of the U.S.-Panama TPA would require that hearings be open and public, that the public has access to the legal submissions of the parties to the panel, and that the public and interested parties have the opportunity to submit views to the panel. The major obligations of the TPA would be subject to the dispute settlement provisions of the TPA. The dispute settlement provisions emphasize the use of consultations and trade-enhancing remedies to promote compliance. The enforcement mechanism includes the use of monetary compensation, as well as trade retaliatory measures under certain circumstances.

Summary of Provisions

Under the provisions of this chapter, the parties would commit to consult and cooperate on TPA matters; however, one party could invoke dispute settlement if it believes that the other has a TPA-inconsistent measure or has failed to carry out a TPA obligation or that a benefit it reasonably expected has not been given. The complaining party could choose the forum for arbitration, including the Free Trade Commission (established in annex 19.1), the WTO, or other dispute settlement bodies available to both parties. Any party could request consultations with the other. If the consultation failed to resolve the matter by a prescribed deadline, either party could request a meeting with the Free Trade Commission, followed by a request for an arbitral panel, if necessary. Once a panel constituted under the chapter supplies its final report, the report would be made public and the parties would be obliged to agree on the resolution of the dispute in question in a manner which conforms with the determinations of the panel. If the parties are unable to agree on a resolution, compensation could be negotiated. If the parties could not agree on the terms of compensation, an actual suspension of benefits of equivalent effect could be undertaken in accord with the panel's report, or the party complained against could pay a monetary assessment in U.S. dollars of an amount equal to 50 percent of the total benefit the panel deems to have been involved.

The TPA dispute settlement chapter provides for compliance reviews and 5-year reviews. The chapter also states that parties would utilize arbitration and alternate dispute resolution to the maximum extent possible to settle international commercial disputes between private parties in the free trade area and would authorize the Commission to establish an advisory panel on private commercial disputes. Actions relating to excepted matters could not be taken. The chapter contains administrative procedures for requesting a panel, establishing a roster of panelists, selecting panelists, and issuing reports.

Views of Interested Parties

Industry responses to the dispute settlement provisions were generally favorable. The Advisory Committee for Trade Policy and Negotiations (ACTPN) stated that the provisions fully meet the requirements of U.S. law and that the procedures are fully transparent, including public release of submissions of interested parties and open hearings. ACTPN also indicated that it supports the provisions to settle disputes through consultation rather than through the use of trade retaliatory measures.[359]

The Trade and Environmental Policy Advisory Committee (TEPAC) expressed support for the panel selection procedures, which ensure that panelists dealing with environmental issues have the requisite expertise. TEPAC also said that it supports the provision allowing the panel to accept public submissions from both the private sector and NGOs in dispute settlement proceedings.[360]

The Intergovernmental Policy Advisory Committee (IGPAC) said that it recommends the creation of a federal-state international trade commission that would provide an infrastructure to facilitate cooperation and understanding of trade issues across all levels of government and address state and local interests in such issues, including dispute settlement proceedings.[361] IGPAC said that it recommends that such a committee be based on U.S. constitutional federalism, and it pointed to the Canadian Federal-Provincial committee for trade consultations (C-Trade) as a potential model. IGPAC also recommended that the USTR and the U.S. Department of Justice request that the federal government cover expenses that state governments might incur in the course of defending state laws or regulations in the dispute settlement process established under this TPA.[362] Moreover, IGPAC said that it recommends that, in the event of a finding by the dispute settlement panel against the actions of a U.S. state or local entity, such state or local entity would not be held liable to compensate the U.S. government for sanctions imposed as a result.[363]

The Industry Trade Advisory Committee on Automotive Equipment and Capital Goods (ITAC 2) expressed support for the side letter to the TPA covering used passenger cars, under which the United States would agree not to initiate dispute settlement proceedings on restrictions that Panama places on the importation of used passenger cars prior to the date of entry into force of the agreement.[364]

LITERATURE REVIEW AND SUMMARY OF HEARING TESTIMONY AND WRITTEN SUBMISSIONS

Literature Review

In examining the literature from academic, public sector, and private sector institutions, the Commission found no studies directly examining the quantitative impact of the U.S.-Panama Trade Promotion Agreement (TPA) or a similar agreement.[365] The Commission found two studies that modeled the potential impact of regional FTAs which would include the United States and Panama, as well as many other countries, as members. In both studies, Panama was modeled as part of a large group of countries, so that results or conclusions apply to the aggregate group of countries, not just to Panama.

Hinojosa-Ojeda[366] used a computable general equilibrium model called the Greater North America Free Trade Agreement (GNAFTA-CGE) to analyze eight different regional trade liberalization scenarios. One scenario, a free trade agreement which would encompass all of North and Central America, was the only scenario which included both the United States and Panama. Hinojosa-Ojeda found that this scenario would have positive impacts on GDP for all Central American countries (including for a group of countries referred to as "the rest of

Central America," which includes Panama). The impact of various free trade scenarios on U.S. GDP was not discussed.

Monteagudo and Watanuki[367] employed a CGE model with variables that represented three kinds of trade barriers: ad valorem tariff equivalents, export subsidies, and domestic supports. The effects of three FTAs were analyzed, one of which was a Free Trade Area of the Americas (FTAA). The FTAA produced benefits for CAC (Central America and the Caribbean, which includes Panama) in terms of both real GDP and total exports. Specifically, real GDP and total exports for this region as a whole were expected to increase by 2.2 percent and 8.5 percent, respectively.[368] With regard to the United States, an FTAA was expected to produce a real GDP increase of 0.6 percent and a gross exports increase of 1.9 percent. Gross U.S. imports were expected to increase 1.1 percent, yielding a positive net trade balance effect of 0.8 percent.

Summary of Hearing Testimony and Written Submissions

The American Chamber of Commerce and Industry of Panama[369]

The American Chamber of Commerce and Industry of Panama (AmCham Panama) stated that it is a nonprofit association with over 385 members representing businesses and individuals interested in strengthening the commercial ties between the United States and Panama and that its members represent 76 percent of the U.S. direct investment in Panama ($5.2 billion). AmCham Panama, on behalf of the Panama Pro-TPA Coalition, said that it strongly supports the U.S.-Panama TPA. It said that the TPA is a front-loaded and comprehensive agreement that is a critical step in U.S. efforts to promote sustainable economic growth in the Western Hemisphere through trade rather than aid. Additionally, AmCham Panama stated that the TPA would increase the mutual benefits of the bilateral U.S.-Panama trading relationship. AmCham noted that as a result of the Caribbean Basin Initiative of 1983, fully 95 percent of all imports from Panama already enter the U.S. market duty free, while U.S. exports to Panama face an average weighted tariff of 7 percent. AmCham Panama stated that the TPA would cut Panamanian tariffs on U.S. consumer and industrial products on a graduated timetable. AmCham Panama stated that U.S. farmers and ranchers would receive significant benefits under the TPA, as more than half of U.S. agricultural exports would be duty free upon the TPA's implementation. Further, AmCham Panama stated that the TPA would provide greater protections and increased transparency for U.S. investments in Panama. It stated that the TPA contains critical provisions regarding greater accountability in governance, particularly regarding the issue of corruption. AmCham Panama also noted that the TPA would enhance U.S. efforts to strengthen democratic ideals in the region.

In its posthearing written submission, AmCham Panama stated that trade between the United States and Panama has doubled over the past five years, currently reaching $2.7 billion. It stated that over 80 percent of U.S. firms that export to Panama are small- to medium-size enterprises (SMEs), and that these SMEs account for almost 42 percent of total U.S. exports to Panama. It further noted that despite the comparatively low U.S. trade barriers, U.S. exports to Panama are seven times larger than imports from Panama. AmCham

Panama noted that the U.S.-Panama TPA, within the context of these current trade conditions, would provide U.S. exporters the opportunity to grow in both number and annual revenue.

AmCham Panama also made several sector-specific points in its support of the TPA: (1) according to the American Farm Bureau Federation, implementation of the TPA would provide U.S. agriculture gains of over $190 million per year; (2) the TPA would significantly improve trade facilitation measures by setting a new *de minimis* value for shipments at $100 and calling for the customs clearance of express shipments to be limited to six hours; and (3) in terms of investment, the TPA would allow for the free transfer of capital in and out of Panama, a stipulation not made in previous trade agreements with Peru and Colombia.

American Dehydrated Onion and Garlic Association[370]

The American Dehydrated Onion and Garlic Association (ADOGA) stated that it opposes tariff reductions on dried onions and dried garlic and the powder or flour derived from these products: HTS 0712.20.20.00, HTS 0712.40.00, HTS 0712.90.40, and HTS 0712.90.40. ADOGA, representing two firms that account for the vast majority of U.S. dehydrated onion and garlic production, said that it opposes a U.S.-Panama Trade Promotion Agreement. ADOGA stated that Panama poses a serious threat to the U.S. industry primarily as a country through which Chinese-produced dehydrated onions and garlic may be transshipped, but also because Panama already receives U.S. duty-free treatment for dehydrated onions and garlic through the CBI. ADOGA suppliers reported difficulty in competing against most low-wage supplier countries, such as Panama, and reported that this agreement offers little opportunity for exports of U.S.-produced dehydrated onions and garlic to Panama.

Bumble Bee Foods, LLC[371]

Bumble Bee Foods reported that it is the nation's largest brand of seafood, with U.S. facilities producing canned tuna, among other foods. It stated that it operates the only remaining tuna cannery in the continental United States (in Santa Fe Springs, CA) and the only remaining tuna cannery in Puerto Rico (in Mayaguez). It is one of three U.S. tuna canners (along with StarKist and Chicken of the Sea, which operate canneries in American Samoa) that together supply more than 85 percent of tuna consumption in the U.S. market, the largest tuna market in the world.

Bumble Bee Foods said that it opposes any reductions in U.S. tariffs on tuna from Panama. It said that it supports the current U.S. duty structure for canned tuna (consisting of an ad valorem tariff for tuna packed in oil and a tariff-rate quota for tuna packed in water). It stated that the rise in low-cost imports has led to the demise of the U.S. tuna processing industry (since 1979 at least ten canneries have closed, with a loss of 20,000 jobs). Bumble Bee noted that, with hourly labor rates of $11.50 and $7.50 in California and Puerto Rico, respectively, it cannot compete with Panama labor rates of about $1.75 per hour. Panama, according to Bumble Bee, has tuna canning operations that currently sell their product in the European Union due to tariff preferences in that market, and Panama could easily divert its shipments to the U.S. market should the proposed U.S.-Panama TPA lead to the elimination of the U.S. tariffs on canned tuna from Panama. Bumble Bee stated that any terms regarding canned tuna in the proposed agreement include rules of origin similar to those included in the Andean Trade Preference Act, where tariff preferences were given only for tuna harvested by

Andean and/or U.S.-flag harvesting vessels (thereby offering increased market opportunities for the U.S. tuna fleet, now that most U.S. canneries have closed).

Caterpillar, U.S. Chamber of Commerce, Association of American Chambers of Commerce in Latin America, and the Latin America Trade Coalition[372]

Caterpillar stated that it is the world's leading producer of construction and mining machines as well as diesel and gas turbine engines, and one of the largest U.S. exporters of such products. The U.S. Chamber of Commerce said that it is the world's largest business federation. The Association of American Chambers of Commerce in Latin America said that it represents 23 American Chambers of Commerce in 21 Latin American and Caribbean countries, and that its coalition represents over 80 percent of all U.S. investment in the region. The Latin America Trade Coalition noted that it is a growing, broad-based group of more than 300 U.S. companies, farmers, and business organizations.

These groups stated that they support the TPA and that the agreement would improve market access for American farm products, industrial and other nonagricultural goods, and services in Panama. Further, they asserted that, beyond the purely commercial gains, the TPA would strengthen the U.S.-Panama geostrategic partnership. They stated that because almost 5 percent of world trade passes through the Panama Canal, both the United States and Panama can benefit significantly through increased bilateral trade in the previously mentioned sectors. Caterpillar, in particular, noted the tremendous opportunities it sees in exporting its U.S.-produced products to Panama duty free. With the $5.3 billion Panama Canal expansion set to begin in 2008, Caterpillar stated that the TPA would provide it with a competitive advantage over most products made elsewhere in the world. Additionally, Caterpillar noted that labor rights, investment protections, and protection of trademarks, patents, and copyrights would be enhanced under the TPA.

The Chamber of Commerce, Industry, and Agriculture of Panama[373]

The Chamber of Commerce, Industry, and Agriculture of Panama (Chamber) stated that it is a nongovernmental organization with 14,000 members representing 14 different sectors of the Panamanian economy. On behalf of the Panama Pro-TPA Coalition, it supports the U.S.-Panama TPA and believes that the successful implementation of the agreement would have a significant positive effect on U.S. exporters, particularly at the local level. According to the Chamber, more than 84 percent of Panama's GDP is derived from its services sector. It stated that as a regional trade center, Panama offers attractive and substantial U.S. trade and investment opportunities in sectors such as port and transportation services, energy, telecommunications, tourism, and financial services. The Chamber noted that 15 percent of U.S. ocean-borne trade passes through the Panama Canal and said that the TPA would create new economic opportunities for U.S. commodities exporters, including the opportunity to participate in the $5.3 billion Canal expansion project set for 2008–2014. The Chamber also stated that it will continue to support and promote greater development on issues regarding investment barriers, transparency and government procurement, labor, environment, dispute settlement, electronic business, and the protection of intellectual property rights in Panama. The group asserted that with greater access to U.S. markets, the TPA would reduce Panama's dependence on foreign aid and, through greater prosperity, further suppress proponents of economic and political extremism in the region.

Council of the Americas[374]

The Council of the Americas (Council) stated that it is a business organization representing approximately 175 member companies invested in, and doing business throughout, the Western Hemisphere. The Council expressed strong support for the U.S.-Panama TPA on both economic and national security grounds. The Council said that open markets and steady nvestment will be key to realizing sustainable, equitable growth in the hemisphere. According to the Council, the TPA would provide U.S. investors greater overall transparency and lower risk through protections such as the implementation of fair dispute settlement mechanisms. The Council further noted the upcoming Panama Canal expansion project and the potential competitive advantages U.S. heavy machinery and technological goods firms would have through the lowering of Panamanian tariffs.

The Council also made the following points in its support of the TPA: (1) the TPA would eliminate 88 percent of all duties immediately and phase out the remaining tariffs over the next 10 years; (2) the TPA would provide greater access to government contracts, including bids to the Panama Canal expansion project; (3) under its TPA commitments, Panama would adhere to multilateral environmental agreements and all core ILO labor standards.

International Intellectual Property Alliance[375]

The International Intellectual Property Alliance (IIPA) stated that it is a coalition of seven trade associations, each representing a significant segment of the U.S. copyright-based industries. IIPA stated that these member associations collectively represent more than 1,900 companies producing and distributing materials protected by copyright laws throughout the world and that they include firms producing all types of computer software; theatrical films, television programs, home videos, and digital representations of audiovisual works; music, records, CDs, and audio cassettes; and textbooks, trade books, reference and professional publications, and journals (in both electronic and print media).

IIPA stated that the copyright-based industries are among the fastest growing and most productive sectors of the U.S. economy. IIPA stated that the "core" U.S. copyright industries accounted for an estimated $819 billion, or more than 6 percent of U.S. GDP, in 2005 and employed 5.38 million workers. Estimated foreign sales and exports of the core copyright industries increased to more than $110 billion in 2005, leading other major industry sectors. IIPA stated that it is essential to the continued growth and competitiveness of these industries that trading partners provide free and open markets and high levels of protection to the copyrights on which this trade depends.

IIPA stated that it supports the TPA and looks forward to the prompt and effective implementation of Panama's obligations under the agreement. IIPA stated that the TPA offers a tool for encouraging compliance with evolving international trends in copyright standards and outlines specific enforcement provisions. IIPA said that it believes that the TPA, once fully implemented, will attract new foreign investment in Panama and new trade in valuable digital and other intellectual property-based products, particularly in the area of e-commerce.

National Association of Manufacturers[376]

The National Association of Manufacturers (NAM) stated that it is the largest U.S. industry trade association, representing small and large manufacturers in every industrial sector and in all 50 states. NAM expressed strong support for the U.S.-Panama TPA. NAM asserted that it is in the strong interest of U.S. manufacturers to support this agreement inasmuch as nearly 60 percent (or $1.6 billion) of total U.S. exports to Panama are attributable to the manufactured goods sector, making the United States Panama's largest supplier of such products. NAM stated that the TPA would allow for "zero-for-zero" market access, which would provide U.S. companies immediate duty-free or near duty-free access to important export sectors such as agricultural and construction equipment, medical and scientific equipment, motor vehicles and parts, paper and wood products, and chemicals. NAM also contended that the agreement would enhance and promote democracy and further economic liberalization within the Western Hemisphere.

NAM made the following points in support of the TPA: (1) the agreement's investment provisions provide a comprehensive and transparent set of rights that are consistent with U.S. law; (2) the intellectual property rights (IPR) chapter contains strong enforcement mechanisms and penalties for end-user piracy and counterfeiting; (3) the TPA's customs and trade facilitation provisions support strong measures against the illegal transshipment of goods; and (4) regulatory and technical barriers to trade are reduced through the agreement's clear technical guidelines.

National Corn Growers Association[377]

The National Corn Growers Association (NCGA) stated that it represents over 32,000 corn farmers. NCGA stated that it supports the U.S.-Panama TPA. NCGA noted that the agreement effectively doubles the amount of the TRQ for U.S. corn exports to Panama by granting an initial 298,700 mt initial TRQ in year one with a zero in-quota duty, and that the TRQ would be completely phased out in year 15.

The National Pork Producers Council[378]

The National Pork Producers Council (NPPC) stated that the U.S.-Panama TPA would create important new opportunities for U.S. pork producers. The NPPC stated that live hog prices are positively affected by the introduction of expanded export market access and that recent strength in U.S. pork markets are directly related to increased exports of U.S. pork. NPPC stated that U.S. pork exports to Panama compete with exports from Canada and the European Union. NPPC reported that the TPA, if implemented, would provide U.S. pork products with a competitive advantage in the Panamanian market. Citing Dermot Hayes, an economist at Iowa State University, NPPC said that increased exports to Panama would be worth $20.6 million in additional revenue to the U.S. pork industry and that, when fully implemented, the TPA would lead to a 20-cent per hog price increase.

Sweetener Users Association[379]

The Sweetener Users Association (SUA) said that it represents companies that use nutritive sweeteners, including sugar, in the confectionery, baking, cereal, beverage, dairy product, and other food manufacturing industries, as well as associations that represent these industries.

The SUA reported that it supports the 7,000 mt increase in the sugar TRQ contained in the U.S.-Panama TPA. The SUA stated that analysis of the impact of the TPA must consider the effects on U.S. sugar consumers, other U.S. agricultural producers, and bilateral agricultural and food trade. The SUA stated that the U.S. market requires imported sugar and that the additional access under the TPA represents a minor share of the U.S. sugar market. It said that the increase in sugar imports from Panama would increase competition in the U.S. market, help stem job losses in sugar-using industries, generate foreign exchange for Panama to import other U.S. food and agricultural products, and benefit U.S. sugar consumers.

United States Association of Importers of Textiles and Apparel[380]

The United States Association of Importers of Textiles and Apparel (AITA) stated that the agreement would have a negligible effect on trade in textile products between the United States and Panama. In addition, AITA expressed dissatisfaction regarding the staging of tariff rates on some products to "Free," preferring an immediate elimination, which would go further toward achieving true trade liberalization. Finally, AITA expressed concern that the lack of broad cumulation provisions, restricted single-transformation origin rules, limited short-supply rules, and onerous administrative processes would likely discourage increased trade with Panama with respect to textile and apparel products.

The U.S. Grains Council[381]

The U.S. Grains Council stated that the U.S.-Panama TPA would benefit the U.S. feedgrains industry overall. The Council said that the TPA, once implemented, will provide U.S. corn growers improved access to the Panamanian market under an expanding duty-free, tariff-rate quota and will eliminate other nontariff barriers such as absorption requirements. According to the U.S. Grains Council, this enhanced access would allow the United States to take advantage of future demand increases from Panama's growing poultry sector.

U.S.-Panama Business Council[382]

The U.S.-Panama Business Council (USPA) stated that it is a business organization that supports cooperation between the two countries by creating business opportunities for both U.S. and Panamanian business leaders. USPA said that it supports the U.S.-Panama TPA. USPA stated that with over 150 years of friendship and cooperation between the two countries, a "special relationship" has been developed which should continue to be fostered through the TPA. USPA asserted that the United States would benefit directly from the upcoming expansion of the Panama Canal, as the United States is the origin or destination of 70 percent of all cargo transiting through the Canal. USPA stated that the United States and

Panama share many close social, economic, and political relationships and that recent visits by high-ranking U.S. Government officials to Panama illustrate this welcoming attitude. USPA stated that the TPA between the two countries reflects important economic, historical, and social ties.

APPENDIX A
REQUEST LETTER FROM USTR

The Honorable Daniel R. Pearson
Chairman
U.S. International Trade Commission
500 E Street, S.W.
Washington, DC 20436

Dear Chairman Pearson,

As you know, the United States and Panama have completed the negotiation of the United States - Panama Trade Promotion Agreement ("Agreement"), a comprehensive free trade": agreement. The advice that the U.S. International Trade Commission ("Commission") provided over the course of these negotiations assisted us greatly in bringing the negotiations to a successful conclusion.

The President has notified the Congress of his intent to enter into the Agreement. Pursuant to authority delegated to me by the President and in accordance with section 2104(f) of the Trade Act of 2002 (Trade Act), I request the Commission to prepare a report as specified in section 2 104(f)(2)-(3) of the Trade Act assessing the likely impact of the Agreement on the United States economy as a whole and on specific industry sectors and the interests of U.S. consumers.

I would greatly appreciate it if the Commission could issue its report as soon as possible. USTR staff will provide the Commission with the details of the Agreement and will be available to answer questions or provide additional information. The text of the Agreement that will be the subject of legal review is available on the USTR website.

Thank you for your continued cooperation and assistance in this matter.

Sincerely,

Susan C. Schwab

APPENDIX B
FEDERAL REGISTER NOTICE

of the individual discipline breakout sessions of the previous day and to continue with Committee business.

The meetings are open to the public. Approximately 30 visitors can be accommodated on a first-come-firstserved basis at the plenary session.

Authority: Federal Advisory Committee Act, P.L. 92–463, 5 U.S.C., Appendix I, and the Office of Management and Budget's Circular A–63, Revised. Dated: April 26, 2007.

Chris C. Oynes, *Associate Director for Offshore Minerals Management.* [FR Doc. E7–8331 Filed 5–1–07; 8:45 am]

INTERNATIONAL TRADE COMMISSION
[INVESTIGATION NO. TA–2104–025]

U.S.–Panama Trade Promotion Agreement: Potential Economy-Wide and Selected Sectoral Effects

Agency: International Trade Commission.

Action: Institution of investigation and scheduling of public hearing.

SUMMARY

Following receipt of a request from the United States Trade Representative (USTR) on March 30, 2007, the Commission instituted investigation No. TA–2104–025, U.S.– Panama Trade Promotion Agreement: Potential Economy-wide and Selected Sectoral Effects, under § 2104(f) of the Trade Act of 2002 (19 U.S.C. 3804(f)), for the purpose of assessing the likely impact of the U.S.–Panama Trade Promotion Agreement (TPA) on the U.S. economy as a whole and on specific industry sectors and the interests of U.S. consumers.

Dates

March 30, 2007: Receipt of request.
May 7, 2007: Deadline for receipt of requests to appear at hearing.
May 10, 2007: Deadline for filing prehearing briefs and statements.
May 16, 2007, 9:30 a.m.: Public hearing.
May 23, 2007: Deadline for filing posthearing briefs and statements and all other written submissions.
September 12, 2007: Anticipated date for transmitting report to USTR and the Congress.

Addresses

All Commission offices, including the Commission's hearing rooms, are located in the United States International Trade Commission Building, 500 E Street, SW., Washington, DC. All written submissions, including requests to appear at the hearing, statements, and briefs, should be addressed to the Secretary, United States International Trade Commission, 500 E Street, SW., Washington, DC 20436. The public record for this investigation may be viewed on the Commission's electronic docket (EDIS) at *http://edis.usitc.gov*.

For Further Information Contact:

Project Leader Jennifer Baumert, Office of Industries (202–205–3450; *jennifer.baumert@usitc.gov*) or Deputy Project Leader Alan Treat, Office of Industries (202–205–3426; *alan.treat@usitc.gov*]. For information on legal aspects, contact William Gearhart of the Office of the General Counsel (202–205–3091; *william.gearhart@usitc.gov*. The media should contact Margaret O'Laughlin, Office of External Relations at 202–205–1819 or *margaret.olaughlin@usitc.gov*. Hearing impaired individuals are advised that information on this matter can be obtained by contacting the TDD terminal on 202–205–1810. General information concerning the Commission may also be obtained by accessing its Internet server (*http://www.usitc.gov*). Persons with mobility impairments who will need special assistance in gaining access to the Commission should contact the Secretary at 202–205–2000.

Supplementary Information

As requested by the USTR, the Commission will prepare a report as specified in § 2104(f)(2)–(3) of the Trade Act of 2002 assessing the likely impact of the U.S.–Panama Trade Promotion Agreement on the U.S. economy as a whole and on specific industry sectors, including the impact the agreement will have on the gross domestic product, exports and imports; aggregate employment and employment opportunities; the production, employment, and competitive position of industries likely to be significantly affected by the agreement; and the interests of U.S. consumers.

In preparing its assessment, the Commission will review available economic assessments regarding the agreement, including literature concerning any substantially equivalent proposed agreement, and will provide in its assessment a description of the analyses used and conclusions drawn in such literature, and a discussion of areas of consensus and divergence between the various analyses and conclusions, including those of the Commission regarding the agreement.

Section 2104(f)(2) requires that the Commission submit its report to the President and the Congress not later than 90 days after the President enters into the agreement, which he can do 90 days after he notifies the Congress of his intent to do so. On March 30, 2007, the President notified the Congress of his intent to enter into a TPA with Panama. The USTR requested that the Commission provide its report as soon as possible.

Public Hearing

A public hearing in connection with the investigation will be held beginning at 9:30 a.m. on May 16, 2007, at the U.S. International Trade Commission Building, 500 E Street, SW., Washington, DC. All persons will have the right to appear, by counsel or in person, to present information and to be heard. Requests to appear at the public hearing should be filed with the Secretary no later than 5:15 p.m., May 7, 2007. Any pre-hearing briefs and statements should be filed no later than 5:15 p.m., May 10, 2007, and any posthearing briefs and statements should be filed no later than 5:15 p.m., May 23, 2007; all such briefs and statements must be submitted in accordance with the requirements below under "written submissions." In the event that, as of the close of business on May 7, 2007, no witnesses are scheduled to appear at the hearing, the hearing will be canceled. Any person interested in attending the hearing as an observer or nonparticipant may call the Secretary to the Commission (202–205–2000) after May 7, 2007, for information concerning whether the hearing will be held.

Written Submissions

In lieu of or in addition to participating in the hearing, interested parties are invited to submit written statements concerning the matters to be addressed by the Commission in its report on this investigation. Submissions should be addressed to the Secretary. To be assured of consideration by the Commission, written statements related to the Commission's report should be submitted to the Commission at the earliest practical date and should be received no later than 5:15 p.m., May 23, 2007.

All written submissions must conform with the provisions of § 201.8 of the Commission's Rules of Practice and Procedure (19 CFR 201.8). Section 201.8 of the rules requires that a signed original (or copy designated as an original) and fourteen (14) copies of each document be filed. In the event that confidential treatment of the document is requested, at least four (4) additional copies must be filed, in which the confidential business information must be deleted (see the following paragraph for further information regarding confidential business information). The Commission's rules do not authorize filing submissions with the Secretary by facsimile or electronic means, except to the extent permitted by § 201.8 of the rules (see Handbook for Electronic Filing Procedures, *ftp://ftp.usitc.gov/pub/reports/electronic_filing_handbook.pdf*. Persons with questions regarding electronic filing should contact the Secretary (202–205–2000 or *edis@usitc.gov*.

Any submissions that contain confidential business information must also conform with the requirements of § 201.6 of the Commission's Rules of Practice and Procedure (19 CFR 201.6). Section 201.6 of the rules requires that the cover of the document and the individual pages be clearly marked as to whether they are the "confidential" or "nonconfidential" version, and that the confidential business information be clearly identified by means of brackets. All written submissions, except for confidential business information, will be made available in the Office of the Secretary to the Commission for inspection by interested parties.

The Commission intends to prepare only a public report in this investigation. The report that the Commission sends to the President and the Congress and makes available to the public will not contain confidential business information. Any confidential business information received by the Commission in this investigation and used in preparing the report will not be published in a manner that would reveal the operations of the firm supplying the information.

By order of the Commission.

Issued: April 26, 2007.

Marilyn R. Abbott,
Secretary to the Commission. [FR Doc. E7–8256 Filed 5–1–07; 8:45 am]

DEPARTMENT OF LABOR

Employment and Training Administration

Workforce Investment Act (WIA) Section 167—The National Farmworker Jobs Program (NFJP)

Agency: Employment and Training Administration (ETA), Department of Labor.

Action: Notice of formula allocations for the Program Year (PY) 2007 NFJP, request for comments.

SUMMARY

Under Section 182(d) of the WIA of 1998, ETA is publishing the PY 2007 allocations for the NFJP, authorized under Section 167 of the WIA. The allocations are distributed to the states by a formula that estimates, by state, the relative demand for NFJP services. The allocations in this notice apply to the PY beginning July 1, 2007.

Dates

Comments must be submitted on or before May 29, 2007.

Addresses

Comments should be sent to Alina M. Walker, Program Manager, Division of Adult Services, Room S–4209, Employment and Training Administration, U.S. Department of Labor, 200 Constitution Avenue, NW., Washington, DC 20210, e-mail address: *walker.alina@dol.gov.*

For Further Information Contact:

Alina M. Walker, Program Manager, Division of Adult Services, Room S– \4209, Employment and Training Administration, U.S. Department of Labor, 200 Constitution Avenue, NW., Washington, DC 20210, telephone: (202) 693–2706 (this is not a toll-free number).

SUPPLEMENTARY INFORMATION

I. Background

On May 19, 1999, ETA published a notice establishing new factors for the formula that allocates funds available for the NFJP in the **Federal Register** at 64 FR 27390. This **Federal Register** notice is available at the following Internet address: *http://www.doleta.gov/MSFW/pdf/allocationtable.pdf*

The May 19, 1999, **Federal Register** may also be obtained by submitting a mail, e-mail or telephone request to Alina M. Walker, Program Manager, Division of Adult Services, Room S–4209, Employment and Training Administration, U.S. Department of Labor, 200 Constitution Avenue, NW., Washington, D.C. 20210, e-mail address: *walker.alina@dol.gov,* telephone number (202) 693–2706 (this is not a toll-free number).

The May 19, 1999, notice explained the purpose of the formula, *i.e.*, distributing funds geographically by state service area on the basis of each area's relative share of farmworkers who are eligible for enrollment in the NFJP. The data used to run the formula is comprised of a combination of data sets that were selected to yield the relative share distribution across states of eligible farmworkers. The combined-data set driven formula is substantially more relevant to the purpose of aligning the allocations with the eligible population than the allocations determined by the prior formula.

For PY 2007, the data factors used in the formula remain unchanged since they were first developed in 1999. The data sets used for determining each State's relative share of eligible farmworkers for PY 2007 were last updated in PY 2005 with more recent data available from the 2000 Census, the 2003 National Agricultural Workers Survey (NAWS), and the 2002 Census of Agriculture, and also remain unchanged.

II. Limitations on Uses of Section 167 Funds

In appropriating the funds for PY 2007, Congress provided in the Fiscal Year 2007 Continuing Appropriations Resolution (Pub. L. 110–5) $79,752,000 for carrying out Section 167 of the Workforce Investment Act of 1998, including $74,302,000 for state service area grants, $4,950,000 for migrant and seasonal farmworker housing grants, and $500,000 for Section 167 training, technical assistance and related activities. Additional funding for migrant rest center activities is included in the $500,000 available for technical assistance and training.

III. PY 2007 Allocation Formula

The calculation of the PY 2007 formula allocation distribution incorporates the state-by-state relative shares of eligible farmworkers developed for the PY 2005 formula allocations, using the updated data sets described above, with various adjustments applied since then. The PY 2005 calculation adjusted those state-bystate relative shares of eligible farmworkers by ''hold-harmless'' and ''stop-loss''/''stop-gain'' limits due to the introduction of the updated data. The following year, the PY 2006 formula allocations were proportionately based on the PY 2005 formula allocations and further adjusted by an additional $3.8 million appropriated by Congress for states whose PY 2005 allocation had been reduced as a result of the updated data used for the PY 2005 allocation distribution. Detailed descriptions of the formula methodology for PY 2005 and 2006 are provided in the applicable announcements.

The PY 2007 appropriation for the WIA Section 167 program is $74,302,000, which is $470 less than the corresponding PY 2006 appropriation. To maintain stability of funding for the program and consistency with the PY 2006 congressional directions to the Department, the Department will distribute the $74,302,000 of PY 2007 formula funding among all states in the same proportion as the distribution of the PY 2006 formula allocations.

IV. State Combinations

We anticipate a single plan of service for operating the PY 2007 NFJP in the jurisdiction comprised of Delaware and Maryland and the jurisdiction

APPENDIX C
HEARING PARTICIPANTS

Calendar of Public Hearing

Those listed below appeared as witnesses at the United States International Trade Commission's hearing:

Subject: U.S.-Panama Trade Promotion Agreement: Potential Economywide and Selected Sectoral Effects

Inv. No.: TA-2 104-25

Date and Time: May 16, 2007 − 9:30 a.m.

Sessions were held in connection with this investigation in the Main Hearing Room (room 101), 500 E Street, S.W., Washington, D.C.

Organization and Witness:

The Chamber of Commerce, Industry, and Agriculture of Panama
    Raúl Del Valle, Former President
    Manuel Ferreira, Economic Chief
    American Chamber of Commerce of Panama (AMCHAM)
    Panama

    David Hunt, Executive Director
    U.S. Chamber of Commerce
    Office of Western Hemisphere Affairs
    Washington, D.C.

    Tom Gales, Vice President, Latin America Division,
    Caterpillar, Inc., on behalf of the U.S.-Panama
    Trade Coalition
    U.S.-Panama Business Council
    Washington, D.C.

    Juan B. Sosa, President
    Sweetener Users Association
    Washington, D. C.

    Thomas Earley,
    Economic Consultant, Promar International

APPENDIX D
U.S.-PANAMA TPA: SUMMARY OF SELECTED CHAPTERS

The following sections summarize those chapters of the U.S.-Panama TPA that are not the subject of a discrete overview elsewhere in the report.

TPA Chapter 1 - Initial Provisions

The text states that the parties establish the TPA, consistent with the 1994 General Agreement on Tariffs and Trade (GATT) and article V of the General Agreement on Trade in Services (GATS), and reaffirm that the existing bilateral rights and obligations continue to apply between the parties.

The text also states that, in addition to the principles and rules of national treatment, most-favored treatment, and transparency, the objectives of the agreement are to encourage expansion and diversification of trade between the parties; eliminate barriers to trade in, and facilitate the cross-border movement of, goods and services between the territories of the Parties; promote conditions of fair competition and substantially increase investment opportunities in the free trade area; and provide adequate and effective protection and enforcement of intellectual property rights in each party's territory. Finally, the text outlines the objectives of creating effective procedures for the implementation, application, and joint administration of the Agreement, and procedures for the resolution of disputes; and the establishment of a framework for the expansion and enhancement of further bilateral, regional, and multilateral cooperation.

TPA Chapter 2 - General Definitions

Among the general definitions in the TPA, the term "territory" is defined by each party to include the land, maritime, and air space under its sovereignty and the continental shelf over which it exercises sovereign rights and jurisdiction in accordance with international law and its domestic law. In the case of the United States, foreign trade zones are included as part of the territory of the United States along with the customs territory and certain areas outside the territorial seas in which the United States may control seabed and subsoil and their natural resources. The general definition of "customs duty" indicates that import-related duties or charges are included, including surtaxes or surcharges, but not antidumping or countervailing duties, certain fees equivalent to internal taxes, or customs administrative fees or charges. The chapter also includes definitions of certain terms with respect to Panama, as well.

TPA Chapter 19 - Administration of the Agreement and Trade Capacity Building

Chapter 19 of the TPA establishes a Free Trade Commission of cabinet-level representatives to supervise the implementation of the TPA, consider all types of matters raised under it, resolve disputes that may arise regarding the interpretation or application of this agreement, establish and task working groups, and fulfill other similar duties. The Free Trade Commission includes the USTR and the Panamanian Ministerio de Comercio e Industrias. Under this chapter, each party also designates a TPA coordinator to prepare for Free Trade Commission meetings and follow up on its decisions. The chapter also includes provisions on administering dispute settlement proceedings.

Because trade capacity building is recognized as a catalyst for the reforms and investments needed to foster trade-driven economic growth and reduce poverty, section B of this chapter establishes a Committee on Trade Capacity Building. This committee will seek to prioritize trade capacity building projects at the national or regional level, or both, and invite the participation of international donor organizations, private sector entities, and nongovernmental organizations to encourage trade and reform. The committee will also provide oversight to a working group on customs administration and trade facilitation created under the provisions of this chapter. The committee is directed to focus on implementing the provisions of Chapter 5 – Customs Administration and of Chapter 3 – Market Access (Section G: Textiles and Apparel), as well as any other priority that the Committee designates.

TPA Chapter 21 – Exceptions

The chapter discusses general exceptions to various chapters of the TPA and mentions specific provisions of various WTO agreements, which are incorporated by reference. This chapter exempts the disclosure of essential security, taxation, or other information, which would impede law enforcement or be contrary to the public interest.

TPA Chapter 22 - Final Provisions

This chapter defines the legal scope of the agreement and contains the mechanisms for acceding to the TPA and putting it into force. The parties must consult on any changes made to provisions of the WTO agreement incorporated in this text to determine if the same principle will apply herein, and any reservation to provisions by a party requires the written consent of the other party. The TPA will enter into force 60 days after the exchange of written notifications by the United States and Panama that each has completed its respective domestic legal procedures. The parties agree that "the English and Spanish texts of this Agreement are equally authentic."[383] Any withdrawal from the TPA will take effect 6 months after written notice.

APPENDIX E
PANAMA: ECONOMIC PROFILE AND TABLES

PANAMA
Economic Profile[384]

Economic indicators	2002	2006
Population (m)	3.1	3.3
GDP (US$ bn)	12.3	17.7
GDP per capita (US$)	3,967.7	5,363.6
Real GDP growth (%)	2.2	8.1
Goods exports (US$ m)	5,314.7	8,509.9
Goods imports (US$ m)	6,349.8	10,309.9
Trade balance (US$ m)	-1,035.1	-1,800.0

Panama's main trade commodities, US$ million, 2005			
Exports		Imports	
Melon and watermelon	117.0	Capital goods	1,079.9
Bananas	96.5	Petroleum products	736.6
Sugar	23.7	Food products	636.9
Coffee	13.5		

GDP by sector, 2005

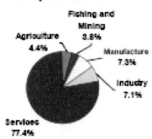

Panama's main trading partners, percent of total, 2005			
Exports		**Imports**	
United States	44.5	United States	27.4
Spain	8.8	Nether. Antilles	11.4
Sweden	5.6	Costa Rica	4.7
Netherlands	4.8	Japan	4.5

Economic Overview

- Panama is an upper-middle-income country located in Central America, bordering both the Caribbean Sea and the North Pacific Ocean, between Colombia and Costa Rica. Its population is approximately one percent that of the United States, and its GDP was less than 0.5 percent of the U.S. GDP in 2005.
- Panama's dollarized economy[385] is primarily export-oriented in the services sector. In the early 1990s, the government adopted trade reform polices that significantly opened its economy, including the conversion of quantitative trade barriers to lower and relatively more uniform ad valorem tariffs.
- The services sector in Panama accounted for 76 percent of the country's GDP and 67 percent of employment in 2005. The country's well developed services sector includes operating the Panama Canal, banking (the International Banking Centre), the Colón Free Zone, insurance, container ports, flagship registry, and tourism.
- Agriculture accounts for about 4 percent of GDP and consists primarily of melon and watermelon, bananas, sugarcane, and coffee production. These products are Panama's main export commodities. Although fishing represents less than 4 percent of the country's GDP, it accounts for approximately one-third of Panama's exports to the United States.

- The Panamanian government has a plan to expand and modernize the Panama Canal that will double its capacity and accommodate giant cargo ships which are too large to currently cross the canal. The expansion and modernization project, approved by Panamanian voters via referendum in October 2006, is expected to be completed by August 2014 with an estimated cost of $5.3 billion.

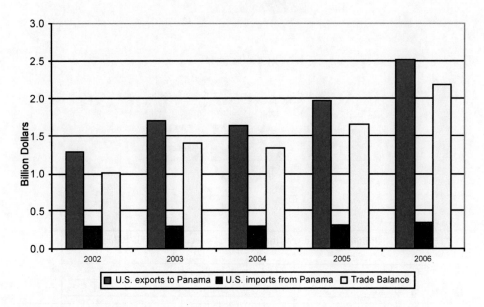

U.S. merchandise trade with Panama, 2002-06

Source: Compiled from officicial statistics of the U.S. Department of Commerce.

Leading U.S. exports to Panama, US$ million, 2006	
Mineral fuels	855.5
Machinery and equipment	383.8
Aircraft	166.1
Pharmaceutical products	131.6
Vehicles, other than railway	89.8
Other	896.7
Total	2,523.6

Leading U.S. imports from Panama, US$ million, 2006	
Fish	101.9
Precious metals and jewelry	35.1
Sugars and sugar confectionery	23.5
Edible fruit and nuts	12.5
Coffee	11.8
Other	152.7
Total	337.6

Source: Compiled from official statistics of the U.S. Department of Commerce.

Preferential trade agreements and U.S. programs

- Panama has signed five FTAs, including the US-Panama TPA. The FTAs with El Salvador, Taiwan, and Singapore entered into force in 2003, 2004, and 2006, respectively. Panama signed an FTA with Chile in 2006 but the agreement has not entered into force. Panama also has partial bilateral trade treaties with Colombia, the Dominican Republic, Mexico, and the countries of Central America.
- Panama is a designated beneficiary of CBERA, CBPTA, and GSP. These programs, together with the provisions under normal trade relations (NTR), allowed 96 percent of U.S. imports from Panama to enter the United States free of duty in 2006.

U.S.-Panama bilateral trade in goods

- U.S. trade with Panama is small, accounting for 0.3 percent of total U.S. goods exports and 0.02 percent of total U.S. goods imports in 2006. Panama ranked as the 45th largest market for U.S. exports and 102nd largest import supplier for the United States in 2006.
- The United States is Panama's largest bilateral trading partner, supplying 27.4 percent of Panama's total imports and purchasing 44.5 percent of Panama's total exports in 2005.
- The U.S. trade surplus with Panama increased from 2002 to 2006, primarily as a result of increased exports to Panama, driven substantially by the increasing value of energy-related exports.
- U.S. exports to Panama in 2006 totaled $2.5 billion and consisted mainly of mineral fuels, machinery and equipment, aircraft, pharmaceutical products, and vehicles, other than railway.
- U.S. imports from Panama in 2006 totaled $337.6 million and consisted mainly of fish, precious metals and jewelry (mainly gold), sugars and sugar confectionery, edible fruit and nuts, and coffee.
- U.S. imports from Panama classified in approximately 5,726 8-digit tariff lines are already eligible to enter duty free or at a reduced tariff under CBERA.

Table E.1. Leading U.S. Exports to Panama, Total U.S. Exports to the World, and Panama Share of Total, 2006

HTS sub-headings	Description	U.S. exports to Panama	U.S. exports to world	Panama share
		1,000 dollars		Percent
2710.19	Petroleum oils & oils (not light) from bitu-minous minerals or preps nesoi 70% + by wt. From petroleum oils or bitum. Min.	774,997	16,033,553	4.8
8802.40	Airplanes and other aircraft nesoi, of an unladen weight exceeding 15,000 kg	111,749	35,876,951	0.3
9880.00	Estimate of non-canadian low value ex-port shipments; compiled low value shipments to canada; and shipments not identified by kind to Canada	102,235	22,909,517	0.4

Table E.1. Continued)

HTS sub-headings	Description	U.S. exports to Panama	U.S. exports to world	Panama share
		1,000 dollars		Percent
3004.90	Medicaments, in measured doses, etc. (excluding vaccines, etc., coated band-ages etc. And pharmaceutical goods), nesoi	97,353	12,381,069	0.8
2710.11	Light oils and preparations from petrole-um oils & oils from bituminous min. Or preps 70%+ by wt. From petro. Oils or bitum. Min.	72,929	6,032,714	1.2
8803.30	Parts of airplanes or helicopters, nesoi	39,738	17,649,186	0.2
8473.30	Parts and accessories for automatic data processing machines and units thereof, magnetic or optical readers, transcribing machines, etc., nesoi	35,241	11,934,426	0.3
1005.90	Corn (maize), other than seed corn	34,638	7,157,295	0.5
3303.00	Perfumes and toilet waters	32,051	808,614	4.0
8703.23	Passenger motor vehicles with spark-ignition internal combustion recipro-cating piston engine, cylinder capacity over 1,500 cc but not over 3,000 cc	29,952	17,872,798	0.2
9009.99	Parts and accessories of photocopying apparatus, nesoi	27,712	266,009	10.4
2304.00	Soybean oilcake and other solid residues resulting from the extraction of soy bean oil, whether or not ground or in the form of pellets	27,528	1,289,179	2.1
2941.90	Antibiotics, nesoi	25,044	708,075	3.5
1001.90	Wheat (other than durum wheat), and meslin	22,406	4,006,867	0.6
4804.11	Kraftliner, uncoated, unbleached, in rolls or sheets	21,758	1,353,247	1.6
8525.20	Transmission apparatus incorporating reception apparatus for radiotelephony, radiotelegraphy, radiobroadcasting or television	18,734	3,575,603	0.5
8471.49	Automatic data processing machines and units thereof presented in the form of systems, nesoi	16,362	3,076,575	0.5
3004.20	Medicaments, in measured doses, etc., containing antibiotics, nesoi	12,841	699,769	1.8
2106.90	Food preparations nesoi	12,463	2,624,136	0.5
8471.50	Processing units other than those of 8471.41 and 8471.49, nesoi	12,039	2,996,730	0.4
	Subtotal	1,527,770	169,252,314	0.9
	Other	995,813	760,223,709	0.1
	Total	2,523,583	929,486,022	0.3

Source: U.S. Department of Commerce.

Table E.2. Leading U.S. imports from Panama, total U.S. imports from the world, and Panama share of total, 2006

HTS sub-headings	Description	U.S. imports from Panama	U.S. imports from world	Panama share
		1,000 dollars		Percent
0306.13.00	Shrimps and prawns, cooked in shell or uncooked, dried, salted or in brine, frozen	39,197	2,998,666	1.3
0302.69.40	Fish, nesoi, excl. fillets, livers and roes, fresh or chilled, not scaled, or scaled in immediate containers weighing over 6.8 kg	23,361	192,291	12.1
1701.11.10	Cane sugar, raw, in solid form, w/o added flavoring or coloring, subject to add. US 5 to Ch.17	17,843	691,066	2.6
0302.69.20	Smelts, cusk, hake, etc. excl. fillets, livers & roes, fresh or chilled, not scaled, or scaled in immediate containers over 6.8 kg	15,472	77,644	19.9
7108.12.10	Gold, nonmonetary, bullion and dore	14,535	4,534,057	0.3
0901.11.00	Coffee, not roasted, not decaffeinated	10,997	2,508,692	0.4
7108.13.55	Gold (incl. gold plated w platinum), not money, semimanufacture, rectangle/near rectangular shape,99.5% or > pure, marked only by wgt/identity	10,643	65,511	16.2
7112.91.00	Gold waste and scrap, including metal clad with gold but excluding sweep-ings contain-ing other precious metals	7,678	447,589	1.7
0302.34.00	Bigeye tunas (Thunnas obesus), fresh or chilled, excluding fillets, other meat portions, livers and roes	7,563	36,548	20.7
0807.19.70	Other melons nesoi, fresh, if entered during the period from December 1, in any year, to the following May 31, inclusive	6,426	65,013	9.9
7602.00.00	Aluminum, waste and scrap	6,301	857,250	0.7
0302.32.00	Yellowfin tunas, fresh or chilled, excluding fillets, other meat portions, livers and roes	5,506	126,466	4.4
1701.11.20	Cane sugar, raw, in solid form, to be used for certain polyhydric alcohols	5,446	121,374	4.5
7010.90.30	Glass containers for convey/pack perfume /toilet preps & containers with/ designed for ground glass stopper, not made by automatic machine	5,422	7,763	69.8
0304.20.60	Frozen fillets of fresh-water fish, flat fish, nesoi	5,122	1,422,667	0.4
9999.95.00	Estimated imports of low valued transactions	3,798	20,194,073	([a])

Table E.2. (Continued)

HTS sub-headings	Description	U.S. imports from Panama	U.S. imports from world	Panama share
		1,000 dollars		**Percent**
7404.00.30	Copper spent anodes; copper waste & scrap containing less than 94% by weight of copper	3,273	177,651	1.8
2202.90.36	Single fruit or vegetable juice (other than orange), fortified with vitamins or minerals, not concentrated	2,683	3,141	85.4
3303.00.30	Perfumes and toilet waters, containing alcohol	2,588	1,269,347	0.2
0804.30.40	Pineapples, fresh or dried, not reduced in size, in crates or other packages	2,320	278,215	0.8
	Subtotal	196,173	36,075,024	0.5
	Other	141,392	1,808,978,158	([a])
	Total	337,565	1,845,053,181	([a])

Source: U.S. Department of Commerce.
[a]Less than 0.5 percent.

Table E.3. U.S. Imports for Consumption from Panama, by Duty Treatment, 2004–6

Item	2004	2005	2006
	1,000 dollars		
Total imports	297,529	319,915	337,565
Dutiable[a]–total	31,446	7,706	13,612
Item	**2004**	**2005**	**2006**
	1,000 dollars		
Duty free[b]–total	266,083	312,208	323,953
Duty free by program:			
NTR[c]	227,182	251,771	265,876
GSP[d]	6,107	19,786	24,232
CBTPA	340	321	339
CBERA	32,449	40,330	33,467
Other duty free[e]	4		39
	Percent		
Total imports	100.0	100.0	100.0
Dutiable–total	10.6	2.4	4.0
Duty free–total	89.4	97.6	96.0
Duty free by program:			
NTR	76.4	78.7	78.8
GSP	2.1	6.2 7.2	
CBPTA	0.1	0.1	0.1
CBERA	10.9	12.6 9.9	

Other duty free	(^{f})		(^{f})

Source: Compiled from official statistics of the U.S. Department of Commerce.

Note: Because this table corrects entries reported in inappropriate categories of dutiability, it includes data that differ from their counterparts in the other tables. Data in all other tables are based on entries as reported. Also, total imports in this table may not reflect total imports in other tables because U.S. imports from CBERA countries that enter through the U.S. Virgin Islands are excluded.

Note: Figures may not add to totals shown because of rounding.

[a] Dutiable value excludes the U.S. content entering under HTS heading 9802.00.80 and heading 9802.00.60, and misreported imports.

[b] Calculated as total imports less dutiable value.

[c] Value of imports which have an NTR duty rate of free.

[d] Reduced by the value of NTR duty-free imports and ineligible items that were misreported as entering under the GSP program.

[e] Calculated as a remainder, and represents imports entering free of duty under column 1-special and non-dutiable U.S. value of imports entering under HTS 9802.00.60 and 9802.00.80.

[f] Less than 0.5 percent.

APPENDIX F
TECHNICAL APPENDIX

MODEL FOR EVALUATING THE EFFECT OF ELIMINATING TARIFFS

This appendix describes the data and modeling framework used to analyze the effects of immediate tariff elimination for selected products on total Panamanian and U.S. imports of affected products.

Introduction

Commission staff used partial equilibrium modeling to estimate economic effects of immediate tariff elimination on total Panamanian and U.S. imports. The model used in this study is a nonlinear, imperfect substitutes model for most sectors.[386] Trade and production data were taken from official statistics of the U.S. Department of Commerce. Import substitution and other elasticities were estimated by USITC industry analysts in consultation with the assigned economist based on relevant product and market characteristics and were generally chosen to give upper-bound estimates of trade effects. Trade and production data and tariff rates are for 2006.

The following model illustrates the case of granting a product TPA duty-free status. The illustration is for a product for which domestic production in the importing country, TPA imports, and non-TPA imports are imperfect substitutes and shows the basic results of a tariff removal on a portion of imports.

Consider the market for imports ports illustrated in fig. F-1, panel (a). The line labeled D_b is the demand for imports from the partner country, the line labeled S_b is the supply of imports with the tariff in place, and the line labeled S_b' is the supply of imports without the tariff (i.e., the product is receiving duty-free treatment under the TPA). Point A is the equilibrium with the tariff in place, and point B is the equilibrium without the tariff. Q_b and

Q_b' are equilibrium quantities at A and B, respectively. P_b and P_b' are equilibrium prices at A and B and P_b'' is the price received by exporting producers when the tariff is in place. The difference between P_b and P_b'' denotes the tariff, t.

In the model, a tariff reduction leads to a decrease in the price of the imported good and an increase in sales of the good in the importing country. The lower price paid for the import leads to a reduction in the demand for domestic production of the good, as well as for imports from non-TPA countries. These demand shifts, along with supply responses to the lower demand, determine the reduction in domestic output and non-TPA imports.

The changes in panel (a) lead to the changes seen in panels (b) and (c), where the demand curves shift from D_d and D_n to D_d' and D_n' , respectively. Equilibrium quantity in the market for domestic production moves from Q_d to Q_d' , and in a similar manner for the market for nonbeneficiary imports, equilibrium quantity falls from Q_n to Q_n'.

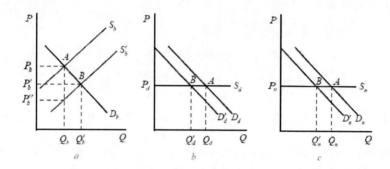

Figure F-1: U.S. markets for TPA beneficiary imports (panel a), domestic production (panel b), and nonbeneficiary imports (panel c)

Derivation of Imports and Net Welfare Effects

The basic building blocks of the model are shown below. Armington shows that if consumers have well-behaved constant elasticity of substitution (CES) utility functions, demand for a good in a product grouping can be expressed as follows:

$$q_i = b_i^\sigma q \left(\frac{p_i}{p} \right)^{-\sigma}$$

(1)

where q_i denotes quantity demanded for good i in the domestic market;[387] p_i is the price of good in the domestic market; is the elasticity of substitution for the product grouping; q is the demand for the aggregate product (that is, all goods in the product grouping); p is a price index for the aggregate product (defined below); and b_i^σ is a constant.[388] As Armington states, the above equation "... can be written in a variety of useful ways."[389] One of these useful ways can be derived as follows. The aggregate price index p is defined as In addition the aggregate quantity index q can be defined as

$$p = \left(\sum_i b_i^\sigma p_i^{1-\sigma} \right)^{\frac{1}{1-\sigma}} .$$

(2)

In addition the aggregate quantity index q can be defined as

$$q = k_A p^{\eta_A}$$

(3)

where k_A is a constant and η_A is the aggregate demand elasticity for the product grouping (natural sign). Substituting equation (3) into equation (1) yields

$$q_i = b_i^\sigma k_A p^{\eta_A} \left(\frac{p_i}{p} \right)^{-\sigma} .$$

Further manipulation and simplification yields which establishes the demand for qi in terms of prices, elasticities, and constants.

$$q_i = b_i^\sigma k_A \frac{p^{(\sigma+\eta_A)}}{p_i^\sigma} ,$$

The supply of each good in the product grouping is represented in constant supply elasticity form:

$$q_i = K_{si} p_i^{\varepsilon_{si}} ,$$

where K_{si} is a constant and ε_{si} is the price elasticity of supply for good .

Excess supply functions are set up for each good in the product grouping with the following general form:

$$K_{si} p_i^{\varepsilon_{si}} - b_i^\sigma k_A \frac{p^{\sigma+\eta_A}}{p^\sigma} = 0.$$

(4)

The model is calibrated using initial trade and production data and setting all internal prices to unity in the benchmark calibration. It can be shown that calibration yields $k_{si} = b_i^\sigma k_A$ for the ith good so that equation (4) can be rendered as

$$p_i^{\varepsilon_n} - \frac{p^{\sigma+\eta_A}}{p_i^{\sigma}} = 0 \ .$$

(4')

If there are n goods, the model consists of n equations like (4') plus an equation for the price aggregator p, which are solved simultaneously in prices by an iterative technique.

For the case of a product eligible for TPA duty-free treatment, the equations are as follows:

$$\left[p_b(1+t)\right]^{\varepsilon_{sb}} - \frac{p^{\sigma+\eta_A}}{p_b^{\sigma}} = 0$$

for imports from TPA beneficiary countries,

$$p_n^{\varepsilon_{sn}} - \frac{p^{\sigma+\eta_A}}{p_n^{\sigma}} = 0$$

for imports from non-partner countries,

$$p_d^{\varepsilon_{sd}} - \frac{p^{\sigma+\eta_A}}{p_d^{\sigma}} = 0$$

for domestic production, and

$$p = \left(\sum_{i=b,n,d} b_i^{\sigma} p_i^{1-\sigma} \right)^{\frac{1}{1-\sigma}}$$

for the price aggregator

The prices obtained in the solution to these equations are used to calculate trade and production values, and resulting percentage changes in total imports and domestic production are computed relative to the original (benchmark) import and production values.

APPENDIX G
GENERAL EFFECTS OF TRADE AGREEMENTS

General Effects of Trade Agreements

Analysis of the economic impact of an FTA entails investigating static effects such as trade creation and trade diversion, as well as terms of trade (i.e., the price of exports relative to the price of imports). In addition, issues related to scale effects and less tangible effects have to be considered. These issues are discussed below.

Static Effects: Trade Creation and Trade Diversion

Trade liberalization can in general be undertaken in two different manners. First, trade liberalization can be based on the MFN principle, where better market access is granted to all trading partners equally. The classical "gains from trade" argument asserts that such trade liberalization will offer consumers access to more goods at lower prices and offer producers more sources for their inputs and more markets for their products (for which they may receive higher prices). Second, trade liberalization can be done in a *preferential* way, with better market access granted to one partner but not to others. It should be noted that better market access can result not only from bilateral tariff removal, but from other negotiated provisions in the areas of cross-border trade in services, telecommunications, electronic commerce, and government procurement, none of which are readily quantifiable. An FTA such as the one between the United States and Panama is an agreement in which preferential liberalization is undertaken reciprocally between participating countries.[390]

To the extent that FTAs are designed to liberalize trade, they are likely to engender economic gains similar to those of an MFN liberalization. However, given their discriminatory nature, studying the economic impact of FTAs involves additional issues that are not present in an MFN liberalization. The traditional way to assess the economic impact of an FTA is to categorize the FTA-induced trade expansion into trade creation or trade diversion.[391] Trade creation improves net welfare and occurs when partner-country production displaces higher cost domestic production. Trade diversion reduces net welfare and occurs when partnercountry production displaces lower cost imports from the rest of the world.[392] The combined effect of an FTA on intrabloc trade will then reflect trade creation as well as trade diversion. Whether the trade creation (welfare-enhancing) effects or the trade diversion (welfare-reducing) effects dominate depends on a variety of factors, including external trade barriers, cost differences, relative supply and demand responses, and other domestic policies. Thus, the overall welfare impact of an FTA can be empirically determined.

Static Effects: Terms of Trade

The impact of an FTA also can be studied from a "terms-of-trade" (i.e., the price of exports relative to the price of imports) viewpoint. If the participating countries are large enough to be able to affect world import and export prices by their actions, the establishment of an FTA is likely to affect the terms of trade of a given FTA member principally in three ways. First, by increasing the demand for its partner's products, the country's own preferential trade liberalization may increase the (pretariff) price of its imports from the partner country, leading to a deterioration in its terms of trade. Second, tariff reductions by the partner country can increase the demand (and the price) for the FTA member's exports and improve its terms of trade. Third, the decreased demand for imports originating from nonmember countries tends to decrease their price and improve the FTA members' terms of trade. Therefore, the impact on economic welfare will depend on whether the terms of trade have improved or deteriorated for a given partner country.

Nonquantifiable Effects

In addition to the generally more easily quantifiable effects discussed so far, regional integration can provide other potential benefits that are more difficult to evaluate because of data limitations. A World Bank publication discusses a variety of additional effects (or classes of effects) that may result from regional integration agreements.[393] One such effect is enhanced security (either against nonmembers or between members).[394] Another potential benefit is that by forming a unit and pooling their bargaining power, FTA members can negotiate more efficiently in international forums. Regional integration can also be useful in "locking in" domestic (trade or other policy) reforms by raising the cost of policy reversal. Another potential gain is the increased possibilities for cooperation in environmental or technological assistance projects. Effects stemming from these nontariff-related FTA aspects assessed in the Commission's report pertaining to the U.S.-Panama Trade Preference Agreement are associated with market access provisions related to cross-border trade in services, telecommunications, and government procurement; trade facilitation provisions related to customs administration and technical barriers; and regulatory environment provisions related to investment, intellectual property rights, trade remedies, and labor and environment.[395]

APPENDIX H
U.S. SUGAR POLICY

U.S. Sugar Policy

The United States maintains a sugar policy consisting of domestic and import elements. The domestic element consists mainly of a price support loan program that maintains guaranteed floor prices for raw cane and refined beet sugar.[396] If the domestic prices of raw and refined sugar fall below the loan rate, U.S. sugar processors may choose to pledge their sugar as collateral and obtain loans from the USDA. In addition, the USDA imposes marketing allotments, which place restrictions on the amount of sugar domestic producers can ship.[397] These allotments, which the USDA imposes to avoid forfeitures, generally are in effect as long as U.S. sugar imports are less than 1.532 million short tons in a given marketing year.[398] If imports are forecast to exceed this amount, marketing allotments may be suspended.[399] In addition, the USDA administers the loan program at no net cost to the Federal Government, to the maximum extent practicable.[400] The USDA also may utilize a payment-in-kind program, whereby domestic sugar processors can bid for excess raw cane or refined beet sugar in USDA stocks in exchange for reduced production levels. The storage costs for excess production are borne by the industry.

The U.S. trade policy for sugar mainly is determined by U.S. market access commitments made under various FTAs, including NAFTA and CAFTA-DR, as well as the Uruguay Round Agreement on Agriculture (URAA). To keep the U.S. domestic price sufficiently above the loan rates,[401] the United States administers a system of TRQs on U.S. imports of sugar and SCPs from Mexico under NAFTA, from certain Central American and Caribbean countries under CAFTA-DR, and from WTO member countries in accordance with the URAA. The United States scheduled separate TRQs for raw sugar, refined sugar, SCPs, blended sugar syrups,[402] and cocoa powder containing sugar[403] under the URAA. Imports within the quota are dutiable at a low in-quota tariff rate,[404] while imports above the quota are dutiable at a higher (generally prohibitive) over-quota tariff rate. Also, over-quota imports may be subject to additional special safeguard tariffs if certain price levels are triggered.[405]

END NOTES

[1] Under this TPA, duty elimination on some tariff lines is to be phased in over a period of up to 15 years, while some over-quota duties and tariff-rate quotas (TRQs) are to be phased out over a period of up to 20 years. Information on the tariff commitments of the United States and Panama is provided in chapter 2 of this report.

[2] A copy of the *Federal Register* notice is in appendix B of this report.

[3] The Commission held a public hearing for this investigation on May 16, 2007. A calendar of the hearing is included in appendix C of this report, and a summary of hearing testimony and written submissions is provided in chapter 6 of this report.

[4] United *States-Panama Trade Promotion Agreement (TPA)*, July 2007, full text available at http://www.ustr.gov/.

[5] See, for example, testimony before the USITC in connection with inv. No. TA-2104-25, U.S.-*Panama Trade Promotion Agreement: Potential Economy-wide and Selected Sectoral Effects*, May 16, 2007; and Chapter 5 (Customs Administration and Trade Facilitation), Chapter 8 (Trade Remedies), Chapter 10 (Investment, Investor-State Dispute Settlement), Chapter 18 (Transparency), Chapter 19 (Administration of the Agreement and Trade Capacity Building), and Chapter 20 (Dispute Settlement) of U.S.-*Panama TPA*.

[6] *U.S.-Panama TPA*.

[7] In addition, each party has some additional staging periods that are contained in the general notes to their respective schedule of tariff commitments.

[8] Goods that satisfy the rules of origin are called "originating goods."

[9] Appendix E includes an economic profile of Panama.

[10] The term "exports" refers to domestic merchandise exports, f.a.s. basis.

[11] Panama's imports from the United States as reported by Global Trade Atlas were valued at $1.2 billion in 2006. Certain mineral fuels (HS chapter 27), aircraft (HS chapter 88), and pharmaceutical products (HS chapter 30) comprise about 84 percent of the difference between reported U.S. exports to Panama and reported imports into Panama from the United States. U.S. exports to Panama of these products may include re-exports that enter Panama for consumption.

[12] Panama's imports of petroleum oils from the United States as reported by Global Trade Atlas were valued at $32.2 million in 2006.

[13] The term "imports" refers to merchandise imports for consumption, customs value.

[14] CBERA was enacted in 1983 and was expanded in 1990 by the Caribbean Basin Economic Recovery Expansion Act (CBEREA). CBERA was enhanced by CBPTA in 2000 and was further modified by the Trade Act of 2002.

[15] The U.S. Department of Commerce reports that the U.S. dollar's status as legal currency in Panama may contribute to that country's relatively high level of acceptance for U.S. goods. U.S. Department of Commerce, "Country Commercial Guide-Panama," June 6, 2007, found at http://www.buyusainfo.net/docs/x_3421748.pdf, retrieved August 30, 2007. Although this investigation has not identified any academic analyses that specifically address the impact of Panama's dollarized economy on U.S.-Panama trade, several studies suggest that a shared currency may effectively reduce transaction costs between trading partners. See, for example, Huseyin Ozdeser, "European Monetary Union, Euro and Impacts of Euro on Trnc Economy Based on a Possible Membership of TRNC to EMU," *Dogus University Journal* 3, issue 6 (2002): 97-110; and Robert D. Blackwill, "The Future of Transatlantic Relations," Council on Foreign Relations, Task Force Report No. 20, February 1999.

[16] Although most chapters of the U.S.-Panama TPA deal with improving market access by addressing trade facilitation, investment, and regulatory environment aspects, market access provisions described in this chapter specifically refer to chapters 3 (National Treatment and Market Access for Goods) and 4 (Rules of Origin) of the TPA (and related annexes and side letters).

[17] Poultry as described in this report refers to chicken, turkey, and variety meats thereof.

[18] U.S. exports to Panama of the products selected for analysis accounted for 6.5 percent of total U.S. exports to Panama in 2006.

[19] U.S. imports of raw cane sugar from Panama accounted for 6.9 percent of total U.S. imports from Panama in 2006.

[20] The market access provisions are found in chapter 3 (national treatment and market access for goods) and chapter 4 (rules of origin) of the TPA.

[21] Recent examples include U.S.-*Peru Trade Promotion Agreement: Potential Economy-Wide and Selected Sectoral Effects*, USITC publication 3855, June 2006, and U.S.-*Colombia Trade Promotion Agreement: Portential Economy-Wide and Selected Sectoral Effects*, USITC publication 3896, December 2006.

[22] All U.S. imports of sugar and sugar-containing products from Panama subject to TRQs are in the form of raw cane sugar. Thus, although Panama's additional TRQ allocation under the TPA includes raw sugar, refined sugar, sugar syrups, and sugar-containing products classified in chaps. 17, 18, 19, and 21 of the HTS, the Commission only modeled raw cane sugar classified under HS subheading 1701.11.

[23] See appendix F for a description of the model.

[24] Trade data for U.S. exports to Panama in this chapter represent Panama imports from the United States as provided by Global Trade Information Service's *Global Trade Atlas*. Panama imports from the United States were used in lieu of U.S. exports to Panama because U.S. exports may include re-exports that are not officially acknowledged as Panama imports for consumption.

[25] Beef as referred to in this section covers beef, beef variety meats, and beef products classified under the following HS subheadings: 0201.10, 0201.20, 0201.30, 0202.10, 0202.20, 0202.30, 0206.10, 0206.21, 0206.22, 0210.20, and 1602.50. Pork as referred to in this section covers pork, pork variety meats, and pork products classified under the following HS subheadings: 0203.11, 0203.12, 0203.19, 0203.21, 0203.22, 0203.29, 0206.30, 0206.41, 0206.49, 0209, 0210.11, 0110.12, 0210.19, 1602.41, 1602.42, and 1602.49.

[26] Poultry as referred to in this section covers chicken, turkey, and variety meats thereof classified within HS subheadings 0207.13, 0207.14, 0207.25, 0207.27, and 1602.31.

[27] Further discussions of the *United States-Panama Agreement Regarding Certain Sanitary and Phytosanitary (SPS) Measures and Technical Standards Affecting Trade In Agricultural Products* (*U.S.- Panama SPS Agreement*) can be found in chapter 4 of this report.

[28] To reflect the potential impact of the U.S.-Panama TPA on U.S. beef exports to Panama, the Commission model used beef data from 2003 as the base year, absent the disruption from concerns of bovine spongiform encephalopathy (BSE). By the end of 2003, Panama, like many countries, reduced its market access to U.S. beef over concerns of BSE. In May 2007, the World Animal Health Organization designated the United States as a "controlled risk" for BSE, the second-safest rating, which has helped to facilitate the reopening of these markets.

[29] David Hunt, American Chamber of Commerce of Panama (AMCHAM), testimony before the United States International Trade Commission (USITC) in connection with inv. No. TA-2104-25, *U.S.-Panama Trade Promotion Agreement: Potential Economy-wide and Selected Sectoral Effects*, hearing transcript, May 16, 2007, 79.

[30] Global Trade Information Services (GTIS), *Global Trade Atlas*.

[31] Ibid.

[32] Panama's largest import suppliers of pork in 2006 were Denmark (42 percent of the value of Panamanian pork imports), the United States (37 percent), and Canada (13 percent). GTIS, *Global Trade Atlas*.

[33] According to FAO statistics, Panama produces 84.9 percent as much pork as it consumes.

[34] Industry official, telephone interview by Commission staff, May 23, 2007.

[35] Estimates for specific years are based on implementation of the TPA on January 1, 2008.

[36] Under the terms of the TPA, Panama receives immediate duty-free treatment on exports of beef to the United States (subject to the safeguard provisions of Article 3017). Panama currently receives duty-free treatment on its exports of most beef products to the United States under the GSP.

[37] U.S. Department of Agriculture (USDA), Food Safety and Inspection Service (FSIS), "Eligible Foreign Establishments," available at http://www.fsis.usda.gov/Regulations_&_Policies/Export_Information/index.asp.

[38] USDA, Animal and Plant Health Inspection Service (APHIS), "List of USDA Recognized Animal Health Status of Countries/Regions Regarding Specific Livestock or Poultry Disease, or Acceptable Commodities," available at http://www.aphis.usda.gov/.

[39] Agricultural Technical Advisory Committee (ATAC) for Animal and Animal Products, "The United States-Panama Trade Promotion Agreement," report of April 18, 2007.

[40] National Pork Producers Council (NPPC), "Statement of the National Pork Producers Council Before the International Trade Commission on Probable Economic Effect of an FTA between the U.S. and Panama," written submission, May 16, 2007.

[41] USA Poultry and Egg Export Council (USAPEEC), "U.S./Panama Free Trade Agreement," May 22, 2007.

[42] Grain as referred to in this section covers corn and rough rice classified under HTS subheadings 1005.90 and 1006.10. These are two of the leading U.S. grain exports to Panama. Rice is traded as unmilled (rough) form, dehulled (brown) form, and milled or semimilled form. Almost all U.S. rice exports to Panama are rough rice; Panama imports negligible amounts of milled rice. U.S. exports to Panama of both rough and milled rice face a tariff-rate duty of 90 percent, and are subject to TRQs under the TPA. The TPA also addresses barley, sorghum, and oats, all of whose trade is currently negligible with Panama. Corn is the primary grain destined for livestock feed in the world. However, white corn is used solely in food, and yellow corn mainly in animal feed. Corn, barley, and sorghum are called "coarse grains" or "feed grains." Wheat is also a dominant U.S. grain export to Panama but already received duty-free treatment prior to TPA and will not be part of this assessment.

[43] U.S. imports of grain from Panama were zero during 1996-2006, according to official statistics of the U.S. Department of Commerce.

[44] Article 3.14 of the U.S.-Panama TPA states that each party shall ensure that it does not, under its TRQs, allocate any portion of an in-quota quantity to a producer group; condition access to an in-quota quantity on purchase of domestic production; or limit access to an in-quota quantity only to processors.

[45] *U.S.-Panama TPA*, Chapter 3, Section F, "Agriculture," Article 3.14.

[46] United States Trade Representative (USTR), *1997 National Trade Estimate (NTE) Report on Foreign Trade Barriers*, 297.

[47] GTIS, *Global Trade Atlas*.

[48] Ibid.

[49] Compiled from official statistics of the U.S. Department of Commerce (USDOC), and GTIS, *Global Trade Atlas*.

[50] *U.S.- Panama TPA*, Annex 3.3; Tariff Schedule of Panama; and Appendix I, notes 20 (a), 21(a), and 22 (a).

[51] USDA, Foreign Agricultural Service (FAS), "Production, Supply, and Distribution Online," market and trade data, available at http://www.fas.usda.gov/psdonline/psdHome.aspx.

[52] GTIS, *Global Trade Atlas*.

[53] USDA, FAS, "Production, Supply, and Distribution Online."

[54] USDA, FAS, "Panama Grain and Feed Rice Situation 2001," Global Agricultural Information Network (GAIN) Report no. PN1002 (July 12, 2001): 1.

[55] ATAC for Grains, Feed and Oilseeds, "The U.S.-Panama Trade Promotion Agreement," report of April 25, 2007.

[56] Absorption requirements require an importer to first purchase specified quantities of domestic products in order to be able to import those same types of products.

[57] U.S. Grains Council, *Global Update* (December 22, 2006): 1, available at http://www.grains.org/galleries/global_updates/glo-12-22-06.pdf.

[58] Frozen potato products referred to in this section cover frozen French fries under HTS subheading 2004.10.

[59] The Netherlands, Panama's second-largest supplier of frozen potato products, accounted for 27 percent of Panamanian imports of frozen potato products in 2006. GTIS, *Global Trade Atlas*.

[60] Industry official (American Frozen Food Institute), telephone interview by Commission staff, April 20, 2007.

[61] Raúl Del Valle, former president, The Chamber of Commerce, Industry, and Agriculture of Panama, testimony before the USITC in connection with inv. No. TA-2104-25, *U.S.-Panama Trade Promotion Agreement: Potential Economy-wide and Selected Sectoral Effects*, hearing transcript, May 16, 2007, 68.

[62] Del Valle, hearing transcript, 67–68.

[63] Tom Mouhsian, director, MWW Group, on behalf of AmCham Panama, "Post-Hearing Comments on the U.S.-Panama Trade Promotion Agreement," written submission, May 23, 2007.

[64] The processed foods referred to in this section cover mixes and doughs, malt extract, bread and pastry, sauces, soups and broths, and food preparations nesoi classified under the following HTS subheadings: 1901.20, 1901.90, 1905.90, 2103.90, 2104.10, and 2106.90. All of these processed food categories accounted for over $1 million in U.S. exports to Panama in 2005.

[65] Further discussions of the *United States-Panama Agreement Regarding Certain Sanitary and Phytosanitary (SPS) Measures and Technical Standards Affecting Trade In Agricultural Products (U.S.- Panama SPS Agreement)* can be found in chapter 4 of this report.

[66] USTR, "Free Trade with Panama: Summary of the United States-Panama Trade Promotion Agreement," Trade Facts sheet, June 2007, 2, available at http://www.ustr.gov/.

[67] USDA, FAS, "Panama Retail Food Sector 2000," GAIN Report no. PN0011 (June 20, 2000): 2.

[68] Christina Stortz, Timothy Taylor, and Gary Fairchild, "A Primer on Exporting to Panama," (University of Florida, Institute of Food and Agricultural Sciences, February 2005): 2, available at http://edis.ifas.ufl.edu/pdffiles/FE/FE51900.pdf.

[69] USDA, FAS, "Panama Retail Food Sector 2000," 4.

[70] *U.S.-Panama TPA*, Annex 3.3, and Panamanian Agricultural Tariff Schedule.

[71] Stortz, Taylor, and Fairchild, "A Primer on Exporting to Panama," 6.

[72] Further discussions of the *United States-Panama Agreement Regarding Certain Sanitary and Phytosanitary (SPS) Measures and Technical Standards Affecting Trade In Agricultural Products (U.S.- Panama SPS Agreement)* can be found in chapter 4 of this report.

[73] *U.S.-Panama SPS Agreement*.

[74] Agricultural Technical Advisory Committee (ATAC) for Trade in Processed Foods, "The U.S.-Panama Trade Promotion Agreement," report of April 25, 2007.

[75] Peggy S. Rochette, senior director of international policy, Grocery Manufacturers Association (GMA) and Food Production Association (FPA), interview by Commission staff, Washington, DC, May 2, 2007.

[76] Agricultural Policy Advisory Committee for Trade (APAC), "The U.S.-Panama Trade Promotion Agreement," report of April 25, 2007.

[77] The discussion of U.S. imports in this sector includes raw sugar, refined sugar, sugar syrups, and sugarcontaining products classified in chaps. 17, 18, 19, and 21 of the HTS that are subject to TRQs, and all items that are covered by the sugar provision of the TPA. The discussion of U.S. exports in this section is limited to raw sugar, refined sugar, sugar syrups, and sugar-containing products classified in chap. 17, as the other products generally are part of various processed food sectors.

[78] The U.S. sugar-producing sector addressed in this section of the report primarily consists of sugarcane growers, sugarcane millers, raw cane sugar refiners, sugar beet growers, and sugar beet refiners. This section of the report does not generally address producers of corn-based sweeteners, e.g., high-fructose corn syrup. The U.S.

sugar-using sector generally consists of a wide range of food and beverage manufacturers, including manufacturers of nonchocolate confectionery, chocolate and chocolate confectionery, and breakfast cereal.

[79] The net-exporter provision of the TPA reads as follows: "In any year, duty-free tariff treatment under subparagraph (a) for Panama shall be accorded to the lesser of (i) the aggregate quantity set out in subparagraph (a) for Panama, or (ii) a quantity equal to the amount by which Panama's exports to all destinations exceeds its imports from all sources ("trade surplus") for goods classified under the following subheadings: HS 1701.11, HS 1701.12, HS 1701.91, HS 1701.99, HS 1702.40, and HS 1702.60, except that Panama's exports to the United States of goods classified under subheadings HS 1701.11, HS 1701.12, HS 1701.91, and HS 1701.99 and its imports of originating goods of the United States classified under HS 1702.40 and HS 1702.60 shall not be included in the calculation of its trade surplus. Panama's trade surplus shall be calculated using the most recent annual data available." *U.S.-Panama TPA*, Annex 3.3-U.S., and Appendix I, 6.

[80] The TRQ consists of three separate quotas—an aggregate quota beginning at 500 mt; a raw sugar quota beginning at 6,000 mt; and a specialty sugar quota beginning at 500 mt. Only the aggregate quota increases after the phase-in period.

[81] *U.S.-Panama TPA*, Chapter 3, Section F, "Agriculture," 4.

[82] U.S. International Trade Commission (USITC), *Interactive Tariff and Trade Dataweb (Dataweb)*, available at http://dataweb.usitc.gov.

[83] All U.S. imports of sugar and sugar-containing products from Panama subject to TRQs are raw cane sugar classified under HS subheading 1701.11. As such, the Commission modeled raw cane sugar only.

[84] *U.S.-Panama TPA*, Annex 3.3, and U.S. appendix I, 5–7.

[85] The over-quota duty rates are 33.87¢/kilogram for cane sugar and 35.74¢/kilogram for beet sugar.

[86] USDA, World Agricultural Outlook Board, "U.S. Sugar Supply and Use," *World Agricultural Supply and Demand Estimates*, table 446-16 (May 11, 2007); converted to metric tons (mt) at rate of 1 mt = 1.10231123 short tons.

[87] Note that the Commission's estimate is not based on a general equilibrium, economy-wide welfare measure. It does not measure the welfare effect in other downstream or upstream sectors. This impact is expected to be minimal, however, as the magnitude of the total change in U.S. sugar imports is small. Morever, the Commission's estimated welfare measure does not include the potential effects of tariff reductions on other imported goods or the effects of increases in U.S. exports to Panama as a result of the market access provisions of the TPA.

[88] The net exporter provision only applies to the aggregate quota beginning at 500 mt.

[89] Based on Commission staff estimates using *Global Trade Atlas*; and USDA, FAS, "Production, Supply, and Distribution Online."

[90] USDA, FAS, "Production, Supply, and Distribution Online."

[91] USTR, "USTR Announces Revised FY 2006 Tariff-Rate Quota Sugar Allocations, Agreement with Mexico on Market Access on Sweeteners," press release, August 3, 2006, available at http://www.ustr.gov/.

[92] The current U.S. raw sugar price is about 21 cents per pound and the wholesale refined sugar price is 25 cents per pound. USDA, Economic Research Service (ERS), *Sugar and Sweeteners Yearbook* tables 4–5, available at http://www.ers.usda.gov/Briefing/Sugar/Data.htm. The current loan forfeiture price under the U.S. sugar program is 18 cents per pound for raw cane sugar and 22.9 cents per pound for refined sugar. USDA, ERS, "Sugar and Sweeteners: Policy," available at http://www.ers.usda.gov/Briefing/Sugar/Policy.htm. Data on Panama's cost of production are proprietary and are from LMC International, Ltd., *The LMC Worldwide Survey of Sugar and HFCS Production Costs* (Oxford, UK: LMC International, Ltd., December 2005).

[93] USDA, ERS, *Sugar and Sweeteners Yearbook* tables.

[94] Majority view, Agricultural Technical Advisory Committee (ATAC) for Sweeteners and Sweetener Products, "The U.S.-Panama Free Trade Agreement," report of April 25, 2007, 3.

[95] Ibid., majority view, 3–4 and 7.

[96] Ibid., minority view, 7–8.

[97] Sweetener Users Association, "Pre-hearing Brief of the Sweetener Users Association," submitted to the USITC regarding inv. No. TA-2104-25, *U.S.-Panama Trade Promotion Agreement: Potential Economy-wide and Selected Sectoral Effects*, May 10, 2007.

[98] ATAC for Trade in Processed Foods, "The U.S.-Panama Trade Promotion Agreement," 6.

[99] Machinery and equipment primarily refer to motor vehicles and parts, computers and other office equipment, telecommunications equipment, construction and mining equipment, heating and air conditioning equipment, household appliances, process control instruments, and medical goods.

[100] The opportunities created by the ongoing canal enlargement project were not factored into the Commission's assessment of the potential impact of the TPA, as this project is not contingent upon TPA provisions.

[101] Industry Trade Advisory Committee on Automotive Equipment and Capital Goods (ITAC 2), "The U.S.-Panama Trade Promotion Agreement," report of April 25, 2007.

[102] Certain machinery includes major household appliances such as refrigerators and washing machines; and heating, ventilation, and air conditioning (HVAC) equipment.

[103] Passenger cars and light trucks as referred to in this section include all the 8-digit items classified under HTS subheadings 8703.22 through 8703.90, and 8704.21 and 8704.31.

[104] USDOC, International Trade Administration (ITA), Office of Aerospace and Automotive Industries, "Compilation of Foreign Motor Vehicle Import Requirements," April 2006, 29, available at http://ita.doc.gov/td/auto/international/importreq/TBR2006.pdf.

[105] ITAC 2, "The U.S.-Panama Trade Promotion Agreement."

[106] Ibid. A Side Letter on Autos ensures that the United States will not initiate dispute settlement procedures with respect to restrictions that Panama has in place prior to date of entry into force of the agreement on the importation of used passenger vehicles.

[107] Economist Intelligence Unit (EIU), "Country Report Panama—Main Report: December 1, 2006," available to subscribers at http://www.eiu.com.

[108] GTIS, *Global Trade Atlas*. According to the ITAC 2 report, Japanese-based automakers represent 80 percent of new motor vehicle sales in Panama, with Korean automakers representing 10 percent, European automakers representing 7 percent, and U.S. automakers, 2 percent. ITAC 2, "The U.S.-Panama Trade Promotion Agreement."

[109] *La Voz*, "Crece Venta de Automóviles en Panamá," March 28, 2007, available at http://www.azcentral.com/lavoz/spanish/business/articles/business_114808.html.

[110] Panamanian motor vehicle distributor official, e-mail message to Commission staff, May 9, 2007; and Juan Sosa, president, U.S.-Panama Business Council, testimony before the USITC in connection with Inv. No. TA-2104-25, *U.S.-Panama Trade Promotion Agreement: Potential Economy-wide and Selected Sectoral Effects*, hearing transcript, May 16, 2007, 103–04.

[111] *Xinhua Spanish*, "Panamá: Venta de Autos en 2006 Supera Los 500 Milliones de Dolares," January 17, 2007, accessed via http://dialogclassic.com.

[112] Sosa, hearing transcript, 103–04.

[113] Hunt, hearing transcript, 104.

[114] Douglas Goudie, Director of International Trade, National Association of Manufacturers, "U.S.-Panama Trade Promotion Agreement: Potential Manufacturing Sector Effects," post-hearing brief submitted to the USITC, May 22, 2007, 2.

[115] ITAC 2, "The U.S.-Panama Trade Promotion Agreement."

[116] Ibid.

[117] For imported passenger cars of a value up to and including $12,000, the tariff is 15 percent; for vehicles valued at $12,001–$14,500, the tariff is 18 percent; and over $14,500, 20 percent. Pickups are assessed a 10 percent tariff. Ibid.

[118] Ibid. The auto side letter states that, "(T)he United States will not initiate dispute settlement procedures under Chapter Twenty (Dispute Settlement) of the Agreement with respect to any restriction that Panama may apply, prior to the date of entry into force of the Agreement, on the importation of used passenger motor vehicles (cars and light trucks, including four wheel drive vehicles)."

[119] Ibid.

[120] ITAC 4, *The U.S.-Panama Trade Promotion Agreement*, April 25, 2007.

[121] ITAC 8, *The U.S.-Panama Trade Promotion Agreement*, April 25, 2007.

[122] Certain machinery as referred to in this section covers major household appliances and HVAC equipment under the following HS headings: 8414, 8415, 8418, and 8450. HVAC equipment is also referred to as climate control products, which are used in both residential and commercial applications, including housing apartments, office buildings such as skyscrapers and business parks, warehouses, and factories.

[123] The opportunities created by the ongoing canal enlargement project were not factored into the Commission's assessment of the potential impact of the TPA, as this project is not contingent upon TPA provisions.

[124] *Price Smart*, "Why Invest in Panama," May 24, 2007.

[125] *Appliance Magazine*, "12th Annual Portrait of the Latin American Appliance Industry," December 2006.

[126] Grupo Elektra, "Grupo Elektra Company Profile," January 2007, available at http://www.grupoelektra.com.mx.

[127] Industry official, interview by Commission staff, Washington, DC, April 12, 2007.

[128] The Colon Free Zone, located at the Atlantic end of the Panama Canal, is the second largest free zone in the world, after Hong Kong. The zone is used as a distribution and packaging center. No manufacturing is allowed in the zone. Most of the goods passing through the zone are shipped to markets in the Caribbean Basin and Latin America. U.S. Department of Commerce (USDOC), International Trade Administration (ITA), "Panama, Import Regs.: Free Trade Zones," September 28, 2004, found at http://web.ita.doc.gov/ticwebsite/laweb.nsf/504ca249c786ec2of85256284006da7ab/eb1ac737a1df025085256 923006f662b?OpenDocument, retrieved February 13, 2004.

[129] U.S. & Foreign Commercial Service (US& FCS) and U.S. Department of State, *Doing Business in Panama: A Country Commercial Guide for U.S. Companies, 2006*, available at

http://www.buyusa.gov/panama/en/11.html.

[130] Ibid.

[131] Additional categories of machinery and equipment include computer equipment and parts, telecommunications equipment, medical instruments, and materials handling equipment. These products were not modeled using the Commission's partial equilibrium model because these products already generally benefit from a relatively low tariff-rate duty, are free of duty, or are subject to duty waivers.

[132] The Government of Panama typically provides contractors on government-sponsored projects with a waiver of customs duties on equipment imported for use on such projects. As a result, most bulldozers and other earth moving equipment already enter Panama free of duty, thus mitigating the effect of the elimination of tariffs on Panama's imports of such equipment under the TPA. Thomas Gales, Caterpillar, Inc., on behalf of the U.S. Chamber of Commerce, Association of American Chambers of Commerce in Latin America, and the Latin American Trade Coalition, testimony before the USITC in connection with inv. No. TA-2104-25, *U.S.-Panama Trade Promotion Agreement: Potential Economy-wide and Selected Sectoral Effects*, hearing transcript, May 16, 2007, 52.

[133] USDOC, ITA, "Medical Device Regulatory Requirements for Panama," available at http://ita.doc.gov/td/health/panamaregs.html (last accessed July 2, 2007);and "Mission Statement: Medical Device Trade Mission to Panama, Guatemala, and Honduras (July 12-19, 2003)," available at http://.ita.doc.gov/doctm/med_panama_guatemala_honduras_0703.html .

[134] Thomas Gales, Caterpillar, Inc., on behalf of the U.S. Chamber of Commerce, Association of American Chambers of Commerce in Latin America, and the Latin American Trade Coalition, "Comments on the U.S.-Panama Trade Promotion Agreement," submitted to the USITC, May 16, 2007.

[135] Goudie, "U.S.-Panama Trade Promotion Agreement: Potential Manufacturing Sector Effects."

[136] James Maes (Assistant Port Director, Safety and Security, Port of Miami-Dade), interview with Commission staff, Miami, FL, December 6, 2006.

[137] The Government of Panama typically provides contractors on government-sponsored projects with a waiver of customs duties on equipment imported for use on such projects. Gales, hearing transcript, 52.

[138] Gales, "Comments on the U.S.-Panama Trade Promotion Agreement."

[139] Thomas Hunt, on behalf of AMCHAM and the Panama Pro-TPA Trade Coalition, "Comments on the U.S.-Panama Trade Promotion Agreement," submitted to the USITC, May 16, 2007.

[140] Goudie, "U.S.-Panama Trade Promotion Agreement: Potential Manufacturing Sector Effects."

[141] Industry Trade Advisory Committee on Consumer Goods (ITAC 4), "The United States –Panama Trade Promotion Agreement," report of April 25, 2007.

[142] Industry Trade Advisory Committee for Information and Communications Technologies, Services and Electronic Commerce (ITAC 8), "The U.S.-Panama Trade Promotion Agreement," report of April 25, 2007.

[143] J.F. Hornbeck, Congressional Research Service (CRS), "CRS Report for Congress: The U.S.-Panama Free Trade Agreement," updated January 4, 2007, 14.

[144] Panama acceded to the WTO on September 6, 1997, and its schedule of specific commitments under the GATS is dated October 1, 2007.

[145] World Trade Organization (WTO), "Republic of Panama: Schedule of Specific Commitments," GATS/SC/124, October 1, 1997. Prior to the U.S.-Panama TPA, the GATS governed the rights and obligations of U.S. service providers in Panama. The Commission therefore uses Panama's GATS commitments as a baseline from which to measure the benefits of the TPA.

[146] It is not possible to establish an overall quantitative measure of the effect of the U.S.-Panama TPA on total trade in services because of the unavailability of data.

[147] Financial and air transport services are the exceptions. Financial services are covered in chapter 12 of the TPA, while air transport services are covered under separate Open Skies agreements. For more information Open Skies agreements, see http://www.state.gov/e/ecb/tra/c661.htm.

[148] The United States lists nine specific services industries for which it maintains current or potential nonconforming measures (NCMs), whereas Panama lists 26 services industries subject to current or potential NCMs. However, due to the already largely open U.S. market and Panama's relatively small services industry, the commercial impact of these measures on U.S. imports and exports is likely to be small.

[149] The negative list approach used in the TPA tends to yield greater market access and transparency than the "positive list" approach employed in the GATS, wherein market access and national treatment apply only to the provision of specifically listed services. Under a positive list approach, the extension of trade disciplines to newly created services would have to be negotiated individually.

[150] *United States-Panama Trade Promotion Agreement (TPA)*, July 2007, full text available at http://www.ustr.gov/. The covered measures include those adopted or maintained by central, regional, or local governments and authorities and by nongovernmental bodies exercising powers delegated by such governments and authorities.

[151] Industry Trade Advisory Committee on Services and Finance Industries (ITAC 10), "The United States- Panama Trade Promotion Agreement," report of April 25, 2007, 2.

[152] ITAC 10, "The United States-Panama Trade Promotion Agreement," April 25, 2007, 6.

[153] This figure represents exports to "other South and Central America" countries, including Panama, for which data are not individually available. U.S. Department of Commerce (USDOC), Bureau of Economic Analysis (BEA), *Survey of Current Business* 86, no. 10 (October 2006).

[154] Ibid.

[155] bid.

[156] Ibid.

[157] This figure represents imports from "other South and Central America" countries, including Panama, for which data are not individually available. Ibid.

[158] *United States-Panama Trade Promotion Agreement*, July 2007, full text available at http://www.ustr.gov/.

[159] Defined here as risk accepted by a reinsurer which is then transferred to another reinsurance company.

[160] ITAC 10, "The United States-Panama Trade Promotion Agreement," April 25, 2007. A prudential carve-out is an exception taken from the GATS disciplines by financial services authorities "for the protection of investors, depositors, policy holders or persons to whom a fiduciary duty is owed by a financial service supplier, or to ensure the integrity and stability of the financial system." From WTO, "The General Agreement on Trade in Services (GATS): Objectives, Coverage and Disciplines," available at http://www.wto.org/english/tratop_e/serv_e/gatsqa_e.htm.

[161] U.S. industry representative, telephone interview with Commission staff, June 1, 2007.

[162] ITAC 10, "The United States-Panama Trade Promotion Agreement," April 25, 2007.

[163] Ibid.

[164] Ibid.

[165] A standard telephone call is the primary means of cross-border trade between the United States and Panama.

[166] In the schedule of specific GATS commitments associated with Panama's 1997 accession to the WTO, Panama did not schedule any commitments for basic or value-added telecommunication services.

[167] In 2000, the Panamanian telecommunication services markets totaled approximately $492 million. By contrast, the U.S. market was valued at approximately $2.9 billion. The year 2000 is the last year for which revenue figures for both countries are available. International Telecommunications Union, *World Telecommunications Indicators Database*, April 2007.

[168] Commercial mobile services are excluded from paragraphs 2-4 of article 13.3, as well as from article 13.4. Annex 1 to the TPA also contains exemptions related to mobile services.

[169] In 2004, Panama's telecommunications regulator levied fines of approximately $400,000 on CWP for failing to provide adequate interconnection services. In June 2006, CWP was fined an additional $10,000 for consistently failing to honor interconnection agreements with new entrant firm, TeleCarrier. TeleGeography, "Country Profile: Panama," *GlobalComms Database*, June 13, 2006.

[170] Telephone calls from Panama to the United States were subject to an additional $1.00 per minute tax until 2005. TeleGeography, "Country Profile: Panama."

[171] TeleGeography, "Country Profile: Panama," and Grant Seiffert, President, Telecommunications Industry Association, written submission, May 22, 2007.

[172] In 1996, BellSouth Panama, a subsidiary of BellSouth (U.S.), was licensed as Panama's first provider of mobile services. In 2004, Telefónica S.A. (Spain) purchased BellSouth's assets in Panama and 11 other countries in Central/Latin America. In line with Telefónica's global branding strategy, mobile assets worldwide were renamed Telefónica Móviles. Telefónica S.A. owns 99.8 percent of Telefónica Móviles in Panama. Budde, "Panama-Telecoms Market Overview and Statistics"; and Telefónica S.A., "Country Operations: United States," available at http://www.telefonica.es/investors/.

[173] INTEL, Panama's incumbent telecommunication services provider, was renamed Cable & Wireless Panama (CWP) in 1997 following the $652 million purchase of 49 percent of company stock by Cable & Wireless plc (U.K.). CWP's other owners include the Government of Panama (49 percent) and CWP employees (2 percent). Budde, "Panama-Telecoms Market Overview and Statistics"; EIU, "Panama Country Profile 2006"; TeleGeography, "Country Profile: Panama"; and Michelle Lescure, "Panama's Crossed Wires," *World Press Review*, August 1, 2002.

[174] *United States-Panama Trade Promotion Agreement*, July 2007, full text available at http://www.ustr.gov/.

[175] The government of Panama curently controls 49% of Cable & Wireless Panama (CWP). CWP is regarded as Panama's incumnent wire-line telecommunications carrier and , therefore, is subject to interconnection obligations contained in the telecom chapter of the U.S.-Panama FTA. Cable & Wireless Panamá, Acerca de Cable & Wireless Panamá, http://www.cwpanama.net/cwp/NuestraEmpresa/acercacwp.htm and Primetrica, Inc., "Panama," *GlobalComms Database*, June 30, 2007.

[176] Paragraph 2 (Resale), paragraph 3 (Number Portability), and paragraph 4 (Dialing Parity) of article 13.3 (Obligations Relating to Suppliers of Public Telecommunications Services) do not apply to suppliers of commercial mobile services.

[177] Article 13.4 (Additional Obligations Relating to Major Suppliers of Public Telecommunications Services) do not apply to commercial mobile services.

[178] Annex 13.3 states that a state regulatory authority in the United States may exempt a rural local exchange carrier from obligations contained in paragraph 2 (Resale), paragraph 3 (Number Portability), and paragraph 4 (Dialing Parity) of article 13.3 (Obligations Relating to Suppliers of Public Telecommunications Services), and from obligations contained in article 13.4 (Additional Obligations Relating to Major Suppliers of Public Telecommunications Services). Annex 13.3 also states that article 13.4 also does not apply to rural telephone companies in the United States.

[179] This section of annex 1 specifies that telecommunication service providers controlled by a foreign government may not supply telecommunication services in Panama.

[180] This section of annex 1 specifies that cellular mobile services may only be provided by Cable & Wireless Panama and BellSouth Panama on bands A and B, for a period of 20 years. In addition, the annex states that the authorization of 1-2 mobile licenses would be possible starting in October 2008.

[181] This section of annex 1 states that telecommunication services supplied in Panama to Panamanian residents may only be supplied by persons domiciled in Panama.

[182] Industry Trade Advisory Committee for Information and Communications Technologies, Services and Electronic Commerce (ITAC 8), "The U.S.-Panama Trade Promotion Agreement," report of April 25, 2007.

[183] Chapter 11 of the TPA defines professional services as services, the provision of which requires specialized postsecondary education, or equivalent training or experience, and for which parties grant or restrict the right to practice, but not to include services provided by trades-persons or vessel and aircraft crew members.

[184] WTO, GATS, "Republic of Panama: Schedule of Specific Commitments."

[185] For example, Panama's accounting industry numbered 5,000 practitioners (700 Authorized (Certified) Public Accountants) and 100 accounting firms in 2004, compared to approximately 335,000 U.S. CPAs. International Federation of Accountants, "Assessment of the Regulatory and Standard-Setting Framework," surveys submitted by the Colegio de Contadores Públicos Autorizados de Panamá and the American Institute of Certified Public Accountants, May 2005; and World Bank, "Corporate Governance Country Assessment: Panama," *Report on the Observance of Standards and Codes (ROSC)*, June 2004, available at http://www.worldbank.org/ifa/rosc_cg_pan.pdf , 11.

[186] USDOC, "Architectural, Construction and Engineering Services (Panama)," Industry sector analysis, September 2, 2005, available at http://www.stat-usa.gov/mrd.nsf/vwISA_Country ; David Hunt, American Chamber of Commerce of Panama (AMCHAM), testimony before the United States International Trade Commission (USITC) in connection with inv. No. TA-2104-25, *U.S.-Panama Trade Promotion Agreement: Potential Economy-wide and Selected Sectoral Effects*, hearing transcript, May 16, 2007, 86–87; professional services firms' Internet sites; and Trevor Delaney, "How One Small Firm Is Expanding Internationally," *Small Firm Business*, March 20, 2006, available at
http://www.law.com/jsp/law/sfb/lawArticleSFB.jsp?id=1142601438843.

[187] Hunt, hearing transcript, 86.

[188] Such standards and criteria may address accreditation of schools or academic programs; qualifying examinations (including alternative methods of assessment) for licensing; the length and nature of experience required for licensing; standards of professional conduct and the nature of disciplinary action stemming from nonconformity; continuing education and requirements to maintain certification; the extent and limitations on scope of practice; local knowledge requirements such as laws, regulations, language, geography, and climate; and alternatives to residency requirements in order to provide for consumer protection.

[189] *United States-Panama Trade Promotion Agreement*, July 2007, full text available at http://www.ustr.gov/.

[190] The practice of Panamanian law is reserved for Panamanian nationals certified by the country's Supreme Court. Moreover, Panama reserves the establishment of law partnerships to lawyers deemed competent to practice law in Panama.

[191] U.S. nationals licensed to practice law in a U.S. jurisdiction are permitted to engage in cross-border supply or establish in Panama for the purpose of providing advice on international law or home country law.

[192] ITAC 10, "The United States-Panama Trade Promotion Agreement," 3; and Tom Mouhsian, director, MWW Group, on behalf of American Chamber of Commerce and Industry of Panama (AmCham Panama), "Post-Hearing Comments on the U.S.-Panama Trade Promotion Agreement," written submission, May 23, 2007.

[193] Mouhsian on behalf of AmCham Panama, "Post-hearing Comments."

[194] Hunt, hearing transcript, 85–87.

[195] ITAC 10, "The United States-Panama Trade Promotion Agreement," 9.

[196] Mouhsian on behalf of AmCham Panama, "Post-hearing Comments."

[197] ITAC 10, "The United States-Panama Trade Promotion Agreement," 9.

[198] Ibid.

[199] Foreign participation in Panama's retail services market is prohibited in article 288 of the Panamanian constitution of 1972, and Panama has scheduled no WTO commitments in retail services.

[200] Examples of retailers selling exclusively own-brand products include Gap and Liz Claiborne, while retailers primarily engaged in the sale of services include chain-restaurants and automotive service providers.

[201] Market access for foreign-owned retailers selling both goods and services requires amending the Panamanian constitution. Amendments to the Panamanian constitution require approval by two consecutive congresses, a process that cannot be completed until 2010.

[202] Industry Trade Advisory Committee on Distribution Services (ITAC 5), "Report on the U.S.-Panama Trade Promotion Agreement," April 25, 2007; and Industry Representatives, telephone and e-mail interviews by Commission staff, May 17-24, 2007.

[203] Industry Representative, telephone interview by Commission staff, May 17, 2007.

[204] David Hunt, American Chamber of Commerce of Panama (AMCHAM), testimony before the United States International Trade Commission (USITC) in connection with inv. No. TA-2104-25, *U.S.-Panama Trade Promotion Agreement: Potential Economy-wide and Selected Sectoral Effects*, hearing transcript, May 16, 2007, 36.

[205] The cost of doing business in Panama will decline as "additional payments" are eliminated because of strengthened customs rules and as the movement of goods and services is expedited. Hunt, hearing transcript, 36. For an in-depth discussion of the effect of trade facilitation on transaction costs, see Organization of Economic Cooperation and Development (OECD),"The Economic Impact of Trade Facilitation" (Working Paper No. 21, October 12, 2005): 26.

[206] For a summary of some of these recent studies, see OECD, "The Economic Impact of Trade Facilitation" (Working Paper No. 21, October 12, 2005): 14-18.

[207] Panama has demonstrated "marked improvement" in terms of the transparency of customs procedures, with the expectation that the agreement would continue to advance this objective. Tom Gales, Caterpillar, Inc., on behalf of the U.S.-Panama Trade Coalition and U.S. Chamber of Commerce, Office of Western Hemisphere Affairs, testimony before the USITC in connection with inv. No. TA-2104-25, *U.S.-Panama Trade Promotion Agreement: Potential Economy-wide and Selected Sectoral Effects*, hearing transcript, May 16, 2007, 33.

[208] Improved transparency, in part the result of the implementation of e-government in Panama, has accelerated goods processing times. Hunt, hearing transcript, 35.

[209] Hunt, hearing transcript, 36. See also, OECD, "The Economic Impact of Trade Facilitation," 26.

[210] See *U.S.-Panama Trade Promotion Agreement (TPA)* Chapter 19 (Administration of the Agreement and Trade Capacity Building), section B, article 19.4. The Committee on Trade Capacity Building (TCB) is "designed to assist Panama with the transition to freer trade with the United States." The committee will also provide and coordinate technical assistance and provide financing to Panama to speed implementation of its FTA commitments. Panama has identified specific TCB needs and has developed strategies to improve its capabilities in these areas; however, successful implementation " will require resources and coordinated assistance among international and U.S. agencies." J.F. Hornbeck, Congressional Research Service (CRS), "CRS Report for Congress: The U.S.-Panama Free Trade Agreement," updated January 4, 2007, 20–21.

[211] The initial trade-capacity building priorities of this Committee are to be related to implementation of the customs administration and trade facilitation commitments (Chapter 5) and Section G: Textiles and Apparel commitments pertaining to market access (Chapter 3).

[212] *United States-Panama Trade Promotion Agreement (TPA)*, July 2007, full text available at http://www.ustr.gov/.

[213] Parties are committed to release goods from port within 48 hours.

[214] The TPA would strengthen Panama's customs administration procedures and reduce circumvention of the system. Hunt, hearing transcript, 35.

[215] Deferral of certain provisions is provided in the TPA to allow parties to develop the necessary technical capacity through such programs as trade capacity building.

[216] In comparison, the Colombia and Peru TPAs have a higher threshold ($200) for express shipments that would not be subject to duties or taxes. CAFTA-DR, however, did not include an exception for express shipments.

[217] Committee objectives included transparency of rules and regulations and inclusion of a mechanism to maintain "best practices" for the import and export process. Industry Trade Advisory Committee on CustomsMatters and Trade Facilitation (ITAC 14), "The United States-Panama Trade Promotion Agreement," report of April 18, 2007.

[218] Ibid.

[219] Ibid.

[220] ITAC 14, "The United States-Panama Trade Promotion Agreement."

[221] Advisory Committee for Trade Policy and Negotiations (ACTPN), "The U.S.-Panama Free Trade Agreement," report of April 25, 2007.

[222] ITAC 10, "The United States-Panama Trade Promotion Agreement."

[223] United States Trade Representative (USTR), "Free Trade with Panama: Summary of the United States-Panama Trade Promotion Agreement," June 2007, 2, available at http://www.ustr.gov/assets/Document_Library/Fact_Sheets/2007/asset_upload_file172_10234.pdf.

[224] The U.S.-Panama SPS Agreement was concluded and entered into force on December 20, 2006.

[225] Standing Committees have been included in other U.S. FTAs, including those with Chile, Australia, Peru, and Colombia and CAFTA-DR.

[226] United States-Panama Trade Promotion Agreement (TPA), July 2007, full text available at http://www.ustr.gov/.

[227] Codex Committees are established within the Codex Alimentarius Commission to develop internationally recognized food safety standards and guidelines.

[228] U.S. meat and poultry exports must be accompanied by an Export Certificate of Wholesomeness issued by the USDA, Food Safety and Inspection Service.

[229] Accompanied by a USDA Export Certificate of Wholesomeness and subject to certain certification statements specified in the annex to the U.S.-Panama SPS Agreement.

[230] Accompanied by USDA, Animal Plant Health Inspection Service export certificate.

[231] Agricultural Policy Advisory Committee for Trade (APAC), "The U.S.- Panama Trade Promotion Agreement," report of April 25, 2007, 2.

[232] Agricultural Technical Advisory Committee (ATAC) for Animal and Animal Products, "The United States-Panama Trade Promotion Agreement," report of April 18, 2007, 2.

[233] Ibid., 2–3.

[234] Agricultural Technical Advisory Committee (ATAC) for Trade in Processed Foods, "The U.S.-Panama Trade Promotion Agreement," report of April 25, 2007, 4.

[235] Ibid.

[236] National Pork Producers Council, "Statement of the National Pork Producers Council Before the International Trade Commission on Probable Economic Effect of an FTA between the U.S. and Panama," written submission, May 16, 2007, 8.

[237] U.S. industry representatives, telephone interviews by Commission staff, April 17-19, 2007.

[238] On December 20, 2006, the United States and Panama completed a bilateral agreement to further their cooperation in the area of standards-related activities, especially in the area of food safety. *United States-Panama Agreement Regarding Certain Sanitary and Phytosanitary (SPS) Measures and Technical Standards Affecting Trade in Agricultural Products*, December 20, 2006, 1-5, available at http://www.ustr.gov/.

[239] *United States-Panama Trade Promotion Agreement (TPA)*, July 2007, full text available at http://www.ustr.gov/.

[240] U.S. Government official, interview by Commission staff, March 13, 2007; and U.S. industry representatives, telephone interviews by Commission staff, April 17-19, 2007.

[241] U.S. industry representatives, telephone interviews by Commission staff, April 17-19, 2007.

[242] Gary Hufbauer, Barbara Kotschwar, and John Wilson, "Trade Policy, Standards, and Development in Central America" (Table 2), World Bank Policy Research Working Paper No. 2576, April 2001; USTR, *2006 National Trade Estimate Report on Foreign Trade Barriers* 502-03; and USTR, *2007 National Trade Estimate Report on Foreign Trade Barriers*, 452.

[243] Hunt, hearing transcript, 49-50.

[244] However, EU officials indicate that Panama would benefit from cooperating more fully with other Central American countries in the consultation and elaboration of technical regulations and standards to improve its harmonization with international standards. European Commission, Joint Committee Established Under the Political Dialogue and Cooperation Agreement with Central America, "EU-CA Joint Assessment on Regional Economic Integration: Final Report of the Working Group," February 3, 2006, 4, available at http://trade.ec.europa.eu/doclib/docs/2007/march/tradoc_134022.pdf.

[245] U.S. & Foreign Commercial Service (US& FCS) and U.S. Department of State. "Chapter 5: Trade Regulations and Standards," *Doing Business in Panama: A Country Commercial Guide for U.S. Companies*, 2006, available at http://www.buyusa.gov/panama/en/11.html, 41–44.

[246] USTR, 2007 NTE Report, 452.

[247] Hornbeck, "CRS Report for Congress," 13–14; and USTR, *2006 NTE Report*, 502-03.

[248] USTR, 2006 NTE Report, 502-03; and 2007 NTE Report, 452.

[249] US&FCS and U.S. Department of State, *Doing Business in Panama*, 40–44.

[250] Industry Trade Advisory Committee on Standards and Technical Trade Barriers (ITAC 16), "The U.S.- Panama Trade Promotion Agreement," report of April 24, 2007, 1–3.

[251] U.S. industry representatives, telephone interviews by Commission staff, April 17–18, 2007.

[252] Ibid.

[253] ITAC 16, "The U.S.-Panama Trade Promotion Agreement, 1–3; and U.S. Government official, interview by Commission staff, March 13, 2007.

[254] *United States-Panama Trade Promotion Agreement (TPA)*, July 2007, full text available at http://www.ustr.gov. Chapter 14 of the U.S.-Panama TPA emphasizes that the digital products referenced throughout the provisions are those digital products which are transmitted electronically.

[255] Currently, countries use different methods to apply customs duties.

[256] USTR, "Free Trade with Panama: Summary," 2.

[257] Advisory Committee for Trade Policy and Negotiations (ACTPN), "The U.S.-Panama Free Trade Agreement," report of April 25, 2007.

[258] Industry Trade Advisory Committee for Information and Communications Technologies, Services and Electronic Commerce (ITAC 8), "The U.S.-Panama Trade Promotion Agreement," report of April 25, 2007.

[259] Industry Trade Advisory Committee on Intellectual Property (ITAC 15), "The U.S.-Panama Trade Promotion Agreement (TPA) Intellectual Property Provisions," report of April 25, 2007.

[260] ITAC 8, "The U.S.-Panama Trade Promotion Agreement," report of April 25, 2007.

[261] abor Advisory Committee for Trade Negotiations and Trade Policy (LAC), "The U.S.-Panama Free Trade Agreement," report of April 25, 2007, 4.

[262] ndustry Trade Advisory Committee on Distribution Services (ITAC 5), "Report on the U.S.-Panama Trade Promotion Agreement," April 25, 2007, 5.

[263] Industry Trade Advisory Committee on Steel (ITAC 12), "The U.S.-Panama Trade Promotion Agreement," report of April 25, 2007, 2.

[264] United States Trade Representative (USTR), *2007 National Trade Estimate (NTE) Report on Foreign Trade Barriers*, 451. In addition, Panama's strong economic outlook indicates that there will be other opportunities for trade. The International Monetary Fund predicts that Panama's GDP will likely expand by 6.8 percent in 2008, the highest rate of predicted growth in Latin America. *Latin Business Chronicle*, "GDP Outlook 2008: Venezuela Worst, Panama Best," April 16, 2007, available at http://www.latinbusinesschronicle.com.

[265] While Panama committed to become a party to the WTO Agreement on Government Procurement (GPA) at the time of its WTO accession, its efforts to accede to the GPA have stalled. The WTO lists Panama as a country that is presently negotiating accession to the GPA. USTR, *2006 National Trade Estimate (NTE) Report on Foreign Trade Barriers*, 503; and World Trade Organization (WTO), "Government Procurement: the Plurilateral Agreement," available at http://www.wto.org/english/tratop_e/gproc_e/gp_gpa_e.htm.

[266] The TPA chapter on government procurement covers the same major provisions as the WTO Government Procurement Agreement, including such topics as national treatment, tendering procedures, and the awarding of contracts. Slight differences in the language of each article, the depth of coverage, and the specific details of compliance can complicate coordination and adherence for countries that are parties to both agreements. USTR, "Free Trade with Panama: Summary of the United States-Panama Trade Promotion Agreement," June 2007, 2, available at
http://www.ustr.gov/assets/Document_Library/Fact_Sheets/2007/asset_upload_file172_10234.pdf.

[267] One textual difference is that the U.S.-Colombia and U.S.-Peru FTAs both established committees on government procurement comprising representatives of each party but the U.S.-Panama TPA does not establish such a committee.

[268] USTR, 2007 NTE Report on Foreign Trade Barriers, 452-53.

[269] Panama is the 45th largest export market for U.S. goods.

[270] USTR, 2007 NTE Report on Foreign Trade Barriers, 451.

[271] Annex 9.1-11 to 9.1-12.

[272] J.F. Hornbeck, Congressional Research Service (CRS), "CRS Report for Congress: The U.S.-Panama Free Trade Agreement," updated January 4, 2007, 15.

[273] Hornbeck, "CRS Report for Congress," 15.

[274] According to the ACTPN, the $5.25 billion expansion of the Panama Canal will offer significant opportunities for U.S. providers of goods, services, and construction services. Advisory Committee for Trade Policy and Negotiations (ACTPN), "The U.S.-Panama Free Trade Agreement," report of April 25, 2007, 5.

[275] David Hunt, American Chamber of Commerce of Panama (AMCHAM), testimony before the United States International Trade Commission (USITC) in connection with inv. No. TA-2104-25, *U.S.-Panama Trade Promotion Agreement: Potential Economy-wide and Selected Sectoral Effects*, hearing transcript, May 16, 2007, 16; *U.S.-Panama Trade Promotion Agreement (TPA)* Article 18.8, "Anti-Corruption Measures"; and *U.S.-Panama TPA* article 9.13, "Ensuring Integrity in Procurement Practices," mirror the provisions employed in the Colombia and Peru FTAs, making bribery in government procurement a criminal offense.

[276] Raúl Del Valle, former president, The Chamber of Commerce, Industry, and Agriculture of Panama, testimony before the USITC in connection with inv. No. TA-2104-25, *U.S.-Panama Trade Promotion Agreement: Potential Economy-wide and Selected Sectoral Effects*, May 16, 2007, 9.

[277] Specifically, the ITAC 8 report expresses support for the TPA language clarifying that government procurement includes the procurement of digital products as defined in the Electronic Commerce Chapter and encourages future trade agreements to include similar language. Industry Trade Advisory Committee for Information and Communications Technologies, Services and Electronic Commerce (ITAC 8), "The U.S.-Panama Trade Promotion Agreement," report of April 25, 2007.

[278] However, in view of the potentially large purchases of the Panama Canal Authority, ITAC 12 urged the U.S. Government to enforce all U.S. supplier rights under the government procurement provisions of the U.S.-Panama TPA. ITAC 12, "The U.S.-Panama Trade Promotion Agreement," 2.

[279] The "reciprocity policy" was applied for the first time in the U.S.-Peru FTA and subsequently included in the agreements with Colombia and Panama. According to IGPAC, "potential benefits to participating states tend to be weakened by the policy's implementation process, supplier self-certification, and by the overly broad definition of "principal place of business" (defined as "the headquarters or main office of an enterprise, or any other place where the enterprises' business is managed, conducted or operated. This definition would allow a

supplier to have more than one principal place of business.") According to the USTR, the reciprocity approach is based on voluntary state coverage, exclusions for sensitive areas, and selfcertification by suppliers. Intergovernmental Policy Advisory Committee (IGPAC), "The U.S.-Panama Free Trade Promotion Agreement (TPA)," report of April 24, 2007, 17.

[280] The TPA's procurement provisions include coverage of eight states (Arkansas, Colorado, Florida, Illinois, Mississippi, New York, Texas, and Utah) and Puerto Rico; this is the first agreement to include the "reciprocity" policy with respect to subcentral procurement. IGPAC agreed to have some subcentral government procurement covered by the TPA, with thresholds of $526,000 for goods and services and $7,407,000 for construction services. IGPAC, "The U.S.-Panama Free Trade Promotion Agreement (TPA)," 1, 17.

[281] Ibid.

[282] Industry Trade Advisory Committee on Services and Finance Industries (ITAC 10), "The United States- Panama Trade Promotion Agreement," report of April 25, 2007, 5-6.

[283] Ibid., 6.

[284] Ibid.

[285] Ibid.

[286] The threshold value for construction services will be $12 million for the first twelve years of the agreement, dropping down to $10.3 million. Ibid., 5–6.

[287] Ibid.

[288] Industry Trade Advisory Committee on Non-Ferrous Metals and Building Materials (ITAC 9), "The U.S.-Panama Trade Promotion Agreement (TPA)," report of April 25, 2007, 3.

[289] It notes that article 9.1-6 of the draft agreement specifies that "no procuring entity may prepare, design, or otherwise structure or divide any procurement in order to avoid the obligations" of the agreement, but says that this language is not restrictive enough and does not reach the level of detail employed in earlier TPAs with Columbia and Peru. It states that those agreements were more specific and included three detailed prohibitions on valuation practices that could be used to frustrate the agreement's purposes. U.S.-Colombia FTA, article 9.1, "Valuation," and U.S.-Peru FTA, article 9.1, "Valuation." ITAC 9, "U.S.-Panama Trade Promotion Agreement," 4.

[290] The LAC said that the U.S. should retain its ability to invest tax dollars in domestic job creation and to pursue other legitimate social objectives. LAC, "U.S.-Panama Free Trade Agreement," 15.

[291] Thomas Gales, Caterpillar, Inc., on behalf of the U.S. Chamber of Commerce, Association of American Chambers of Commerce in Latin America, and the Latin American Trade Coalition, testimony before the USITC in connection with inv. No. TA-2104-25, U.S.-Panama Trade Promotion Agreement: Potential Economy-wide and Selected Sectoral Effects, hearing transcript, May 16, 2007, 53.

[292] In commenting on the business opportunity that the canal expansion project represents, a Chamber representative said that canal expansion will be accomplished by large contractors who are awarded the construction projects through a bid process in which U.S. contractors are eligible to participate. He said that the winning contractors will be responsible for designing, building, and procuring materials and supplies for the project and will contact vendors or smaller subcontractors to meet their needs. Gales, hearing transcript, 63-65.

[293] Juan Sosa, president, U.S.-Panama Business Council, testimony before the USITC in connection with inv. No. TA-2104-25, U.S.-Panama Trade Promotion Agreement: Potential Economy-wide and Selected Sectoral Effects, hearing transcript, May 16, 2007, 54. Mr. Sosa, explained how Panama's transportation facilities have drawn several U.S. businesses to establish regional headquarters in Panama (with combined assets of approximately $500 billion) and that they will be well positioned to do business in Panama after the canal expansion project is complete.

[294] The following sectors were excluded from the U.S.-Panama BIT: communications, representation of foreign firms; distribution and sale of imported products; retail trade; insurance; state companies; private utility companies, energy production; practice of liberal professions; custom house brokers; banking; rights to the exploitation of natural resources including fishers and hydroelectric power production; and ownership of land allocated within 10 km of the Panamanian border. Annex, "Treaty Between the United States of America and the Republic of Panama Concerning the Treatment and Protection of Investments," October 27, 1982, available at http://www.sice.oas.org/bits/panusatc.asp.

[295] Article XIII, "Treaty Between the United States of America and the Republic of Panama Concerning the Treatment and Protection of Investments," October 27, 1982, available at http://www.sice.oas.org/bits/panusatc.asp.

[296] United States-Panama Trade Promotion Agreement (TPA) , July 2007, full text available at http://www.ustr.gov/.

[297] Investment related to financial services is covered separately in the financial services chapter (TPA chap. 12).

[298] Such provisions may include requirements to export a given level or percentage of goods or services, to purchase goods produced in a party's territory, or to transfer a certain technology or other proprietary information.

[299] Investment-related reservations related to financial services, including insurance, are listed in annex III, and are presented in table 3.2 of this report.

[300] Such retail firms are defined in annex I of the TPA as those whose products are exclusively produced at the direction of the retail firm's owner and bear the label of the firm's owner.

[301] Article 288 of the 1972 Constitution, and article 16 of Executive Decree 35 of May 24, 1996.

[302] Industry Trade Advisory Committee on Automotive Equipment and Capital Goods (ITAC 2), "The U.S.-Panama Trade Promotion Agreement," report of April 25, 2007; ITAC 8, "The U.S.-Panama Trade Promotion Agreement"; and ITAC 10, "The United States-Panama Trade Promotion Agreement."

[303] Carlos M. Urriola, American Chamber of Commerce & Industry of Panama, "President's Letter," March 2007, available at http://www.panamcham.com/about_us/editDetail.asp?id=56; and Gales, hearing testimony, 69.

[304] Latin American Trade Coalition, "About the Agreements: Panama," available at http://www.latradecoalition.org/portal/latc/about/default, accessed April 27, 2007; and Hunt, hearing testimony, 14.

[305] For more information on this provision, see pages 5-15 of this report.

[306] ITAC 2, "The U.S.-Panama Trade Promotion Agreement"; and ITAC 10, "United States-Panama Trade Promotion Agreement."

[307] IGPAC, "The U.S.-Panama Free Trade Promotion Agreement."

[308] ITAC 10, "The United States-Panama Trade Promotion Agreement."

[309] Hunt, hearing testimony, 68.

[310] ITAC 2, "The U.S.-Panama Trade Promotion Agreement"; ITAC 8, "The U.S.-Panama Trade Promotion Agreement"; and Industry Trade Advisory Committee on Energy and Energy Services (ITAC 6), "The U.S.-Panama Free Trade Agreement (FTA)," report of April 25, 2007.

[311] Industry Trade Advisory Committee on Consumer Goods (ITAC 4), "The United States-Panama Trade Promotion Agreement," report of April 25, 2007.

[312] ITAC 5, "Report on the U.S.-Panama Trade Promotion Agreement."

[313] IGPAC, "The U.S.-Panama Free Trade Promotion Agreement."

[314] Center for International Environmental Law (CIEL), "Separate Comments of TEPAC Members on the U.S.-Panama Free Trade Agreement," attachment 3 to the Trade and Environment Policy Advisory Committee report on the U.S. Panama TPA, April 25, 2007.

[315] Trade and Environment Policy Advisory Committee (TEPAC), "The U.S.-Panama Trade Promotion Agreement," report of April 25, 2007.

[316] TEPAC, "U.S.-Panama Trade Promotion Agreement"; and CIEL, "Separate Comments of TEPAC Members on the U.S.-Panama Free Trade Agreement."

[317] CIEL, "Separate Comments of TEPAC Members on the U.S.-Panama Free Trade Agreement."

[318] Trade Promotion Act of 2002, 19 U.S.C. 3802(b)(4)(A).

[319] U.S. Government official, interview by Commission staff, April 24, 2007.

[320] See U.S. House Committee on Ways & Means, "Peru & Panama FTA Changes," accessible through "Congressional Leaders Joined Administration Officials to Announce an Agreement on a New Trade Policy for America," news release, May 10, 2007, available at http://waysandmeans.house.gov/news.asp; and USTR, "Bipartisan Agreement on Trade Policy: Government Procurement," Trade Facts sheet, May 2007, available at http://www.ustr.gov/, 3.

[321] Industry Trade Advisory Committee on Intellectual Property Rights (ITAC 15), "The U.S.-Panama Trade Promotion Agreement (TPA) Intellectual Property Provisions," report of April 25, 2007, 3. ITAC 15 understands, however, that it will have an opportunity to file an addendum to comment on any changes made to the TPA after the filing of its report.

[322] There are, however, several areas in which ITAC 15 prefers the stronger wording of provisions contained in the Morocco, Bahrain and Oman free trade agreements, and believes that these agreements generally should serve as the model for future negotiations. ITAC 15, "U.S.-Panama TPA Intellectual Property Provisions."

[323] International Intellectual Property Alliance, (IIPA) "Re: U.S.-Panama Trade Promotion Agreement: Potential Economy-wide and Selected Sectoral Effects," memorandum , submitted May 22, 2007.

[324] IIPA "Re: U.S.-Panama Trade Promotion Agreement: Potential Economy-wide and Selected Sectoral Effects," 3.

[325] ACTPN, "U.S.-Panama Free Trade Agreement (FTA)," 4.

[326] ITAC 8, "The U.S.-Panama Trade Promotion Agreement," 12.

[327] Industry Trade Advisory Committee for Chemicals, Pharmaceuticals, Health/Science Products and Services (ITAC 3), "The United States-Panama Trade Promotion Agreement," report of 24, 2007, 9.

[328] Generic Pharmaceutical Association (GPhA), "GPhA Says 'New Trade Policy for America' Fosters Pharmaceutical Innovation While Increasing Global Access to Affordable Medicines," press release, May 31, 2007, available at http://www.gphaonline.org/.

[329] "Separate Statement of TEPAC Member Rhoda H. Karpatkin, Consumers Union of U.S., Inc., et al.," attachment 2 to TEPAC, "U.S.-Panama Trade Promotion Agreement."

[330] U.S. House of Representatives, Committee on Government Reform - Minority Staff, Special Investigations Division, "Trade Agreements and Access to Medications Under the Bush Administration," June 2005, 6-9.

[331] Under the Trade Act of 2002, the U.S. Department of Labor is responsible for the preparation of three reports that address the labor issues associated with each new FTA: (1) Laws Governing Exploitive Child Labor Report, (2) Labor Rights Report, and (3) United States Employment Impact Review. As of October 2006, the Department of Labor had not published those reports related to the U.S.-Panama TPA. U.S. Department of Labor (DOL), Bureau of International Labor Affairs (ILAB), "Labor-Related Reports for U.S. Free Trade Agreements," available at http://www.dol.gov/ilab/media/reports/usfta/main.htm.

[332] For example, see AFL-CIO, "Statement by AFL-CIO President John Sweeney on U.S. Trade Policy Developments," May 10, 2007, found at http://www.aflcio.org/mediacenter/prsptmpr05112007a.cfm, retrieved May 21, 2007; U.S. Chamber of Commerce, "Chamber Welcomes Bipartisan Deal to Move Trade Agenda Forward," May 10, 2007, found at http://www.uscahmber.com/press/releases/2007/may/07-86.htm, retrieved May 30, 2007; National Association of Manufactures, "Memorial Day Recess Alert," 2007, found at http://www.nam.org/s_nam/doc1.asp?TrackID=1&SID=1&DID=238685&CID=2-2556&VID=2&RTID=0&CIDQS=&Taxonomy=False&specialSearch=False, retrieved May 30, 2007; and Business Roundtable, "Business Roundtable Praises New Bipartisan Cooperation on Trade Policy," May 10, 2007, found at http://www.businessroundtable.org//newsroom/document.aspx?qs=5886BF807822B0F19D5468122FB51711 FCF50C8, retrieved May 20, 2007.

[333] Under the Trade Act of 2002, U.S. negotiating objectives on labor issues include increasing the observance of core labor standards and eliminating or reducing regulations and measures that comprise sustainable development. USDOC, International Trade Administration (ITA), "The Trade Act of 2002: What Does It All Mean?" *Export America* (November 2002), available at http://www.ita.doc.gov/exportamerica/TechnicalAdvice/ta_tradeAct2002.pdf.

[334] ACTPN, "U.S.-Panama Free Trade Agreement (FTA)," 5-6.

[335] Hunt, hearing transcript, 62.

[336] LAC, "U.S.-Panama Free Trade Agreement," 3-4, 7-14.

[337] AFL-CIO, "Statement by AFL-CIO President John Sweeney on U.S. Trade Policy Developments," May 10, 2007, available at http://www.aflcio.org/mediacenter/prsptm/pr05112007a.cfm.

[338] U.S. Chamber of Commerce, "Chamber Welcomes Bipartisan Deal to Move Trade Agenda Forward," press release, May 10, 2007, available at http://www.uscahmber.com/; and National Association of Manufacturers (NAM), "Memorial Day Recess Alert," *NAM Capital Briefing*, e-newsletter (May 24, 2007), available at http://www.nam.org/s_nam/doc1.asp?TrackID=&SID=1&DID=238685&CID=202556&VID=2&RTID=0& CIDQS=&Taxonomy=False&specialSearch=False.

[339] Business Roundtable, "Business Roundtable Praises New Bipartisan Cooperation on Trade Policy," press release, May 10, 2007, available at http://www.businessroundtable.org/.

[340] In a mandate separate from the Commission's mandate, the USTR is tasked with providing an environmental review of the U.S.-Panama TPA. Although the USTR has not yet released its final environmental review of the U.S.-Panama TPA, it appears unlikely that the agreement will have significant environmental effects in the United States. Pursuant to the Trade Act of 2002 and the environmental review guidelines, the USTR provided an interim report to Congress in June 2004 on the probable environmental effects on the United States of a U.S.-Panama FTA. In its report, the USTR stated that such an FTA would be unlikely to result in any significant economically driven environmental effects in the United States but that it may have positive environmental consequences for Panama. The USTR added that such an FTA would not be expected to have a negative effect on the ability of U.S. government authorities to enforce or maintain U.S. environmental laws or regulations.

[341] USTR, "USTR Notifies Congress of Intent to Initiate FTA Talks With Panama," letter to Congress, November 18, 2003, 5, available at http://www.ustr.gov/.

[342] For more information on such remedies, procedures, and sanctions, please see the section on Dispute Resolution in this Chapter.

[343] USTR, "Final Bipartisan Trade Deal Full Summary," Trade Facts sheet, May 24, 2007, available at http://www.ustr.gov/.

[344] ACTPN, "U.S.-Panama Free Trade Agreement (FTA)," 7.

[345] TEPAC, "U.S.-Panama Trade Promotion Agreement," 2.

[346] This conclusion is unchanged from the March 19, 2004 interim report of the TEPAC. TEPAC, "U.S.- Panama Trade Promotion Agreement," 3.

[347] Ibid., 5.

[348] Ibid., 7.

[349] Ibid.

[350] ITAC 9, "The U.S.-Panama Trade Promotion Agreement (TPA)," 5.

[351] ITAC 7, "The United States Panama Trade Promotion Agreement," 5.

[352] ITAC 3, "The United-States Panama Trade Promotion Agreement," 6.

[353] See, for example, Zdenek Drabek and Warren Payne, "The Impact of Transparency on Foreign Direct Investment." *Journal of Economic Integration*17, no.4 (December 2002): 777-810; and Matthias Helbe, Ben Shepherd and John S. Wilson for the World Bank Development Research Group, *Transparency and Trade Facilitation in the Asia-Pacific: Estimation the Gains From Reform*, September 2007, available at http://econ.worldbank.org/projects/trade_costs.

[354] USTR, "Free Trade with Panama: Summary of the United States-Panama Trade Promotion Agreement," Trade Facts sheet, June 2007, 2, available at http://www.ustr.gov/.

[355] ITAC 10, "The United States-Panama Trade Promotion Agreement."

[356] Ibid.

[357] ACTPN, "The U.S.-Panama Free Trade Agreement (FTA)."

[358] ITAC 8, "The U.S.-Panama Trade Promotion Agreement."

[359] ACTPN, "U.S.-Panama Free Trade Agreement (FTA)," 4.

[360] Ibid.

[361] IGPAC, "The U.S.-Panama Free Trade Promotion Agreement (TPA)," 11.

[362] IGPAC notes that California, under NAFTA chapter 11, will be the state most frequently involved in such proceedings. IGPAC, "The U.S.-Panama Free Trade Promotion Agreement (TPA)," 21.

[363] IGPAC, "The U.S.-Panama Free Trade Promotion Agreement (TPA)," 20.

[364] ITAC 2, "The U.S.-Panama Trade Promotion Agreement," 6.

[365] Section 2104(f)(3) of the Trade Act of 2002 requires the Commission to review available economic assessments regarding the agreement, to provide a description of the analyses used and conclusions drawn in such literature, and to discuss areas of consensus and divergence among reviewed literature, including that of the Commission.

[366] Raul A. Hinojosa-Ojeda, "Regional Integration Among the Unequal: A CGE Model of US-CAFTA, NAFTA and the Central American Common Market," *North American Journal of Economics and Finance* 10, no. 1 (1999): 235–92.

[367] Josefina Monteagudo and Masakuza Watanuki, "What Kind of Trade Integration Helps Latin America the Most?" United Nations Development Programme, *Cooperation South*, no. 2 (2003): 19–32.

[368] The effect on exports and imports is measured by changes in trade in goods and excludes trade in services.

[369] avid Hunt, executive director, American Chamber of Commerce and Industry of Panama (AmCham Panama), testimony before the U.S. International Trade Commission (USITC), May 16, 2007; and written submission to the USITC, May 16, 2007; and Tom Mouhsian, director, MWW Group, on behalf of AmCham Panama, "Post-Hearing Comments on the U.S.-Panama Trade Promotion Agreement," written submission, May 23, 2007.

[370] rene Ringwood, Ball Janik LLP, counsel to the American Dehydrated Onion and Garlic Association, "Regarding the United States-Panama Trade Promotion Agreement: Potential Economy-Wide and Selected Sectoral Effects," posthearing brief to USITC, submitted May 22, 2007.

[371] hristopher D. Lischewski, president and CEO, Bumble Bee Foods LLC, "Written Comments Regarding Canned Tuna Harmonized Tariff Schedule of the U.S. 1604.14.10 to 1604.14.30," submitted to USITC May 21, 2007.

[372] om Gales, vice president, Latin American Division, Caterpillar, Inc., on behalf of the U.S.-Panama Trade Coalition and U.S. Chamber of Commerce, Office of Western Hemisphere Affairs, testimony before the USITC in connection with inv. No. TA-2104-25, *U.S.-Panama Trade Promotion Agreement: Potential Economy-wide and Selected Sectoral Effects*, May 16, 2007; and written submission, May 16, 2007.

[373] aúl Del Valle, former president, The Chamber of Commerce, Industry, and Agriculture of Panama, testimony before the USITC in connection with inv. No. TA-2104-25, *U.S.-Panama Trade Promotion Agreement: Potential Economy-wide and Selected Sectoral Effects*, May 16, 2007; and written submission, May 16, 2007.

[374] Eric Farnsworth, vice president, Council of the Americas, "Submission for the Record Before the U.S. International Trade Commission Hearing on U.S.-Panama Trade Promotion Agreement," submitted May 24, 2007.

[375] Maria Strong, vice president and general counsel, on behalf of the International Intellectual Property Alliance, "Re: U.S.-Panama Trade Promotion Agreement: Potential Economy-wide and Selected Sectoral Effects," memorandum , submitted May 22, 2007.

[376] Douglas Goudie, director of international trade, National Association of Manufacturers, "U.S.-Panama Trade Promotion Agreement: Potential Manufacturing Sector Effects," post-hearing brief submitted to the USITC, May 22, 2007, 2.

[377] Ken McCauley, president, National Corn Growers Association, written comments on U.S.-Panama Trade Promotion Agreement, submitted May 23, 2007.

[378] Nicholas Giordano, vice president and counsel, international trade policy, National Pork Producers Council, "Statement of the National Pork Producers Council Before the International Trade Commission on Probable Economic Effect on an FTA Between the U.S. and Panama," written submission, May 16, 2007.

[379] Sweetener Users Association, pre-hearing brief submitted to the United States International Trade Commission regarding the U.S.-Panama Trade Promotion Agreement: Economy-Wide and Selected Sectoral Effects," submitted May 10, 2007.

[380] Julie Hughes, senior vice president, U.S. Association of Importers of Textiles and Apparel, letter dated May 23, 2007.

[381] U.S. Grains Council, *Global Update*, (December 22, 2006): 1.

[382] Juan B. Sosa, president, U.S.-Panama Business Council, testimony before the USITC in connection with inv. No. TA-2104-25, *U.S.-Panama Trade Promotion Agreement: Potential Economy-wide and Selected Sectoral Effects*, May 16, 2007; and written submission, May 16, 2007.

[383] U.S.-Panama TPA, art. 22.6.

[384] Economic profile sources: U.S. International Trade Commission, *Dataweb*; Economist Intelligence Unit (EIU), "Panama Country Profile 2006"; EIU, "Country Report Panama - Main Report," 2007; International Monetary Fund (IMF), *Balance of Payments Statistics Yearbook 2006*; IMF, "Panama: Recent Economic Developments," Country Report No. 01/41 (Feb 2001); IMF, "Panama: Recent Economic Developments," Country Report No. 99/07 (March 1999); Central Intelligence Agency, *The World Factbook, 2007*; World Bank, *Panama Country Brief, 2007*; and World Bank, *World Development Indicators Online*.

[385] In Panama, the U.S. dollar serves as legal tender and is used as local currency.

[386] For derivations, see Paul S. Armington, "A Theory of Demand for Products Distinguished by Place of Production," *IMF Staff Papers*, vol. 16 (1969), 159-76; and J. Francois and K. Hall, "Partial Equilibrium Modeling," in J. Francois and K. Reinert, eds., *Applied Methods for Trade Policy Analysis, A Handbook* (Cambridge: Cambridge University Press, 1997). In the case of sugar, the domestic and imported products are assumed to be perfect substitutes, so that their prices change by the same amounts.

[387] The product grouping consists of similar goods from different sources. For example, goods *i*, *j*, and *k* would indicate three similar goods from three different sources. See Armington (1969) for further discussion of the concept.

[388] Armington (1969), 167.

[389] Ibid., 168.

[390] It should be noted that, although negotiated bilaterally, some FTA provisions such as those related to customs administration, labor, or environment tend to be applied in a nondiscriminatory manner and are closer to the MFN principle.

[391] The seminal works on this issue are Jacob Viner, *The Customs Union Issue* (New York: Carnegie Endowment for International Peace and London: Steven & Sons, Ltd., 1950); and J.E. Meade, *The Theory of Customs Unions* (Amsterdam: North-Holland Publishing, Co., 1955).

[392] Losses from trade diversion occur when lost tariff revenue associated with changes in the pattern of trade exceeds efficiency gains from the decline of the prices paid by consumers. These losses will be larger the higher the FTA's margin of preferences (i.e., the trade barriers facing nonmembers relative to intra-FTA barriers).

[393] World Bank, *Trade Blocs*, (Oxford University Press, 2000): 66.

[394] For additional information, see Schiff and Winters, "Regional Integration as Diplomacy," 271–96. As has been mentioned above, the data necessary to estimate the potential impact of negotiated commitments of an FTA related to, for example, intellectual property rights and customs administration and services, are not readily available.

[395] Qualitative assessments of the impact of the U.S.-Panama TPA on these negotiated objectives are provided in chaps. 4 through 6 of this report.

[396] The current nominal loan rate is fixed at 18.0 cents per pound for raw sugar and 22.9 cents per pound for refined sugar. However, the rates vary by location and may effectively be higher as a result of factors such as interest expense, transportation costs, and location discounts.

[397] Production in excess of this amount must be held as stocks by the industry. Such stocks vary over time.

[398] Raw value basis, excluding imports under a sugar re-export program. Marketing year is from October through September.

[399] The marketing allotments are suspended (restrictions are lifted) if the overall allotment quantity must be reduced as well. The overall allotment quantity is the total amount of sugar that is permitted to be marketed by domestic producers. The suspension of marketing allotments is to allow domestic producers to compete with imports. However, the USDA is still obligated to purchase domestically-produced sugar at the loan rates in the event marketing allotments are suspended.

[400] Effectively, this means no forfeitures of sugar to the USDA.

[401] U.S. sugar policy, mainly implemented by a system of import quotas and the domestic price support loan program described above, contributed to a domestic wholesale price for raw sugar of 21.42 cents per pound and refined sugar of 26.21 cents per pound in 2003. By comparison, the world wholesale price for raw cane sugar averaged 7.51 cents per pound and for refined sugar 9.74 cents per pound that year. USDA, Economic Research Service, "Sugar and Sweeteners Yearbook Tables," available at

http://www.ers.usda.gov/Briefing/Sugar/Trade/.

[402] These TRQs are all provided for in the additional U.S. notes 5, 7, 8, and 9 to chapter 17 of the HTS and pertinent subheadings.

[403] This TRQ is provided for in additional U.S. note 1 of chapter 18 of the HTS.

[404] Zero for the subject countries under preferential trade arrangements.

[405] The NAFTA and certain other FTAs exempt the relevant countries from these special safeguard duties. See HTS subheadings 9904.17, 9904.18, 9904.19, and 9904.21.

In: Panama: Politics and Economics
Editor: Ricardo Colson

ISBN: 978-1-60692-403-7
© 2009 Nova Science Publishers, Inc.

Chapter 2

THE PROPOSED U.S.-PANAMA FREE TRADE AGREEMENT*

J. F. Hornbeck

SUMMARY

On June 28, 2007, the United States and Panama signed a free trade agreement (FTA) after two and half years and ten rounds of negotiations. Negotiations were formally concluded on December 16, 2006, with an understanding that further changes to labor, environment, and intellectual property rights (IPR) chapters would be made pursuant to detailed congressional input. These changes were agreed to in late June 2007, clearing the way for the proposed FTA's signing in time to be considered under Trade Promotion Authority (TPA), which expired on July 1, 2007. TPA allows Congress to consider trade implementing bills under expedited procedures. Panama's legislature approved the FTA on 58 to 4 on July 11, 2007. The 110th Congress may take up implementing legislation in 2008.

Significant changes from previous bilateral FTAs include the adoption of enforceable labor standards, compulsory adherence to select multilateral environmental agreements (MEAs), and facilitation of developing country access to generic drugs. In each case, the proposed U.S.-Panama FTA goes beyond provisions in existing multilateral trade rules and even those contemplated in the Doha Development Round negotiations.

There is one highly sensitive issue that remains to be resolved. In September 2007, the Panamanian National Assembly elected Pedro Miguel González Pinzón to a one-year term as President of legislative body. Although a deputy in the National Assembly since 1999, he is known in the United States for his alleged role in the June 10, 1992 murder of a U.S. serviceman in Panama. A Panamanian court acquitted him of the charge in 1995, but the United States does not recognize the verdict and maintains an outstanding warrant for his arrest. His continued presence as National Assembly President has been one factor delaying

---

* This is edited, reformatted and augmented version of a Congressional Research Service Report Order Code RL32540 Updated January 19, 2008.

consideration of the FTA by the U.S. Congress. This situation could change if he is not re-elected to a second term in a September 1, 2008 election.

The proposed U.S.-Panama FTA is a comprehensive agreement. Some 88% of U.S. commercial and industrial exports would become duty-free right away, with remaining tariffs phased out over a ten-year period. About 50% of U.S. farms exports to Panama would achieve duty-free status immediately. Tariffs and tariff rate quotas (TRQs) on select farm products are to be phased out by year 17 of the agreement. Panama and the United States agreed to a separate bilateral agreement on SPS issues that would recognize U.S. food safety inspection as equivalent to Panamanian standards, which would expedite entry of U.S. meat and poultry exports. The FTA also consummates understandings on services trade, telecommunications, government procurement, and intellectual property rights (particularly with respect to pharmaceutical products), while supporting trade capacity building.

This report will be updated periodically. Related information may be found in CRS Report RL30981, *Panama: Political and Economic Conditions and U.S. Relations*, by Mark P. Sullivan.

THE PROPOSED U.S.-PANAMA FREE TRADE AGREEMENT

On June 28, 2007, the United States and Panama signed a free trade agreement (FTA) after two and a half years and ten rounds of negotiations (see **Appendix 1** for a chronology of events). Negotiations formally concluded on December 16, 2006, with an understanding that changes to labor, environment, and intellectual property rights (IPR) chapters would be made pursuant to congressional input, which were agreed to in late June 2007. The FTA was signed in time to be considered underTrade Promotion Authority (TPA), which expired on July 1, 2007. TPA allows Congress to consider certain trade implementing bills under expedited procedures.[1] Panama's legislature ratified the FTA 58 to 4 on July 11, 2007, and the U.S. Congress may consider implementing legislation sometime in 2008.

The FTA incorporates changes based on principles outlined in the "New Trade Policy for America,"[2] a bipartisan policy crafted jointly by congressional leadership and the Bush Administration. It requires adoption as fully enforceable commitments, the five basic labor rights defined in the International Labor Organization's *Fundamental Principles and Rights at Work and its Follow-up (1998) Declaration*, select multilateral environmental agreements, and new pharmaceutical IPR provisions that may facilitate Panama's access to generic drugs. A congressionally mandated report by the United States International Trade Commission (USITC) concluded that the likely main trade effect of the FTA would be to increase U.S. exports given that 96% of U.S. imports from Panama already enter duty free. The small size of the Panamanian economy, however, suggests that the overall effect on the U.S. economy would be very small.[3]

Although many economic policy issues were addressed in a bipartisan compromise, albeit not to the satisfaction of all Members, the FTA now also faces a political issue between the two governments that has delayed congressional action on the FTA. On September 3, 2007, following an election of his peers, Pedro Miguel González Pinzón assumed the office of President of the National Assembly for a one-year term. Although a deputy in the National Assembly since 1999, he is known in the United States for his alleged role in the June 10,

1992, murder of a U.S. serviceman in Panama. A Panamanian court acquitted him of the charge in 1995, but the United States does not recognize the verdict and maintains an outstanding warrant for his arrest.[4]

Both the Bush Administration and Members of Congress have indicated that his continued presence in the National Assembly leadership position posed a problem for congressional action on the FTA.[5] Panama, for its part, faces a sensitive situation given it does not wish to appear as if it is compromising its national sovereignty to accommodate political concerns in the United States. At this juncture, it appears as though González Pinzón will serve out his one-year term, with a possibility that he may not be re-elected. Congressional action on the U.S.-Panama FTA could occur at any time in 2008, but this situation may encourage a delay until after a new National Assembly president is elected on September 1, 2008, should that happen. This report will be updated periodically.

PANAMA'S CANAL AND ECONOMIC RELATIONS WITH THE UNITED STATES

The United States and Panama have entered into many agreements over the past 150 years, the most prominent ones defining their relative stake in the famous canal that traverses the Central American isthmus, bisecting Panamanian territory (see **Figure 1**). The canal has been a critical factor influencing Panamanian domestic and foreign affairs, and like earlier U.S.-Panama agreements, the FTA's significance is tied to a Panamanian economy that has formed largely around the canal.

Figure 1. Map of Panama

Source: Map Resources adopted by CRS (5-25-06)

Early U.S.-Panama Economic Relations

Since first explored by the Spanish at the turn of the sixteenth century, interest in Panama has centered on its unique geographic characteristic: the slender distance separating the

Atlantic and Pacific Oceans. Because of the transit possibilities this presented (first for Peruvian gold and other colonial trade), Panama was a natural crossroads for the movement of commerce, a strategic position that grew as the world became ever more traveled and integrated. In fact, Panama's destiny became fused to its geography and, over time, to the vagaries of foreign interests that sought to take advantage of it, particularly the United States.

Panama was swept to independence from Spain on November 28, 1821, becoming part of the Gran Colombia regional group. By this point, both the United States and Britain had openly coveted the prospect of an inter-oceanic connector. Well before construction of a canal could begin, the United States displaced Britain as the dominant foreign influence and completed a cross-isthmian railroad in 1855. This project was driven by the westward expansion of the United States, which included an anticipated southern water route to the west coast. To secure this transit system, as well as the safety of goods and people using it, the United States resorted to armed intervention in Panama some 14 times in the 19th century. By the time the United States sought permission to construct a canal, a precedent had already been set to use military force for defense of U.S. interests in Panama.[6]

The initial U.S. effort to build a canal required a concession from Colombia allowing the United States to complete the bankrupt French project abandoned in 1889. In early 1903, the details were set down in a treaty ratified by the U.S. Senate, but unanimously rejected by the Colombian legislature. The United States responded by reaching out to the growing Panamanian successionist movement. On November 3, 1903, in a quick and bloodless move encouraged by the offshore presence of U.S. warships, Panama separated from Colombia. The United States immediately recognized Panama as an independent state, and in return, Panama signed the Hay-Buneau-Varilla Treaty, ceding to the United States the rights to construct a canal and to control it "in perpetuity."[7]

The Panama Canal opened in 1914, leading to U.S. dominance in the economic and, at times, political life of Panama. Although both countries benefitted from its operations, the relationship was far from equal, which along with the perpetual U.S. presence, generated a nagging resentment, frequent protests, and periodic violence over the tangible loss of national sovereignty. This tension remained a dominant feature of U.S.-Panamanian relations until the canal was ceded back to Panama in 1977 under terms defined in the Panama Canal Treaties signed by Presidents Jimmy Carter and Omar Torrijos. Although tensions flared again in 1989 when the U.S. military invaded Panama to arrest then-chief of state General Manual Noriega on narcotics trafficking charges and for threatening U.S. personnel and property, the incursion proved to be a catalyst for the return of democracy. Perhaps not coincidentally, Panama's decision to promote trade liberalization followed soon thereafter.[8]

The Canal and U.S. Trade Policy

The canal solidified Panama as a maritime economy and its return to control by Panama raised expectations of greater economic benefits from its ownership. The canal operations by themselves account for approximately 6% of Panama's GDP, with the largest and fastest growing traffic volume generated along the U.S. East Coast-to-Asia trade route (especially U.S.-China). About one-third of all cargo passing through the canal has its origin or destination in the United States. The canal's total economic impact, however, is far greater, supporting income and jobs in various services industries including warehousing, ship registry and repair, salvage operations, insurance, banking, and tourism. The two major ports at either end of the canal have been privatized and modernized, a portion of the canal was widened in 2001, but Panama faces a difficult and expensive challenge to enhance the capacity of the entire canal to accommodate much larger post-Panamax ships.[9] Panama held a national referendum on the proposed $5.25 billion expansion on October 22, 2006, which passed by a wide margin.

With transfer of the canal and its operations to Panama, the country also inherited a substantial amount of land and physical assets. The conversion of these assets to private use has been a boon to the Panamanian economy, but not without considerable costs and investment, as well. Privatization efforts eased the transformation of former U.S. government facilities to productive Panamanian use, which has included refurbishing the Panamanian railroad by Kansas City Southern Railways, transforming the former Albrook base into residential housing, and developing a small foreign processing zone in the former Ft. Davis.[10]

The Panama-Pacific Special Economic Area (PPSEA) is perhaps the most ambitious of these projects. This public-private partnership, established in law, aspires to convert the former Howard Air Force Base into a "world class business center," with an emphasis on the export sector. Existing assets include housing and office buildings, a hospital, transportation infrastructure, fiberoptic cable network, an 8,500-foot runway, and four hangar facilities. The government offers businesses various fiscal incentives and a streamlined regulatory process. Firms are required to commit to state-of-the-art practices that include adopting internationally accepted environmental and labor standards.[11]

With the assistance of the International Finance Corporation (IFC) of the World Bank, Panama is seeking a large global financing package to cover the initial investment needs. The project aims at developing various businesses including computer technology, cell phone manufacturing, international call centers (Dell already operates one on site), aeronautical industry support, and others that require a well-trained work force. The IFC supports this project not only for its prospects as a business venture, but because it is forward looking rather than relying on the "maquiladora" business model common in much of the region.[12]

At the start of the 21st century, the canal and close ties with the United States are still the defining features of Panama's economy, but in the past these traits have hindered Panama's participation in regional integration. Although part of the Central American Integration System, a broadly focused political arrangement, Panama has declined to join the Central American Common Market, relying instead on the canal and the large U.S. economy as its economic anchors. Panama has always had a fully dollarized monetary system and is a beneficiary of U.S. unilateral trade preferences defined in the Caribbean Basin Economic Recovery Act (CBERA), the Caribbean Basin Trade Partnership Act (CBTPA), and the Generalized System of Preferences (GSP).[13] Under these circumstances, there has been little external incentive for Panama to become a more open economy. Only since joining the World Trade Organization (WTO) in 1997 did Panama begin to reduce tariff rates, an important step in preparing Panama for an FTA with the United States.

Panama's subregional independence and reliance on U.S. economic ties has suited the United States as well, given its continuing interest in the Canal. An FTA with Panama may be seen as one way for the United States to support longestablished commercial interests and deepen bilateral relations, particularly if accepted as a mutually beneficial pact with reasonably balanced political and economic outcomes. Although many ships have outgrown the canal, its locale and prospects for enlarging the passageway continue to reinforce

Panama's historic, albeit currently diminished, importance for the United States as a strategic trade passage.

A bilateral FTA with Panama is also part of the Bush Administration's "competitive liberalization" trade strategy, in which negotiations are taking place on multilateral, regional, and bilateral levels. This multi-tiered negotiation strategy is predicated on an expectation that gains on one level of negotiation may encourage, if not compel, similar breakthroughs on others. Because of slow progress in negotiations at the WTO Doha Round and the Free Trade Area of the Americas (FTAA), the United States has moved ahead aggressively with bilateral talks, of which the Panama FTA is one. Some, however, have questioned the bilateral approach for the asymmetrical negotiation power the United States wields, the effects it may have on non-participating countries, and the one-sided trading system that is developing around a U.S. hub, as opposed to a truly regional or multilateral system.

For Panama, the proposed FTA reinforces its varied trade liberalization goals and supports continued U.S. foreign direct investment. The services sector is already globally competitive, but the manufacturing sector is small and agricultural remains protected and uncompetitive (see below). For Panama, the chief concern was crafting an FTA that would balance the need to pursue openness for services, export growth and promotion for manufacturing, and adjustment time for agriculture to become more competitive, while minimizing social displacement. The incentive to negotiate was perhaps also enhanced by the desire to keep pace with other Latin American countries that have or are negotiating FTAs with the United States.

PANAMANIAN TRADE RELATIONS

Panama is a country of 3.2 million people with a stable, diversified economy that has rebounded briskly from the 2001-2002 global economic downturn. Panama's gross domestic product (GDP) expanded by 4.2% in 2003, 7.6% in 2004, 6.9% in 2005, and 7.1% in 2006 (see **Appendix 2** for selected macroeconomic data). With the exception of Costa Rica, Panama has the highest per capita income in the Central American region, but income distribution is highly skewed, poverty remains a nagging problem, especially in rural areas, and unemployment is high, but declining. Unlike any other Latin American country, 77% of Panama's GDP is in services, developed around the transportation and commerce generated by canal traffic and the Colón Free Zone (CFZ). Industry is the second most important sector, contributing 17% to GDP followed by agriculture at 6%.[14]

Structure and Direction of Panamanian Trade

Trade is an increasingly important part of this services-based economy. As seen in **Table 1**, Panama's balance of payments points to a sizeable trade deficit in goods compared to a large services trade surplus. Panama's merchandise trade deficits ranged from $700 million to $1.6 billion from 2001 to 2006. In each year, the merchandise deficit was offset by a services trade surplus of between $900 million to $1.7 billion, unusual for a Latin American economy.

Table 1. Panama's Current Account Balance

	2001	2002	2003	2004	2005	2006
Balance on Merchandise Trade ($ million)	-696	-1,037	-1,113	-1,538	-1,316	-1,576
Balance on Services Trade ($ million)	899	979	1,254	1,278	1,415	1,715

Data Source: United Nations Economic Commission on Latin America and the Caribbean (ECLAC). *Preliminary Overview of the Economies of Latin America and the Caribbean*, years 2003-2006.

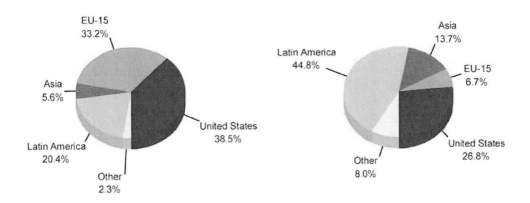

Figure 2. Panama Direction of Trade, 2006

Source: CRS from World Trade Atlas.

Overall, the current account deficit has remained relatively high in recent years due in part to the sharp rise in oil prices, which has also negatively affected Panama's inflation rate and terms of trade (**Appendix 2**). Panama places a strong emphasis on increasing exports as a driver of economic growth, pointing to the Panama Pacific Special Economic Area, Colón Free Zone (see below), and, to a lesser extent, the small export processing zones and nontraditional agricultural products as opportunities to execute this vision. As a global trader, it has completed FTAs with El Salvador (2002), Taiwan (2004), and Singapore (2005). In addition to the United States, it is negotiating FTAs with Guatemala, Nicaragua, Costa Rica, and Honduras. Panama nonetheless remains closely tied to the United States as its dominant trading partner, which as a single country is a larger trading partner than any of the world's major regions.

In 2006, the United States accounted for some 38.5% of Panamanian exports and 26.8% of its imports (see **Figure 2**). The European Union is the second largest export market with a 33.2% export share, but accounts for only 6.7% of Panamanian imports. The Latin American countries collectively are Panama's third largest export market with 20.4%, but has the largest import share at 44.8%.

Panama is one of the few Latin American countries with which the United States has a merchandise trade surplus, and although relatively small, it is by far the largest in the region. Panama runs a sizeable trade deficit with Latin America; its largest Latin American trade partners are Mexico, Costa Rica, and Brazil. Panama also imports significant quantities of oil from Peru, Venezuela, and Ecuador. Asia accounts for 5.6% of Panama's exports, but 13.7% of its imports, dominated by Japan, South Korea, and more recently, China.

The Colón Free Zone

A distinct feature of Panama's trade regime is the Colón Free Zone (CFZ), which with the exception of Hong Kong, is the largest duty free zone in the world. The vast trade volume that traverses the Panama Canal, multimodal transportation infrastructure, modern financial sector, and Panama's central location in the Americas make Colón a logical place for a duty free zone. It serves as a "one stop shop" for both Latin American buyers, and sellers from the rest of the world, including Asia and the United States. Sellers operate showrooms targeted at small- and medium-sized buyers, who make wholesale purchases of goods for retail sale in their respective countries. Goods are typically repackaged in smaller lots, priced in the local market currency, and transferred to the purchasing country without incurring income, value added, or transfer taxes. Most CFZ trade is in electronics, clothing, jewelry, and other consumer goods.

Buyers benefit from the ability to purchase small lots, reduced travel costs, consolidated shipping and improved shipping times, and credit offered by sellers. The sellers benefit from reaching smaller Latin American markets in one location and reduced tax and similar reductions in transaction costs. Panama benefits from the 20,000 direct jobs the CFZ creates and the public revenue they generate. CFZ trade is reported as a separate component of Panama's trade statistics and only those goods entering the Panamanian economy are recorded as imports. In 2005, nearly $5 billion worth of goods passed through the CFZ, with $500 million added to the Panamanian trade balance.[15]

The CFZ is frequently associated with a number of illicit activities including money laundering, illegal transshipment, trademark and other intellectual property violations. In part, this is a reputation that Panama as a whole has been fighting since the military dictatorship, which was widely known for its flagrant disrespect of the law, if not outright corruption. Panama's proximity to Colombia and headquarters as a transshipment point helped fuel this perception.

The CFZ has attempted to counter this reputation. The zone itself is an enclosed commercial area, encircled by, and under the supervision of, customs and other law enforcement agencies of the Republic of Panama. In addition, both the Colón Free Zone User's Association and the CFZ Administration have a strict code of conduct and argue that illegal activity is also policed by individual companies because a bad reputation hurts those dedicated to making the CFZ a world class trading center. Even the accusation of an infraction can lead to a suspension of the license needed to operate in the zone. Cash accounts for only 10% of transactions and there is careful monitoring of all goods that move in and out of the zone through electronic tracking systems.[16]

U.S.-Panama Merchandise Trade

U.S.-Panamanian merchandise trade is small.[17] In 2006, the United States exported $2,706 million worth of goods and imported $323 million, producing a U.S. trade surplus of

$2,383 million, the largest in the Western Hemisphere. Still, Panama ranked as only the 45th largest export market for U.S. goods and 98th for imports. Major U.S. exports, as seen in **Table 2**, include oil and mostly capital- and technology-intensive manufactured goods such as aircraft, pharmaceuticals, machinery, medical equipment, and motor vehicles.

Table 2. U.S.-Panama Merchandise Trade, 2006
(top ten U.S. exports and imports by $ value)

U.S. Exports	$ Value million	% of Total	U.S. Imports	$ Value million	% of Total
1. Oil (not crude)	855.6	31.6%	1. Fish/Seafood:	101.9	26.9%
2. Machinery	291.8	10.8%	2. Repaired Goods	79.6	21.0%
- Computers	(65.1)				
- Office mach.	(41.8)				
3. Electrical mach.	183.6	6.8%	3. Gold	35.0	9.3%
4. Aircraft	166.1	6.2%	4. Crude Oil	32.3	8.6%
5. Pharmaceuticals	132.4	4.9%	5. Sugar (cane)	23.5	6.2%
6. Vehicles	93.4	3.5%	6. Edible Fruit	12.2	3.3%
7. Optical/Medical Equipment	93.4	3.5%	7. Coffee	11.8	3.1%
8. Perfume	77.3	2.9%	8. Electrical mach.	9.0	2.4%
9. Paper	67.2	2.5%	9. Aluminum	8.8	2.3%
10.Cereals	69.0	2.6%	10.Glass	5.2	1.4%
Other	676.9	24.7%	Other	59.0	15.4%
Total	2,706.7	100.0%	Total	378.3	100.0%

Data Source: U.S. Department of Commerce.

The United States imports relatively little from Panama, accounting for the growing U.S. merchandise trade surplus. Most imports are primary products; over one-quarter is seafood, mostly fresh fish and shrimp. Repaired goods are number two accounting for 22% of total imports.[18] Commodity trade includes crude oil, precious metal (mostly gold), fruit, sugar, and coffee, which together account for 30.5% of total imports. Unlike the Central American countries, where U.S. sensitivities to textile and apparel trade run high, Panama trades little in this sector. Panama's agricultural exports, particularly sugar, presented the more difficult negotiation issues.

U.S. Foreign Direct Investment

Panama has no formal restrictions on capital flows, does not discriminate between foreign and domestic investment, and maintains bilateral investment treaties with the United States and many European countries. Critics have pointed out, however, that the legal environment can be cumbersome and that Panama's relatively high labor costs (for the hemisphere) and inflexible labor laws can be a frustration if not an impediment to U.S. foreign direct investment (FDI).[19] Still, U.S. companies are well represented in Panama, including the largest container port facility in the region, multiple financial institutions, transportation firms, and manufacturing facilities from various sectors. Like other countries pursuing an FTA with the United States, Panama seeks closer ties for the continued FDI that may be generated from having a permanent rules-based trade relationship with a large trading partner.

Table 3. U.S. Investment in Panama, Mexico, and Central America ($ millions)

Sector	2001	2002	2003	2004	2005	2006
Panama	5,141	5,842	5,409	5,631	5,777	5,728
Mexico	52,544	56,303	59,851	63,502	75,106	84,699
Central America	2,994	3,199	2,333	2,857	3,242	3,568

Data Source: U.S. Department of Commerce. Bureau of Economic Analysis. BEA website. Data are stock of foreign direct investment (FDI) presented on an historical-cost basis.

U.S. FDI represents over a third of total FDI in Panama. **Table 3** compares U.S. FDI in Panama to other regional destinations, and although the dollar value of U.S. investment in Panama exceeds that in the five Central American countries combined, it actually amounts to 40% of Panama's GDP compared to only 4% for Central America. Plans to widen and improve the canal will likely provide an opportunity for some $5 billion of investment in the canal itself, and perhaps related large amounts of FDI for other sectors of the economy with a significant U.S. presence.

SUMMARY OF TRADE NEGOTIATIONS AND THE PROPOSED U.S.-PANAMA FTA[20]

Panama approached the United States for a stand-alone FTA, preferring to avoid a direct link to the U.S.-Dominican Republic-Central America Free Trade Agreement (CAFTA-DR).[21] Panama wanted to maximize an FTA's potential to win U.S. congressional approval by emphasizing the historical and strategic nature of the U.S.-Panamanian relationship, while separating the negotiations from the divisive CAFTA-DR accord. Panama's service economy, small textile and apparel industry, and limited integration with the Central American economies also bolstered the case for separate negotiations.[22] Another unique feature of the FTA negotiations was the treatment of business issues with respect to the Panama Canal Area. Its status as an autonomous legal entity under the Panamanian Constitution required separate negotiations for government procurement, labor, investment, and other areas. The United States is the only country with which Panama has been willing to negotiate issues related to the canal area in an FTA.

The proposed agreement was completed in ten rounds of negotiation, concluding on December 16, 2006 and in general follows the text framework of earlier FTAs. It was signed on June 28, 2007 following some significant last minute changes to the labor, environment, intellectual property rights, and government procurement chapters to accommodate new commitments agreed to by the USTR and bipartisan congressional leadership. Market access schedules, drawn from previous FTA templates, reflect both U.S. and Panamanian interests, as do other market access provisions.

Congress requires that the United States International Trade Commission (USITC) make an economic assessment of the potential impact of an FTA on the U.S. economy. The analysis usually is done with both a general equilibrium model to estimate economy-wide changes and a partial equilibrium model to estimate sectoral or industry-level changes. In Panama's case, there was insufficient data to make a meaningful estimate from a general equilibrium model, and so detailed estimates of how the FTA might affect U.S. economic growth, employment, trade, and income were not offered. In general, however, through other quantitative and qualitative indicators, the USITC concluded that because Panama's economy is very small relative to that of the United States, the likely overall effect on the U.S. economy also will be similarly very small.[23]

At the sectoral level, the USITC finds that the "main effect" of the FTA would likely be to increase U.S. exports, while causing little growth in U.S. imports from Panama. In general, the estimates are in line with general expectations based on (1) the small amount of goods imported from Panama, (2) the small production capacity of Panama, and (3) the fact that most imports from Panama (96% by value) already enter the United States duty free through either normal trade relations (NTR) or preferences provided by the Caribbean Basin Initiative (CBI) programs or the Generalized System of Preferences (GSP).[24]

Specific estimates suggest that when fully implemented, the largest growth potentially will accrue to U.S. exports of rice (145%), pork (96%), beef (94%), and passenger vehicles (43%). Again, these would amount to a very small dollar value increase given that, with the exception of rice, the U.S. exports of these goods to Panama represent less than two-tenths of one percent (0.2%) of U.S. exports to the world and even a smaller portion of U.S. production. With respect to the services provisions in the FTA, they exceed WTO commitments, but the gains for U.S. providers are also expected to be small, with the potential for further gains once the Panama Canal expansion project is underway.[25]

Below is a more detailed discussion of the major negotiation areas and a description of the issues that have been of particular interest to Panama and the United States, including the U.S. Congress. Where relevant, changes made pursuant to the May 10, 2007 bipartisan "New Trade Policy for America" are discussed.

Market Access

Market access (chapter 3 of the FTA) covers provisions that govern barriers to trade such as tariffs, quotas, safeguards, other nontariff barriers, and rules of origin (chapter 4). The proposed U.S.-Panama FTA would replace unilateral trade preferences provided to Panama under the Caribbean Basin Economic Recovery Act (CBERA), the Caribbean Basin Trade Partnership Act (CBTPA), and the Generalized System of Preferences (GSP), under which most imports from Panama enter the United States duty free along with those entering under the normal trade relations schedule (see **Appendix 3** for selected tariff rates). Panamanian agricultural products face some of the highest barriers, particularly sugar, which is subject to a tariff rate quota (TRQ). U.S. exports face tariffs, with most falling in the range of 3-10%, plus the additional 5% transfer tax, which applies to domestic goods as well.

Market access provides for national treatment for traded goods of both parties, with a detailed schedule defining the progressive elimination of customs duties for manufactured and agricultural goods. There are nine staging categories that classify each country's goods based on the time to tariff elimination, with the most sensitive products given lengthier phase out of tariffs. The USTR reports that tariffs on 88% of industrial and commercial goods would go to zero immediately, with the remaining tariffs phased out over a ten-year period. Similarly, over half of U.S. farm exports would receive immediate duty free treatment.[26] Tariffs on some agricultural goods would remain in place longer, with some taking up to 17 years to be completely eliminated. Safeguards have been retained for many products only for the period of duty phase out, but antidumping and countervailing duties were not addressed, leaving these trade remedy laws fully operational, as required under TPA.

Rules of origin define which goods would be eligible for duty-free treatment based on the country of origin of their content. Rules of origin are intended to prevent transshipment of goods made from materials originating in countries outside the agreement. They are particularly pertinent to apparel and textile trade. Apparel products made in Panama would be given duty-free treatment if they are made from U.S. or Panamanian fabric and yarns (the yarn forward rule).

Agricultural Trade

U.S. domestic agricultural support programs are not addressed in the proposed FTA, which focused on reducing tariffs, adjusting quota levels, and cooperating more closely on sanitary and phytosanitary (SPS) rules and enforcement. Market access was particularly difficult for four highly protected products: pork; poultry; rice; and sugar. The United States was basically "offensive" on pork, poultry, and rice, expecting to open further Panama's markets as soon as possible. It was "defensive" on sugar, attempting to limit increases in the sugar quota that might disrupt operations of the sugar program as defined in legislation. Panama's position was the reverse, pressing to minimize increases in U.S. exports of pork, poultry, and rice, and to increase its U.S. sugar export quota.

In the United States, the sugar program reflects an historical commitment to protect the income of sugar beet, sugar cane, and sugar processing firms with belowprime-rate loans, limitations on sales in the domestic market, and tariff rate quotas (TRQs). TRQs restrict imports with prohibitively high tariffs on imports above a defined quota amount, as defined in WTO rules agreed to by the United States. In 2003, the above-quota tariff on sugar was 78%.[27] On average, Panama harvests only a quarter of the sugar produced by each of the five Central American countries, but it still plays a disproportionally important role in the agricultural sector. Sugar constitutes: 1) a third of Panama's total agricultural exports, compared to less than 10% for the Central American countries, and; 2) 41% of agricultural exports to the United States. The U.S. market consumes 76% of Panamanian sugar exports, compared to less than 10% of sugar exports from Central America.

Given the dependence of sugar producers on the U.S. market, in part driven by Panama's relatively high wage rates that make it cost prohibitive to produce for the world market, the Panamanians argued that even a relatively small quantitative increase in their portion of the U.S. sugar quota would have a large benefit for their industry. The U.S. sugar industry, however, continued to resist the inclusion of sugar in bilateral FTAs, arguing that the WTO is the forum for addressing domestic support programs and TRQs in the agricultural sector.

In Panama, pork, rice, and poultry were the most sensitive products. These are also protected by TRQs, with in-quota tariffs of 15% and out-of-quota tariffs rising to 74%, 103%, and 273%, respectively. Pork and poultry have a special issue related to the consumption of white versus dark meat. The United States consumes considerably more white meat than dark, leaving a disproportional amount of dark cuts for export, which face the highest tariffs. In Panama, as with much of the world, dark meat is preferred. The concern revolved around U.S. producers' willingness to sell dark meat cuts at a low price in foreign markets, putting downward pressure on prices and hurting domestic producers in those countries. The Panamanians argued that because of the relatively high profit margins on white meat in the United States, on a cost allocation basis, U.S. producers can actually afford to sell the dark meat at below cost. The cost accounting can be debated, but concerns over the price effect in the Panamanian market remained unchanged.

Panama's rice industry, which supplies over 90% of the domestic demand, also argued that opening their market to U.S. subsidized rice would decimate their industry, which, because of its protection, sells rice considerably above the world price. In fact, the USITC report estimates that when fully implemented, the FTA will have the greatest impact on U.S. rice exports. The rice provisions, however, will not be fully implemented until year 17 of the agreement.[28]

Panamanian agriculture represents only 6% of GDP, but 17% of employment. These numbers point to both an inherent inefficiency, due in part to protection, but also the strong role agriculture plays in supporting rural employment and social stability. Agriculture's 17% of national employment actually supports 40% of the country's population living in rural areas, most of whom exist at or below the poverty line. Given the potential to dislocate much of the poor in the country, the Panamanians argued that opening the agricultural sector too quickly to the large production capacity of the United States would have been highly detrimental to the social structure of the rural economy, leading to increased unemployment, poverty, and rural-urban migration. For these reasons, Panama wanted a slow transition to open markets in the agriculture sector, as well as, an increase in the sugar quota to boost employment. This would also buy time for Panama to develop its non-traditional export crops, such as melons, palm oil, and pineapples, which some view as the future of this sector.

The compromise struck in the proposed FTA would provide duty-free treatment for over half of U.S. farm exports to Panama including high quality beef, poultry products, soybeans, most fresh fruits, and a number of processed goods. Remaining tariffs would be phased out between 7 and 17 years after the FTA takes effect. Rice tariffs, which protect one of Panama's most sensitive products, would remain in place for the full 17 years, as would tariffs on pork, chicken leg quarters, dairy products, and corn, among others. These products would receive expanded quotas under the Panamanian tariff rate quota system. The United States agreed to give Panama an additional 7,000 metric tons of sugar imports in the first year under a three-tiered TRQ system, which would grow by 1% per year, capped eventually for some types of sugar. The American Sugar Alliance apparently has agreed not to come out against the agreement.[29]

Other protective measures for agriculture were negotiated. Whereas export subsidies, voluntary restrain agreements (VREs), and import licensing are generally prohibited, TRQs, safeguards, and a sugar compensation mechanism would be allowed. The sugar mechanism gives the United States the option to compensate Panamanian sugar producers in lieu of giving Panamanian their exports duty-free treatment. This provision might be used if the U.S. sugar program were threatened with disruption.

Sanitary and Phytosanitary Standards (SPS)

SPS was one of the most difficult issues to resolve. Although understood as necessary to ensure the safety of agricultural imports, SPS standards can be a burden, and are often denounced as a veiled form of protectionism. Panama's SPS standards, on the whole, are considered to be very high and meet or exceed WTO standards. The USTR, however, has long raised concerns over procedural transparency with respect to phytosanitary permits and also Panama's requirement that imports of poultry, beef, and pork, its most protected products, come from processing plants that have been individually inspected by Panamanian officials. The United States contends that this process has often been cumbersome, drawn out, and ultimately very costly to U.S. producers.[30]

The United States wanted Panama to recognize the USDA certification process as equivalent to Panamanian standards for the purpose of securing unimpeded entry of U.S. meat exports. This issue became highly controversial during the ninth round of negotiations, when U.S. negotiators proposed this agreement be put into a formal side letter. Panama responded by noting that the SPS chapter had already been closed, that its meat inspection standards are among the highest in the world, and that a last minute effort to change SPS provisions raised sovereignty issues in Panama by potentially requiring Panama to lower its standards in some cases.[31]

As part of the resolution, Panamanian officials visited the United States to review the food safety inspection system for meat and poultry and found that accepting the U.S. system would pose no sanitary threat to Panama. This understanding was formalized in a separate bilateral agreement between the two countries, along with a streamlined import documentation system. Signed and entered into force on December 20, 2006, the agreement states that for meat, poultry, dairy, and other processed products, Panama agrees to accept U.S. sanitary, phytosanitary, and regulatory systems as equivalent to those of Panama and will no longer require individual plant inspections. Panama has since amended its laws accordingly.[32]

Textiles and Apparel

In general, textiles and apparel make for difficult market access negotiations, but Panama produces very little of these goods. The proposed FTA would provide immediate duty-free access for all textile and apparel goods, subject to rules of origin. The permanence of the provisions and more accommodating measures provide a benefit to the small Panamanian industry. Safeguard measures would allow duties to increase on imports in which a sudden increase in volume either threatens or actually harms U.S. producers. The text also provides for short supply lists of fabrics, yarns, and fibers that otherwise would face duties. The market access provisions were not the major apparel issue. Because Panama is a huge transshipment point for international trade and has its own duty free zone, the main concern was to assure U.S. apparel producers that there would be effective customs cooperation to deter illegal transshipment of goods that do not meet rules of origin. There is an extensive provision on consultation, monitoring, and onsite visit procedures in support of adhering to the rules of origin.[33]

Government Procurement

Transparency in the bidding process for government contracts was listed as one of the most important issues by the U.S. Chamber of Commerce in Panama.[34] Some of the concerns expressed were addressed in the 2006 amendments to the procurement law, which modernized (e.g., through the use of Internet procurement system) and made more transparent procurement regulations and government purchasing information. A separate administrative court for public contracting disputes was also created. These changes enhanced Panamanian laws that already require transparency in the bidding process. Panama has not acceded to the WTO Government Procurement Agreement, which the United States has encouraged.[35]

The government procurement chapter differs from earlier FTAs by stating that a firm's adherence to "acceptable" environmental and labor standards may be included as a standard in the bidding and procurement process. The technical specifications article states that it is not intended to preclude a procuring entity from using technical specifications to promote conservation of natural resources, or to require a supplier to comply with generally applicable laws regarding fundamental principles and rights to work; and acceptable conditions of work with respect to minimum wages, hours of work and occupation safety and health in the territory in which the good is produced or the service is performed.

Government procurement takes on a greater importance when considered in light of the proposed expansion of the Panama canal and related prospects for large long-term investments. The Panama Canal Authority (PCA) operates independently of the national government and Panama required separate negotiation apart from the regular government procurement chapter. Panama negotiated to maintain the canal authority dispute settlement system within the proposed FTA, as well as to keep small business set aside provisions for Panamanian firms. In addition, for 12 years after the agreement takes effect, Panama may set aside contracts let by the PCA to Panamanian firms subject to clear notice of intent to do so and limitations on the size of contracts. The text otherwise addresses U.S. concerns over nondiscriminatory, fair, and open government procurement procedures for all national government authorities. Like the PCA, subnational governments (e.g. states and municipalities) are not required to uphold the government procurement provisions, but those willing to do so appear in an appendix of the proposed FTA.

Investment

Panama has a well-developed financial services industry to support the flow of capital and is a regional financial center. U.S. firms invest heavily in Panama relative to other Latin American countries and a permanent rules-based trade agreement may be seen as enhancing this relationship. Panama signed a bilateral investment treaty with the United States in 1991, the first in the region, which includes investor-state provisions and further guarantees of the free flow of transfers under a 1998 law. Although the Panamanian government has been responsive to U.S. foreign investment interests, concerns have arisen in particular cases involving investment in highly regulated industries. Resolution of these concerns facilitated the FTA negotiations and the potential exists for further significant foreign investment in Panama, including the canal expansion and reverted areas of the former canal zone.[36]

The text provides for clear and enforceable rules for foreign investments, which is largely accomplished by "standard" language (identical to the CAFTA-DR) requiring national and most-favored-nation (nondiscriminatory) treatment. It further clarifies rules on expropriation and compensation, investor-state dispute settlement, and the expeditious free flow of payments and transfers related to investments, with certain exceptions in cases subject to legal proceedings (e.g., bankruptcy, insolvency, criminal activity). Transparent and impartial dispute settlement procedures provide recourse to investors.

Two investment issues stand out. First is the investor-state provision, which was controversial during the CAFTA-DR debate, but is commonly used in U.S. bilateral investment treaties (BITs) and in earlier FTAs. It allows investors alleging a breach in investment obligations to seek binding arbitration against the state through the dispute settlement mechanism defined in the Investment Chapter. U.S. investors have long supported the inclusion of investor-state rules to ensure that they have recourse in countries that may lack the institutional capacity to adequately protect the rights of foreign investors. Since bilateral investment treaties are usually made with developing countries that have little foreign investment in the United States, it was not anticipated that these provisions would be applied in the United States. Circumstances changed under NAFTA, when investor-state provisions gave rise to numerous "indirect expropriation" claims against subnational (state) governments in the United States, Mexico, and Canada over environmental and other regulations.[37]

Although none of the claims filed against the United States has prevailed, Congress instructed in TPA legislation that future trade agreements ensure "that foreign investors in the United States are not accorded greater substantive rights with respect to investment protections than United States investors." In response, Annex 10-B of the proposed U.S.-Panama FTA states that "except in rare circumstances, nondiscriminatory regulatory actions by a Party that are designed and applied to protect legitimate welfare objectives, such as public health, safety, and the environment, do not constitute indirect expropriations." This provision, along with one that allows for early elimination of "frivolous" suits, is intended to address congressional concerns.

Second, Annex 10-F of the proposed FTA seeks to reserve certain rights with respect to disputes filed under Section - B of the investment chapter that may affect the Panama Canal Authority (PCA). First, it clarifies that Panama has sole authority over the canal and its operations, and should a claim be made against the PCA, the dispute tribunal "may not order attachment or enjoin the application of a measure that has been adopted or maintained by the Panama Canal Authority in pursuance of ..." its responsibility for the canal. Second, a claim arising from acts of the PCA that alleges a breach of the investment agreement must first be made to the PCA, where it will have three months to respond before the claim may be made to the dispute settlement panel under the proposed FTA.

Services

Services trade was negotiated in multiple chapters and includes financial services, shipping, telecommunications, professional services, and e-commerce. Panama is a service-based economy, has many competitive services industries, and is known for its "open regulatory environment for services." In general, the FTA provides for market access commitments in services that exceeds the WTO General Agreement on Trade in Services (GATS). With the possible exception of future canal expansion projects, the USITC estimates that the new commitments, although important changes, will have only a small economic impact on U.S. provides.[38]

Panama does require local licensing for many professionals to practice in the country, which the United States wanted to change, but was only partially successful in some cases (e.g., lawyers). Panama was the first country in Latin America to pass e-commerce legislation. It recognizes the legal standing of electronic transactions and provides for the creation of an oversight agency. The United States pressed for even greater transparency in regulatory procedures and U.S. business groups identified services as a critical negotiating area given U.S. competitive advantages and the large services sector in Panama.[39]

Equal ability to compete in retail trade, express delivery, and financial services, including insurance and portfolio management, was achieved in the proposed FTA, an issue of primary importance to the United States. In particular, restrictions on investment in retail trade and access to contracts let by the Panama Canal Authority were either eliminated or reduced. Greater access to other professional services and ransparency in licensing and other accreditation were clarified. To the extent that restrictions in these areas are reduced, U.S. firms are better able to compete in the largest sector of the Panamanian economy, the one most likely to grow with canal expansion and increased merchandise trade through the canal. Panama wanted greater transparency in the U.S. state-level financial services regulatory system to help ease the possible opening of Panamanian banks in select U.S. states. The United States government argued, however, that it was unable to make commitments on state-level financial services regulatory matters.

Intellectual Property Rights

Clarifying intellectual property rights (IPR) was a major U.S. priority, in particular by having Panama's standards approximate more closely those of the United States and by securing Panama's commitment to join an array of international agreements related to IPR protection. The most contentious IPR issues revolved around patent and data exclusivity issues related to pharmaceutical products.

The USTR reports that Panama's IPR laws and institutional support have improved with the creation of courts dedicated specifically to IPR cases. Panama updated its patent law in 1996 and has a law governing trademark protection. Panama signed on to the World Intellectual Property Organization (WIPO) Copyright Treaty and Performances and Phonographs Treaty. The 1994 copyright law improved protection and increased the options to prosecute violators. The United States continues to encourage Panama to accede to additional IPR treaties, as now required in the proposed FTA, and to remain vigilant in its antipiracy commitment, a primary concern given the large amount of goods that are shipped through the Canal Free Zone.[40]

IPR provisions in the proposed FTA exceed those in the WTO. They provide that all businesses receive equal treatment and that Panama ratify or accede to various international IP agreements. Trademark registration is better enforced through a transparent online process and special system to resolve disputes over internet domain issues, among other requirements. Copyright provisions clarify use of digital materials (exceeding TRIPS standards) including rights over temporary copies of works on computers (music, videos, software, text), sole author rights for making their work available online, extended terms of protection for copyrighted materials, strong anti-circumvention provisions to prohibit tampering with technologies, the requirement that governments use only legitimate computer software, the prohibition of unauthorized receipt or distribution of encrypted satellite signals, and rules for liability of internet service providers for copyright infringement. Patents and trade secrets rules conform more closely with U.S. norms. End-user piracy is criminalized and all parties are required to authorize the seizure, forfeiture, and destruction of counterfeit and pirated goods. The text also mandates statutory damages for abuse of copyrighted material.[41]

Pharmaceutical Issues

Three patent-related issues generated the major IPR debate. The first, and perhaps most sensitive and complicated, issue was *data exclusivity*. To bring a patented drug to market, a drug company must demonstrate through clinical trials that the drug is both safe and effective, a time-consuming and costly process. Under U.S. law, the data used to establish these claims are protected from use by generic manufacturers to certify their own products for a period of five years from the time the patented drug is approved for use in a country's market, the so-called data exclusivity term. This issue was raised by Members of Congress during the CAFTA-DR debate, but was only partially addressed in a side agreement assuring that relevant WTO rules would be in force. Critics, however, wanted the side agreement to include an explicit exception to the data protection requirement for cases where compulsory licencing under the WTO rules might be invoked.[42]

Congressional input led to significant changes to the Panama text. The IPR chapter provides that if a company files to bring to market a new drug in a second country (e.g., Panama) after making an initial filing in the first country (e.g., the United States), and Panama approves the drug within six months of that filing, the data exclusivity term begins at the time the drug was approved in the United States, not Panama. This provision is intended to encourage both drug companies and foreign governments to engage in the approval process as efficiently as possible, thereby speeding the entry of generic drugs into developing countries (Panama). Because the six-month rule effectively reduces the data exclusivity term in Panama, drug companies are encouraged to file as soon as feasible to maximize the time their data may be protected in Panama after getting market approval. Because countries must approve within the sixth-month rule to benefit from it, they are encouraged to put in place an efficient drug certification process.

In addition, there is language in the IPR chapter stating that in the case of epidemics, a waiver from the data exclusivity laws would be allowed. In the past, the WTO public health provisions have allowed for compulsory licensing, circumventing patents in public health emergencies, but in the case of the U.S.-Panama FTA, the waiver is extended to the data exclusivity term, as well.

A second issue is *patent term restoration*, which allows for the retroactive application of patents in cases where the approval process for a patent extends beyond some legal- or regulatory-determined standard period of time. Although there are provisions that require term restoration for patents in general, in the case of pharmaceutical products, term extension is only optional.

The third issue is *patent linkage*. This term refers to linking the sanitary registration process (done, for example, by the Food and Drug Administration in the United States) with the patent registration process. U.S. firms would like to see a ransparent, preferably administrative process that would automatically check for patent infringement when an application for bringing a drug to market is made in a foreign country sanitary registration office. The Panama agreement allows for both administrative and judicial procedures, which could increase the chances of a country employing a cumbersome and costly process.

Public health advocates have long pushed for re-balancing international rules in ways that would facilitate the introduction of lower cost generic equivalents into developing countries. The revised IPR chapter in the Panama FTA supports congressional interest in pursuing this goal. Pharmaceutical companies, however, argued against these changes because they bear the full cost through cumbersome administration and lost revenue by the earlier introduction of generic competition. They count on this revenue to offset the high costs of research and development that allows new drugs to be properly tested and approved in the first place. Also, in developing countries with less than robust patent laws, data exclusivity, for example, is often the only recourse drug companies have to provide some protection of their investment, and so changing the terms of the data exclusivity term has a direct financial cost for drug companies.

Labor and Environment

Labor and environment provisions have been highly contentious issues in trade agreements, with considerable disagreement in Congress and elsewhere over how aggressive language in trade agreements should be in accommodating these concerns. An important aspect of the proposed U.S.-Panama FTA is that it adopts new standards for both the labor and environment chapters that reflect a bipartisan understanding as developed by congressional leadership and the USTR in the "New Trade Policy for America." Despite the bipartisan nature of the agreement, many Members continue to express reservations about the benefits of bilateral FTAs.

The debate over labor and environmental standards reflect differences in both economic and political perspectives. From an economic perspective, labor and environment advocates in the United States have argued that developing country firms may have an "unfair" competitive advantage because their lower standards are a basis for their lower costs, which in turn are reflected in lower prices for goods that compete with those produced in developed countries.[43] It follows from this argument that the difference in costs may be an inducement to move U.S. investment and jobs abroad. In addition, critics have also argued that trade agreements should not support a status quo in production standards that leads to unacceptable working conditions and severe environmental degradation.

On the other hand, some studies have suggested that cost differentials are usually not high enough to determine business location alone, and that productivity is the more important factor.[44] Further, many economists view trade liberalization as part of the overall development process that, in and off itself, can promote improved social and economic conditions over the long run.[45] Developing countries are concerned with the loss of sovereignty should specific standards be defined in trade agreements, as well as with the possibility that such provisions can be misused as a disguised form of protectionism.

Labor Issues

Preliminary drafts of the U.S.-Panama FTA adopted the CAFTA-DR labor chapter language verbatim. Many Members of Congress and others objected to four key aspects of this language. First, it emphasized that a country must effectively "enforce its own labor laws," rather that define specific labor standards to be codified and enforced. Second, this was the only provision in the labor chapter subject to the FTA's labor dispute resolution process (other commitments are unenforceable). Third, labor (and environment) provisions had their own dispute settlement process separate from the process used for commercial and other disputes. Critics argued that the labor dispute mechanism was inferior for many reasons. Fourth, for other commitments in the labor chapter, language requiring that the Parties to the agreement "strive to ensure" that basic labor principles as defined in the International Labor Organization (ILO) *Fundamental Principles and Rights at Work and its Follow-up (1998) Declaration* was an inadequate commitment and unenforceable.

In short, there existed a basic criticism that the labor provisions in the bilateral FTAs did not reflect the intent of Congress in defining labor negotiating objectives in Trade Promotion Authority (TPA) legislation, were a step backward in U.S. policy on this issue that conditions trade benefits on meeting basic ILO labor commitments as defined in the Caribbean Basin Initiative (CBI) and the Generalized System of Preferences (GSP), and were effectively meaningless without a credible enforcement mechanism.[46]

Although supporters of the CAFTA-DR model prevailed in earlier agreements, a new bipartisan consensus emerged with the 110th Congressional leadership that led to a significantly changed model for bilateral FTA labor chapters. The principles of this change, as defined in the May 10, 2007, "New Trade Policy for America," were incorporated into the labor chapters for proposed U.S. bilateral FTAs with Panama Peru, and Colombia. The major changes from the CAFTA-DR model state that each country:

- shall adopt and maintain in its statutes, regulations and practices as rights, the five core ILO labor principles: freedom of association; the effective recognition of the right to collective bargaining; the elimination of all forms of compulsory or forced labor; the effective abolition of child labor and, for purposes of this Agreement, a prohibition on the worst forms of child labor; and, the elimination of discrimination in respect of employment and occupation;
- not waive or otherwise derogate from, or offer to do so, in a manner affecting trade or investment between the countries in implementing the above commitment;
- shall not fail to effectively enforce its labor in accordance with the above commitment and that each party retains the right to the reasonable exercise of discretion in using resources to achieve this goal, provided the exercise of such discretion is not inconsistent with the obligations of the chapter, and;
- will be required to use the dispute settlement process defined for the entire agreement (rather than a separate process for labor disputes as defined in the CAFTA-DR).

The change in language is intended to make commitments to ILO basic principles binding and enforceable to the same extent as all other commitments in the proposed FTA, including having recourse to trade sanctions. The rest of the labor chapter conforms largely to commitments in previous bilateral FTAs that include procedural guarantees of transparency and fairness in the use of tribunals to enforce a Party's labor laws and institutional arrangements that include creation of a joint Labor Affairs Council to oversee implementation and review of commitments made in the Labor Chapter. These commitments include establishing a Labor Cooperation and Capacity Building Mechanism.

Panama's Labor Conditions

Panama has higher wage rates, stronger labor laws, and fewer impediments to union formation compared to many countries in the region. The business community, including U.S. firms operating in Panama, argue that the labor laws are too generous with respect to firing or downsizing the labor force, which can actually encourage unintended responses by business, such as extended use of temporary workers. In 1970, Panama created the Tripartite Council on Union Freedom and Participation in Economic and Social Development with representatives from the government, labor, and business. Its primary function is to oversee that worker rights are being observed in Panama.

The U.S. Department of State has pointed out that Panama's labor laws guarantee all five of the ILO basic principles. In general, major violations have not been found. Nonetheless, concerns still exist over the widespread use of temporary workers in the general and child labor in the informal sector and rural areas, particularly during harvest times. Lax enforcement of health and safety standards was also cited as a problem.[47]

The Colón Free Zone and the small export processing zones are all subject to national labor laws. The Panama Canal Area presents a unique issue. Although the Canal Zone has separate statutes governing labor, they tend to be more generous with respect to workers' rights and compensation, and jobs in the Canal Zone are highly coveted. Workers may organize and exercise their rights to collective bargaining, but the prohibition on striking goes to Panama's commitments under the Panama Canal Treaties, which stipulate that the canal must be operated without interruption.[48]

Environmental Issues

Major environmental goals in FTAs include protecting and assuring strong enforcement of existing domestic environmental standards, ensuring that multilateral environmental agreements are not undermined by trade rules, promoting strong environmental initiatives to evaluate and raise performance, developing a systematic program of capacity-building assistance, and assuring that environmental provisions in FTAs are subject to the same dispute resolution and enforcement mechanisms as are other aspects of the agreements.[49]

Advocates raise the issue of the environmental effects of trade, particularly in developing countries that may have weak laws and lax enforcement mechanisms. Some of these same advocates, however, have indicated that thus far trade agreements have not led to catastrophic pollution nor encouraged a "regulatory race to the bottom." There has also been a certain acknowledged degree of success in having environmental issues addressed in the body of FTAs, in side agreements on environmental cooperation, and through technical assistance programs, the latter of which developing countries can use to respond to specific problems. Advocates and many Members of Congress still note that much can be improved, such as clarifying obligations, tightening enforcement language, and ensuring that the United States allocates financial resources to back up promises of technical assistance.[50]

As with the proposed FTA labor chapter, revisions made pursuant to ideas outlined in the "New Trade Policy for America," reflect a bipartisan sense of that although the text recognizes sovereign rights and responsibilities with respect to the management of natural resources, that trade and environmental policies should be mutually supportive and dedicated to the objective of sustainable development. The new language, therefore, strengthens the commitments to environmental obligations and their enforcement, requiring that each country:

- adopt, maintain, and implement laws, regulations, and other measures to fulfill their obligations under selected multilateral environmental agreements (MEAs) listed in Annex 18.2;
- shall not fail to effectively enforce environmental laws and regulations, including those adopted as signatories to the MEAs;
- shall not waive or otherwise derogate from, or offer thereto, from such laws (replacing the "strive to ensure" with "shall not");
- adopt a commitment to policies that will promote conservation and sustainable use of biological diversity;
- subject disputes to the FTA's overall dispute settlement mechanism rather that an mechanism developed solely to deal with labor and environmental disagreements that was used in previous FTAs, and;
- meet obligations for formal cooperation among governments on environmental issues and use of the consultation and dispute resolution mechanism in a way that is transparent and involves public input.[51]

As required under TPA, the USTR conducted an environmental review of the potential environmental effects possibly attributable to the proposed FTA. It noted that Panama "faces a number of challenges in protecting its environment as it supports its economic and population growth." Deforestation, land degradation, loss of wildlife, and threats to water quality and wetlands, among other problems are serious issues for Panama. The Panama Canal also places severe water use requirements on the country. Panama has responded through the public policy process, establishing environmental standards in law and entering into international and U.S. bilateral environmental cooperation agreements.[52] These issues were already factors in Panama's development process prior to the negotiation of the proposed FTA. Thus, the environmental review maintains that the marginal effects of the proposed FTA on environmental standards would be small, whether in terms of projected impacts on the United States or on Panama.

The environmental review further notes that Panama's service-oriented economy and the small trade volume with the United States are unlikely to be greatly affected by the proposed FTA and so will change marginal production and trade little. The FTA, however, may have both positive and negative effects. The negative effects of pollution, environmental degradation, and endangering wildlife would come mostly from increased agricultural trade and production, which might be addressed with increased environmental oversight and policies. The positive effect of the FTA could include improvements in environmental standards that may be encouraged by the provisions of the agreement and the consultative and cooperation agreements attached to the proposed FTA.[53] Panama's environmental regulatory agency (Autoridad Nacional de Ambiente — ANAM) points out that Panama is increasingly using environmental impact studies, but realizes it has enforcement capacity issues that may require time to remedy, which could be accommodated in the FTA.

Trade Capacity Building

The proposed FTA would create a Committee on Trade Capacity Building (TCB), designed to assist Panama with the transition to freer trade with the United States. In general, the committee's mission includes providing technical assistance and coordinating financing to accelerate the transition period in expectation of increasing the gains of trade while minimizing the adjustment costs. The TCB Committee would help coordinate technical assistance provided by U.S., regional, and multilateral agencies in helping Panama meet its obligations under the FTA.

Panama prioritized TCB needs in its national trade capacity building strategy. The overriding goal is to formulate a strategy that would allow Panama to assume all the commitments under the proposed FTA, in the context of meeting the country's development needs. The National TCB Strategy places strong emphasis on sectoral adjustment strategies, recognizing that some industries are already competitive by international standards (e.g., financial services), whereas others will need considerable assistance when faced with increased competition from the United States (e.g., agriculture). Emphasis is also placed on supporting existing and potentially new micro, small, and medium-sized businesses, which may need the most assistance and constitute a significant portion of the Panamanian economy, as well as government capacity to administer trade-related activities.[54]

The major goals identified include inter-sectoral coordination, increasing exports to the United States, enhancing the investment climate, better integrating education and innovation into the business community, and improving government trade facilitation (processing imports and exports.) The strategy identifies 18 action plans covering major trade and trade-related issues, ranging from market access and rules of origin, to labor, environment, transparency, and trade agreement administration. In each case, the status of Panama's commitments under the proposed FTA is identified along with action items that may need to be pursued to improve capacity in the respective area.

Successfully implementing the strategy, however, requires financial and technical resources coordinated among international and U.S. aid agencies. Already in place is a U.S. Agency for International Development (USAID) project to support Panama's transition to more open trade. It has two major initiatives: supporting implementation of the proposed FTA and assisting Panama with sectoral adjustment to the increased competitiveness arising from international trade. In the first case, the USAID project has helped prepare and disseminate a product that explains the benefits of the proposed FTA and how Panama might better access the U.S. market with its specific products.

The second initiative focuses on helping three major sectors of the economy, each with a differing level of product complexity, to increase their exposure and market share in the United States. Specifically, agro-industry, information and communications technology, and artisan products were identified as sectors with potential to benefit from the proposed FTA. Sectoral strategies range from targeted product design, to "hands on" assistance in participating in trade fairs, and building contacts and linkages with venture capitalists and other key business facilitation professionals.[55]

OUTLOOK

Panama's legislature ratified the revised FTA 58-4 on July 11, 2007, but it cannot take effect until the U.S. Congress passes implementing legislation. The 110th Congress may consider such a bill in 2008, but the election of Pedro Miguel González as President of the National Assembly is one factor that has delayed congressional action on the FTA. The debate over FTAs is frequently contentious for other reasons as well, given their increased complexity and Members' broadly held concerns over the negative effects of globalization that have increased substantially in a post-CAFTA-DR environment. To address some of these concerns, the proposed U.S.-Panama FTA, in addition to supporting U.S. commercial and economic interests, incorporates significant changes initiated by the Democrats and ultimately agreed to by congressional leadership as part of a bipartisan congressional understanding arrived at with the Bush Administration.

The most significant changes include the adoption of enforceable labor standards, compulsory adherence to select multilateral environmental agreements (MEAs), and an easing of restrictions to developing country access to generic drugs. In each of these cases, the proposed U.S.-Panama FTA goes beyond provisions in existing multilateral trade rules and even those contemplated in the Doha Round. In this case, along with the broader arguments both for and against FTAs, Congress perhaps now faces an even more difficult choice given that the recent changes to this proposed FTA may set a precedent in U.S. trade policy. As significant as these changes may be, perhaps portending a shift in U.S. trade policy, it is still not clear that they are sufficient to ease the concerns many Members have over bilateral free trade agreements.

APPENDIX 1. CHRONOLOGY OF U.S.-PANAMA FTA

Date	Milestone
November 18, 2003	The USTR notifies Congress of President George W. Bush's intent to enter into negotiations on a free trade agreement (FTA) with the Republic of Panama.
April 26-29, 2004	First round of negotiations occurs in Panama City.
June 11-15, 2004	Second round of negotiations takes place in Los Angeles.
July 12-16, 2004	Third round of negotiations held in Panama City.
August 9-12, 2004	Fourth round of negotiations held in Tampa.
October 18-22, 2004	Fifth round of negotiations takes place in Panama City.
December 6-10, 2004	Sixth round of negotiations held in Washington, DC.
January 10-15, 2005	Seventh round of negotiations held in Washington, DC.
Jan. 31-Feb. 6, 2005	Eighth round of negotiations occurs in Washington, DC.
Jan. 17-20, 2006	Ninth round of negotiations held in Washington, DC.
Dec. 16, 2006	Tenth and final round of negotiations concludes in Washington, D.C. Chapters on labor and environment left open.

March 27, 2007	Bipartisan "New Trade Policy for America" released.
March 30, 2007	President Bush formally notifies Congress of his intention to sign the proposed U.S.-Panama FTA.
April 27, 2007	USTR transmits to the White House and Congress 27 trade advisory reports on the U.S.-Panama FTA.
May 10, 2007	Congressional leadership and Bush Administration agree to change labor, environment, and intellectual property rights chapters in this and other FTAs based on principles outlined in the bipartisan "New Trade Policy for America."
June 29, 2007	The United States and Panama sign a free trade agreement at the Organization of American States in Washington, D.C.
July 2, 2007	USTR releases final text of proposed U.S.-Panama FTA.
July 11, 2007	Panamanian legislature approves U.S.-Panama FTA 58-4.

APPENDIX 2. PANAMA: SELECTED ECONOMIC INDICATORS

	2000	2001	2002	2003	2004	2005	2006
GDP Growth (%)	2.7	0.6	2.2	4.2	7.5	6.9	7.5
Per Capita GDP Growth (%)	0.8	-1.3	0.4	2.3	5.6	5.1	5.7
Urban Unemploy. Rate (%)	15.2	17.0	16.5	15.9	14.1	12.1	10.4
Inflation (%)	0.7	0.0	1.9	1.5	1.5	3.4	2.0
Current Acct. Bal. (% GDP)	-5.8	-1.4	-0.8	-3.9	-7.5	-5.0	-4.2
Terms of Trade (2000=100)	100.0	102.7	101.6	97.2	95.3	93.59	0.8
Foreign Direct Invest. ($ mil)*	624	467	99	771	1,004	1,027	2,500

Source: United Nations Economic Commission on Latin America and the Caribbean. *Preliminary Overview of the Economies of Latin American and the Caribbean, 2006.* December 2006.

*Net investment = direct foreign investment in Panama minus Panamanian direct investment abroad.

APPENDIX 3. U.S.-PANAMA TARIFF RATES FOR SELECTED PRODUCTS (% OF TOTAL DOLLAR VALUE)

Major U.S. Exports[a]	% of Total	Tariff Rate	Major U.S. Imports[a]	% of Total	NTR Tariff Rate[b]	Free under CBI[c]
Oil (2710)	31.6	5%[d]	Fish/Seafood (0302)	26.9	Free	
Aircraft (8802)	6.2	10%	Repaired Goods (9801)	21.0	Free	
Machinery	10.8	3-5%	Precious Metals (7112) - gold/scrap	9.3	Free	

Appendix 3 – (Continued)

Electrical Machinery (8517)	6.8	5%	Crude oil (2710)	8.6		Free under CBTPA
Pharmaceuticals (3004)	4.9	Free	Sugar (1701) - under quota - over quota (avg. 2003)	6.2	0 78%	
Optical/Medical Instruments	3.5	10%	Coffee	3.1	Free	
Cereals	2.8		Fruit	3.3		
- corn (1005)	(1.8)		- bananas			Free under CBI and GSP
- under quota		3%	- papaya			
- over quota		58%	- watermelon			
- mesline (1001)		Free				
- rice (1006)	(1.0)					
- under quota		15%				
- over quota	(0.2)	103%				
Other	33.4		Other	21.6		
Total	100%		Total	100%		

Data Source: U.S. Department of Commerce.

Note: all Panamanian imports are subject to a 5% transfer tax, which is also collected on domestic products. This tax is considered similar to a nondiscriminatory sales or value added tax (VAT).

a. By HTS number = Harmonized Tariff Schedule of the United States.

b. NTR is the general or normal tariff rates (also known as most favored nation rates) applied to products not given preferential tariff treatment.

c. CBI = Caribbean Basin Initiative provides unilateral preferential tariff treatment to select Caribbean and Central American country products. Petroleum enters duty free under the Caribbean Basin Trade Partnership Act (CBTPA — P.L. 106-200), a related program.

d. Tariffs on oil vary depending on end use. Discussions with U.S. Department of Commerce officials suggest most U.S. oil exports to Panama (for automotive use) face a 5% tariff. Some oil for maritime use has tariffs as high as 30%.

END NOTES

[1] For details, see CRS Report RL33743, *Trade Promotion Authority* (TPA): *Issues, Options, and Prospects for Renewal*, by J. F. Hornbeck and William C. Cooper.

[2] Agreed to on May 10, 2007 and available on the websites of the House Ways and Means Committee and the United States Trade Representative (USTR).

[3] USITC. U.S.-*Panama Trade Promotion Agreement: Potential Economy-wide and Selected Sectoral Effects. eptember 2007.* Publication 3948. pp. 1-1 and 1-5.

[4] U.S. Department of State. Press Statement. *Election of Panamanian National Assembly President Pedro Miguel González-Pinzón.* September 1, 2007.

[5] Inside U.S. Trade. *Committee Chairs Signal FTA Problem Over Panama Assembly Head.* September 21, 2007 and Yerkey, Gary G. Gutierrez Says Panama Must 'Resolve' Fugitive Issue or Put Free Trade Pact at Risk. *International Trade Reporter.* September 20, 2007. p. 1322.

[6] Conniff, Michael L. *Panama and the United States: The Forced Alliance.* Athens: the University of Georgia Press, second edition. 2001. pp. 30-35.

[7] Woodward, Ralph Lee. *Central America: A Nation Divided*. New York: Oxford University Press, third edition. 1999, pp. 187-191 and ibid., pp. 63-70.

[8] Conniff, *Panama and the United States*, pp. 134-39 and CRS Report RL30981, *Panama: Political and Economic Conditions and U.S. Relations*, by Mark P. Sullivan.

[9] The Economist Intelligence Unit. *Panama: Country Profile 2003*. London, 2003. pp. 16-17 and U.S. Department of Energy. Energy Information Administration. *Panama: Country Analysis Briefs*. October 2003; and [http://www.pancanal.com].

[10] Ibid.

[11] Government of Panama. *Panama-Pacifico Special Economic Area Agency*.

[12] bid., and discussion with IFC official.

[13] Panama's dollarized economy has been a cornerstone of its long-term economic stability. It has safeguarded Panama against exchange rate risk, currency mismatches, and speculative attacks experienced in other developing economies, and eliminated the monetizing of deficits, thereby reinforcing fiscal constraint and price stability. See Moreno-Villalaz, Juan Luis. Financial Integration and Dollarization: The Case of Panama. *Cato Journal*, Winter 2005. For more on trade preferences, see CRS Report RL33951, *U.S. Trade Policy and the Caribbean: From Trade Preferences to Free Trade Agreements*, by J. F. Hornbeck.

[14] Republic of Panamá. Controller General's Office. 2005.

[15] U.S. Department of Commerce. U.S. Commercial Services. *Doing Business In Panama: A Country Commercial Guide for U.S. Companies 2005*. April 7, 2005. p. 3 and author's interviews with CFZ representatives, September 21, 2005.

[16] Colón Free Zone User's Association. *Rules of Conduct for the Members of the Colón Free Zone Users' Association*, 1995; and author's interviews with representatives from agencies mentioned.

[17] Services trade data are not available for smaller U.S. trading partners, including Panama.

[18] Technically classified in the Harmonized Tariff System (HTS) as "products of the United States when returned after having been exported, without having been advanced in value or improved in condition by any process."

[19] U.S. Department of Commerce, *Doing Business in Panama*, pp. 3-4.

[20] This summary reflects information in the final text of the proposed FTA, released on July 2, 2007.

[21] For a discussion of the CAFTA-DR and a deeper understanding of the regional economic implications of freer trade, see CRS Report RL31870, *The Dominican Republic-Central America-United States Free Trade Agreement (CAFTA-DR)*, by J. F. Hornbeck.

[22] Inside U.S. Trade. Panama FTA Unlikely To Be Docked Into CAFTA as Talks Set to Begin. April 23, 2004.

[23] USITC, U.S.-*Panama Trade Promotion Agreement: Potential Economy-wide and Selected Sectoral Effects*, pp. 1-1 and 1-5.

[24] Ibid., pp. 1-5, 2-1, and 2-7.

[25] Ibid., pp. 2-1 and 2-7.

[26] Office of the United States Trade Representative. *Free Trade with Panama: Summary of the Agreement*. January 2007.

[27] The economic effect is to raise the price of sugar in the United States above the world price, increasing income to sugar-producing industries, but raising costs to sugar-using firms and consumers. CRS Report RL33541, *Sugar Policy Issues*, by Remy Jurenas.

[28] USITC, U.S.-*Panama Trade Promotion Agreement: Potential Economy-wide and Selected Sectoral Effects*, pp. 2-7 and 2-10.

[29] Inside U.S. Trade. *Panama FTA Offers Limited Sugar Access; Labor Changes Possible*. December 22, 2006.

[30] United States Trade Representative. 2007 *National Trade Estimate Report on Foreign Trade Barriers*. Washington, D.C. March 2007. p. 452.

[31] Berrocal, Rafael E. Panamá Reconoce Sistema Sanitario de Estados Unidos. Presna.com. February 22, 2006 and *Inside U.S. Trade*. Dispute Over Agriculture Inspections Holding up U.S.-Panama FTA Talks. January 23, 2006. Also see USTR Press Release, February 13, 2006.

[32] *United States-Panama Agreement Regarding Certain Sanitary and Phytosanitary Measures and Technical Standards Affecting Trade in Agricultural Products*. December 20, 2006.

[33] Inside U.S. Trade. *U.S. Panama FTA Includes Restrictive Textile Rules of Origin*. January 5, 2007 and USTR, Free Trade with Panama, p. 2.

[34] Panamcham. *Issues of Importance in the U.S.-Panama FTA Negotiations*, March 12, 2004. [http://www.panamcham.com/business_center/FTA.asp].

[35] USTR, 2007 *Foreign Trade Barriers*, p. 503.

[36] Ibid., p. 475.

[37] Indirect expropriation refers to regulatory and other actions that can adversely affect a business or property owner in a way that is "tantamount to expropriation." This issue and many cases are discussed in CRS Report RL31638, *Foreign Investor Protection Under NAFTA Chapter 11*, by Robert Meltz.

[38] USITC, *U.S.-Panama Trade Promotion Agreement: Potential Economy-wide and Selected Sectoral Effects*, p. 3-1.

[39] USTR, *2007 Foreign Trade Barriers*, pp. 455-456.

[40] USTR, *2007 Foreign Trade Barriers*, p. 454.

[41] U.S.-Panama FTA, Chapter 15.

[42] U.S. Congress. House of Representatives. Committee on Ways and Means. *Dominican Republic-Central America-United States Free Trade Agreement Implementation Act*. H.Rept. 109-182. pp. 50-51. The side agreement is available at [http://www.ustr.gov] and for a summary of the debate, see Brevetti, Rosella. CAFTA Opponents Blast U.S. Stance on Guatemalan Data Protection Law. *International Trade Reporter*. BNA, Inc. March 10, 2005. See also: CRS Report RS21609, *The WTO, Intellectual Property Rights, and the Access to Medicines Controversy*, by Ian F. Fergusson.

[43] The difference is that in most developing countries, the social costs associated with environmental degradation, pollution, and poor working conditions may not be captured in the market price of goods (so-called *external* costs). Through legal and regulatory measures, developed countries require that businesses correct for many of these social costs, thereby *internalizing* them to the business, where they are then reflected in the final (relatively higher) price of the good in the market place.

[44] See Perkins, Dwight H., Steven Radelet, and David L. Lindauer. *Economics of Development, Sixth Edition*. New York: W. W. Norton Company. 2006. pp. 745-746. Productivity and wage levels are highly correlated, suggesting that lower productivity jobs gravitate toward countries with a relative abundance of low-skilled (and hence low-wage) workers. See also Rodrik, Dani. *Sense and Nonsense in the Globalization Debate*. Foreign Policy. Summer 1997. pp. 30-33.

[45] Some broader evidence suggests that FTAs have not "forced a race to the bottom of regulatory standards," but rather to the contrary, that policy convergence is affected more by countries agreeing to "norms of governance" via cooperation through international agreements. See Drezner, Daniel W. Globalization and Policy Convergence. *International Studies Review*. Vol. 3, Issue 1, Spring 2001. pp. 75 and 78.

[46] U.S.-Panama Free Trade Agreement. *Report of the Labor Advisory Committee for Trade Negotiations and Trade Policy (LAC)*. April 25, 2007. pp. 3-7, and U.S. Congress. House of Representatives. Committee on Ways and Means. *Dominican Republic-Central America-United States Free Trade Agreement Implementation Act*. H.Rept. 109-182. pp. 47-50.

[47] U.S. Department of State. *Panama: Country Report on Human Rights Practices - 2006*. Washington, D.C. March 6, 2007, the Economist Intelligence Unit. Country Report -Panama. London, June 2004. p. 14, and American Federation of Labor and Congress of Industrial Organizations (AFL-CIO). *Panama: Labor Rights and Child Labor Reports*. Washington, D.C. August 9, 2004. p. 3.

[48] Panama Legislative Assembly. *Law No. 19 — "Whereby the Panama Canal Authority is Organized."* Chapter V — Personnel Administration and Labor Relations. June 11, 1997.

[49] See [http://www.sierraclub.org/trade/fasttrack/letter.asp], *Principles for Environmentally Responsible Trade*. Another important issue for the United States is ensuring that its higher environmental standards defined in law and regulation not be compromised by challenges of protectionism. See CRS Report RL31638, *International Investor Protection: "Indirect Expropriation" Claims Under NAFTA Chapter 11*, by Robert Meltz.

[50] See Audley, *John. Environment and Trade: The Linchpin to Successful CAFTA Negotiations?* Carnegie Endowment for International Peace. Washington, D.C. July 2003.

[51] U.S.-Panama FTA, Chapter 17, The Environment.

[52] Office of the United States Trade Representative. *Interim Environmental Review: U.S.-Panama Free Trade Agreement*. June 2004. pp. 7-9.

[53] Ibid., pp. 15-20.

[54] Government of Panama. Ministry of Trade and Industry. *Panama's National Strategy for Trade Capacity Building (TCB) in Light of the Free Trade Agreement with the United States*. Panama, March 4, 2005. pp. 20-23.

[55] Miller, Eric. *USAID/Panama-Supported TCB Programs*. Summary chapter. Nathan and Associates. May 9, 2007.

In: Panama: Politics and Economics
Editor: Ricardo Colson

ISBN: 978-1-60692-403-7
© 2009 Nova Science Publishers, Inc.

Chapter 3

PANAMA: POLITICAL AND ECONOMIC CONDITIONS AND U.S. RELATIONS*

Mark P. Sullivan[1] & Justin Rivas[2]

SUMMARY

With four successive elected civilian governments, the Central American nation of Panama has made notable political and economic progress since the 1989 U.S. military intervention that ousted the regime of General Manuel Noriega from power. The current President, Martín Torrijos of the Democratic Revolutionary Party (PRD), was elected in May 2004 and inaugurated to a five-year term in September 2004. Torrijos, the son of former populist leader General Omar Torrijos, won a decisive electoral victory with almost 48% of the vote in a four-man race. Torrijos' electoral alliance also won a majority of seats in the unicameral Legislative Assembly.

The most significant challenges facing the Torrijos government have included dealing with the funding deficits of the country's social security fund; developing plans for the expansion of the Panama Canal; and combating unemployment and poverty. In April 2006, the government unveiled its ambitious plans to build a third lane and new set of locks that will double the Canal's capacity. In an October 2006 referendum on the issue, 78% of voters supported the expansion project, which officially began in September 2007. Panama's service-based economy has been booming in recent years, but income distribution remains highly skewed, with large disparities between the rich and poor.

The United States has close relations with Panama, stemming in large part from the extensive linkages developed when the canal was under U.S. control and Panama hosted major U.S. military installations. The current relationship is characterized by extensive counternarcotics cooperation, assistance to help Panama assure the security of the Canal, and negotiations for a bilateral free trade agreement (FTA). The United States is providing an estimated $7.7 million in foreign aid FY2008, and could receive up to almost $4 million in FY2008 supplemental assistance under the Mérida Initiative. For

---

* This is edited, reformatted and augmented version of a Congressional Research Service Report Order Code RL30981 Updated July 31, 2008.
[1] Mark P. Sullivan, Specialist in Latin American Affairs, Foreign Affairs, Defense, and Trade Division
[2] Justin Rivas, Research Associate, Foreign Affairs, Defense, and Trade Division

FY2009, the Administration requested $11.6 million in bilateral foreign aid, not including an additional $8.9 million under the Mérida Initiative.

The United States and Panama announced the conclusion of a FTA in December 2006, although U.S. officials stated the agreement was subject to additional discussions on labor. Subsequently, congressional leaders and the Bush Administration announced a bipartisan deal in May 2007, whereby pending FTAs, including that with Panama, would include enforceable key labor and environmental standards. On June 28, 2007, the United States and Panama signed the FTA, which included the enforceable labor and environmental provisions. Panama's Legislative Assembly overwhelmingly approved the agreement in July 2007. The U.S. Congress had been likely to consider implementing legislation in the fall of 2007, but the September 1, 2007 election of Pedro Miguel González to head Panama's legislature for one year delayed consideration. González is wanted in the United States for his alleged role in the murder of a U.S. serviceman in Panama in 1992. His term expires September 1, 2008, and González has said that he will not stand for re-election. This could increase the chance that Congress will consider FTA implementing legislation. For more on the bilateral FTA, see CRS Report RL32540, *The Proposed U.S.-Panama Free Trade Agreement*, by J.F. Hornbeck.

Most Recent Developments

On September 1, 2008, Panama's Legislative Assembly is scheduled to select a new Assembly president for a one-year term. Current Assembly president Pedro Miguel González, wanted in the United States for his alleged role in the murder of a U.S. serviceman in Panama in 1992, has said that he will not stand for re-election. His tenure as president resulted in the delay of U.S. congressional consideration of implementing legislation for a free trade agreement with Panama.

On July 6, 2008, Juan Carlos Varela easily won the presidential primary election as a candidate for the Panameñista Party (PP, formerly the Arnulfista Party) in the May 6, 2009 presidential election. A primary for the Democratic Change (CD) party is scheduled for August 3, 2008, with businessman and former government official Ricardo Martinelli the only candidate. The ruling Democratic Revolutionary Party (PRD) is scheduled to hold a primary on September 7, 2008, with former housing minister Balbina Herrera competing against the mayor of Panama City Juan Carlos Navarro.

On May 19, 2008, lawyers for former Panamanian leader Manuel Noriega asked a U.S. appeals court to block his extradition to France on drug-money laundering charges. In January, a U.S. federal judge denied a request to block his extradition. Noriega was scheduled to be released on September 9, 2007, from federal prison in Miami after being imprisoned for nearly 18 years on drug trafficking charges, but will remain in U.S. custody until he exhausts his appeals. Noriega wants to be returned to Panama, where he faces 20 years for conviction on a variety of charges.

On September 3, 2007, Panama officially launched its Canal expansion project, with a ceremony led by former President Jimmy Carter, whose Administration negotiated the Panama Canal Treaties.

On September 1, 2007, Panama's Legislative Assembly elected Pedro Miguel González of the ruling PRD as head of the legislature for a one-year term. The State Department issued a statement expressing deep disappointment about the election of González because of his indictment in the United States for the murder of U.S. Army Sergeant Zak Hernández and the attempted murder of U.S. Army Sergeant Ronald Marshall in June 1992. According to the State Department, there is an outstanding U.S. warrant for his arrest. Although González was acquitted for the Hernández murder in 1997, observers maintain that the trial was marred by jury rigging and witness intimidation. The selection of González has delayed U.S. congressional consideration of the FTA with Panama.

On July 11, 2007, Panama's unicameral Legislative Assembly overwhelmingly approved the bilateral U.S.-Panama free trade agreement by a vote of 58 to 3, with 1 abstention.

On June 28, 2007, Panama and the Unites States signed a bilateral free trade agreement, which includes enforceable labor and environmental provisions pursuant to the bipartisan trade deal negotiated between congressional leaders and the Bush Administration in May 2007.

From June 3-5, 2007, the General Assembly of the Organization of American States (OAS) held its 37th regular session in Panama City focused on the theme of "Energy for Sustainable Development."

On May 10, 2007, congressional leaders and the Bush Administration announced a bipartisan trade deal whereby pending free trade agreements, including the Panama free trade agreement, would include enforceable key labor and environmental standards.

On February 16, 2007, President George W. Bush met with President Torrijos in Washington D.C., with talks focused on the pending free trade agreement and the Canal expansion project.

On February 12, 2007, Panama and the United States signed a declaration of principles intended to lead to Panama's participation in the Container Security Initiative (CSI), operated by the Department of Homeland Security, and the Megaports Initiative, run by the Department of Energy.

On December 19, 2006, the United States and Panama announced the conclusion of negotiations for a free trade agreement, but the United States Trade Representative maintained that the agreement would still be subject to additional discussions on labor in order to ensure bipartisan support in the 110th Congress.

On November 7, 2006, Panama was elected to hold a two-year rotating Latin America seat on the U.N. Security Council. The country had emerged as a consensus candidate on November 1, 2006, after 47 rounds of voting between Guatemala and Venezuela. During those rounds, Guatemala, the U.S.-backed candidate, had received about 25-30 votes more than Venezuela, but neither country received the two-thirds vote needed for the seat. Many observers attribute Venezuela's defeat, at least in part, to President Hugo Chávez's strong anti-American speech before the U.N. General Assembly in September. In the context of Panama's close relations with the United States, the election of Panama to the seat bodes well for U.S. interests at the United Nations compared to the potential of Venezuela winning the seat.

On October 22, 2006, Panamanians approved the Torrijos government's Canal expansion project with over 78% support in a national referendum.

In mid-October 2006, the Centers for Disease Control and Prevention (CDC) helped Panama solve the mystery of recent deaths ultimately traced to contaminated cough syrup from China. At least 100 deaths were traced to the contaminant.

POLITICAL CONDITIONS

Panama has made notable political and economic progress since the December 1989 U.S. military intervention that ousted the military regime of General Manual Antonio Noriega from power. The intervention was the culmination of two and a half years of strong U.S. pressure against the de facto political rule of Noriega, commander of the Panama Defense Forces. Since that time, the country has had four successive civilian governments, with the current government of President Martín Torrijos elected in May 2004 to a five-year term. Inaugurated on September 1, 2004, Torrijos is the son of former populist leader General Omar Torrijos. His electoral alliance, led by the Democratic Revolutionary Party (PRD), also won a majority of seats in the unicameral Legislative Assembly. Jockeying has already begun for Panama's next presidential and legislative elections scheduled for May 2009.

From the Endara to the Moscoso Administration

Endara Government (1989-1994)

Before the U.S. intervention, Panama had held national elections in May 1989, and in the presence of a large number of international observers, the anti-Noriega coalition, headed by Guillermo Endara, prevailed by a three-to-one margin. The Noriega regime annulled the election, however, and held on to power. By the fall, the military regime was losing political power and relied increasingly on irregular paramilitary units, making the country unsafe for U.S. forces and U.S. citizens. On December 20, 1989, President George H.W. Bush ordered the U.S. military into Panama "to safeguard the lives of Americans, to defend democracy in Panama, to combat drug trafficking, and to protect the integrity of the Panama Canal Treaty." Noriega was arrested on January 3, 1990, and brought to the United States to stand trial on drug trafficking charges.

As a result of the intervention, the opposition coalition headed by Guillermo Endara that had won the May 1989 election was sworn into office. During his term, President Endara made great progress in restoring functioning political institutions after 21 years of military-controlled government, and under his administration, a new civilian Public Force replaced Noriega's Panama Defense Forces. But Endara had difficulties in meeting high public expectations, and the demilitarization process was difficult, with some police and former military members at times plotting to destabilize, if not overthrow, the government.

Pérez Balladares Government (1994-1999)

In May 1994, Panamanians went to the polls to vote in presidential and legislative elections that observers called the freest in almost three decades. Ernesto Pérez Balladares, candidate of the former pro-Noriega Democratic Revolutionary Party (PRD), who led a coalition known as "United People", won with 33% of the vote. Placing a surprisingly strong second, with 29% of the vote, was the Arnulfista Party (PA) candidate, Mireya Moscoso de Gruber, heading a coalition known as the "Democratic Alliance."

In the electoral race, Pérez Balladares campaigned as a populist and advocated greater social spending and attention to the poor. He stressed the need for addressing unemployment, which he termed Panama's fundamental problem. Pérez Balladares severely criticized the Endara government for corruption, and he was able to overcome attempts to portray him as someone closely associated with General Noriega. (Pérez Balladares served as campaign manager during the 1989 elections for candidate Carlos Duque, who the Noriega regime had tried to impose on the electorate through fraud.) Instead, Pérez Balladares focused on the PRD's ties to the populist policies of General Omar Torrijos, whose twelve-year (1969-1981) military rule of Panama ended when he died in a plane crash in 1981.

President Pérez Balladares implemented an economic reform program and worked closely with the United States as the date of the Panama Canal turnover approached. Under his government, Panama and the United States held talks on the potential continuation of a U.S. military presence in Panama beyond the end of 1999 (the date Panama was to assume responsibility for defending the Canal). Ultimately negotiations ended without such an agreement. (For more see "Former U.S. Military Presence in Panama" below.)

Although Panama's constitution does not allow for presidential reelection, President Pérez Balladares actively sought a second term in 1999. In 1997, the PRD had begun studying the possibility of amending the constitution to allow a second bid for the presidency in the May 1999 elections. Ultimately, a referendum was held on the issue in August 1998 but failed by a large margin.

Late in his administration, Pérez Balladares became embroiled in a scandal involving the illegal sale of visas to Chinese immigrants attempting to enter the United States via Panama. As a result, U.S. officials cancelled the former president's U.S. tourist visa in November 1999.[1]

Moscoso Government (1999-2004)

In her second bid for the presidency, Arnulfista Party (PA) candidate Mireya Moscoso was victorious in the May 1999 elections. Moscoso, who was inaugurated September 1, 1999, for a five-year term, captured almost 45% of the vote and soundly defeated the ruling PRD's candidate Martin Torrijos (son of former populist leader Omar Torrijos), who received almost 38% of the vote. Until March 1999, Torrijos had been leading in opinion polls, but as the election neared, the two candidates were in a dead heat. A third candidate, Alberto Vallarino, heading a coalition known as Opposition Action, received about 17% of the vote.

President Moscoso, a coffee plantation owner and Panama's first female president, ran as a populist during the campaign, promising to end government corruption, slow the privatization of state enterprises, and reduce poverty. She also promised to ensure that politics and corruption did not interfere with the administration of the Canal. The memory of her husband Arnulfo Arias, a nationalist who was elected three times as president, but overthrown each time, was a factor in the campaign, particularly since Arias was last overthrown in 1968 by General Omar Torrijos, the father of the PRD's 1999 and 2004 presidential candidate.

Although Moscoso took the presidency, the PRD-led New Nation coalition won a majority of 41 seats in the 71-member unicameral Legislative Assembly. Just days before her inauguration, however, Moscoso was able to build a coalition, with the support of the Solidarity Party, the Christian Democratic Party (which later became the Popular Party), and the National Liberal Party, that gave her government a one-seat majority in the Assembly. In

August 2000, the Christian Democrats deserted the coalition and formed an alliance with the principal opposition, the PRD. However, corruption scandals in 2002 led to five PRD legislators defecting to support the Moscoso government, once again giving the President majority support in the Legislative Assembly.

As noted above, Moscoso was elected as a populist, with pledges to end government corruption and reduce poverty, but her campaign pledges proved difficult to fulfill amid high-profile corruption scandals and poor economic performance. As a result, the President's popularity declined significantly from a 70% approval rating when she first took office in 1999 to only 15% in 2004.[2]

Torrijos Government (2004-2009)

On May 2, 2004, Panama held elections for president, as well as for a 78-member Legislative Assembly. In the presidential race, Martín Torrijos of the PRD won a decisive victory with 47.5% of the vote, defeating former President Guillermo Endara, who received 30.6% of the vote, and former Foreign Minister José Miguel Alemán, who received 16.4% of the vote. Torrijos' electoral alliance also won a majority of seats in the unicameral Legislative Assembly, 43 out of 78 seats, which should provide him with enough legislative support to enact his agenda. Elected at 40 years of age, Torrijos spent many years in the United States and studied political science and economics at Texas A&M University. He served four years under the Pérez Balladares government as deputy minister of interior and justice, and as noted above, became the PRD's presidential candidate in the 1999 elections.

Leading up to the election, Torrijos had been topping public opinion polls, with 42%-49% support. In the campaign, he emphasized anti-corruption measures as well as a national strategy to deal with poverty, unemployment, and underdevelopment. He was popular among younger voters and had a base of support in rural areas. Torrijos maintained that his first priority would be job creation.[3] He called for the widening of the Canal, a project that would cost several billion dollars, and would seek a referendum on the issue. During the campaign, all three major candidates supported negotiation of a free trade agreement with the United States, maintaining that it would be advantageous for Panama. Endara and Alemán appeared to emphasize the protection of some sensitive Panamanian sectors such as agriculture, while Torrijos stressed that such an agreement would make Panama's economy more competitive and productive.[4]

The most significant challenges facing the Torrijos government have included dealing with the funding deficits of the country's social security fund (Caja de Seguro Social, CSS); developing plans for the expansion of the Panama Canal; and combating unemployment and poverty. After protests and a protracted strike by construction workers, doctors, and teachers in June 2005, the Torrijos government was forced to modify its plans for reforming the social security fund. After a national dialogue on the issue, Panama's Legislative Assembly approved a watered-down version of the original plan in December 2005. The enacted reform did not raise the retirement age but will gradually increase required monthly payments into the system and introduces a dual pension system that combines aspects of privatization with the current system.[5] In mid-December 2007, an almost six-week strike by doctors in the public healthcare system was resolved, with the government offering a 26.7% increase in salaries equivalent and a commitment not to privatize the system.[6]

The government unveiled in April 2006 its ambitious plans to build a third set of locks that will allow larger post-Panamax ships to transit the Canal. Panama's Cabinet approved the expansion plan on June 14, and the Legislative Assembly approved it on July 10, 2006. A referendum on the expansion project took place on October 22, 2006, with 78% supporting the project. The referendum was viewed as a victory for the Torrijos government, which advanced the project as integral to Panama's future economic development, and one that helped restore the President's popularity.[7]

The Torrijos government's agenda also has included judicial, penal and anticorruption reforms, as well as an economic development strategy to target poverty and unemployment. In May 2008, a new penal code went into effect that takes a tougher stance on crime by increasing sentences on serious crimes and introducing new categories of crimes, including environmental crimes and thefts of energy, water, or telecommunications services.[8] In early July 2008, Panama's Legislative Assembly gave President Torrijos powers to carry out security sector reforms over the next two months. Some critics fear that the action could remilitarize the country.[9] In terms of tackling poverty, in June 2008, the government Torrijos extended its "Red de Oportunidades" social support program to include the elderly living in extreme poverty, and in July 2008, the government announced that monthly cash payments under the program would increase.[10]

The popularity of the Torrijos government has declined significantly in 2008. A June 2008 poll showed support for the President at 34%, down from 51% in April.[11] Increasing inflation and violent crime are significant challenges that reportedly have contributed to the President's decline in popularity. Consumer price inflation was 6.4% at the end of 2007, and is forecast to reach 9.7% at the end of 2008.[12]

May 2009 Elections

Panama is scheduled to hold legislative and presidential elections on May 6, 2009. Since the Constitution does not allow for re-election, President Torrijos cannot be a candidate. As a result, jockeying began in early 2008 among presidential aspirants.

On July 6, 2008, Juan Carlos Varela easily won the presidential primary election for the Panameñista Party (PP, formerly the Arnulfista Party) as a candidate for the 2009 presidential election. A primary for the smaller Democratic Change (CD) party is scheduled for August 3, 2008, with businessman and former government minister Ricardo Martinelli running unopposed. The ruling Democratic Revolutionary Party (PRD) is scheduled to hold a primary on September 7, 2008, with former housing minister Balbina Herrera competing against the mayor of Panama City Juan Carlos Navarro. Former President Guillermo Endara will run as the candidate of the Fatherland's Moral Vanguard Party

Human Rights

The Panamanian government generally respects human rights, but, as noted by the State Department in its 2007 human rights report (issued in March 2008), serious human rights problems continue in a number of areas. Prison conditions overall remain harsh, with reported abuse by prison guards, and prolonged pretrial detentions remained a problem. According to the report, the judiciary is marred by corruption and ineffectiveness, and is subject to political manipulation. Other serious problems include discrimination and violence against women, trafficking in persons, discrimination against indigenous people and other ethnic minorities, and child labor.

Panama had been criticized by the State Department and international human rights groups for vestiges of "gag laws" used by the government to silence those criticizing policies or officials, but the legislature repealed these laws in May 2005. Nevertheless, as noted in the State Department human rights report, the legislature approved penal code amendments in May 2007 that establish fines or arrests of journalists who violate the privacy of public officials, recognize criminal libel against journalists, and allow the government to prosecute journalists for publishing classified information. The new penal code went into effect in May 2008. The State Department's human rights report maintains that 15 past libel cases against journalists remain pending. It also cites concerns of journalists and human rights organizations that the government attempts to manipulate the free flow of information by using advertising funding to reward news organizations that carry stories favorable to the government.

In an attempt to redress human rights abuses that occurred under military rule and to prevent their reoccurrence, the Moscoso government established a Truth Commission in 2001 to investigate violations under the military regime. The Commission recommended that the government investigate 33 cases of killings or disappearances committed during the 1968-1989 period of military rule, some of which were under review by the end of 2007, however little progress has been made. In July 2006, just as one of the first human rights trials was approaching an end, a former military officer implicated in the 1970 killing of activist Heliodoro Portugal died from an apparent heart attack. There are reportedly 110 human rights cases involving the torture, incarceration, murder, or disappearance of political activists under the period of military-dominated government.[13]

In recent years, violence from the civil conflict in neighboring Colombia has resulted in hundreds of displaced persons seeking refuge in the neighboring Darién province of Panama. The Office of the U.N. High Commission for Refugees (UNHCR) reports that there are some 900 displaced Colombians in Panama under temporary humanitarian protection. Their presence is restricted to a small area in the Darién. According to the State Department's human rights report, many of the Colombians have lived in Panama for years, have given birth to children in Panama, and do not want to return to Colombia because of family and cultural ties to local Panamanian communities. While many of the displaced are Afro-Colombians, there have also been indigenous people from Colombia who have fled to Panama because of the violence. In December 2006, Panama recognized 42 members of Colombia's Wounaan indigenous group as refugees.[14]

According to UNHCR, there are almost 1,000 recognized refugees in the country. In April 2008, UNHCR lauded Panama for the approval of a new law that will allow long-standing refugees (those residing 10 years or more) the opportunity to apply for permanent residency. According to UNHCR, the new law will largely affect refugees from Nicaragua and El Salvador who arrived in Panama during the Central American conflicts of the 1980s, and will not affect the more recent refugees from Colombia.[15]

With regard to worker rights in Panama, the State Department's 2007 human rights report noted that unions and collective bargaining are permitted in export processing zones (EPZs), but that the International Labor Organization's Committee of Experts questioned the government as to whether these workers have the right to strike. Panama's law regulating the EPZs does not include arbitration or specify procedures to resolve labor disputes in the courts. The State Department report also noted that child labor was a problem, with violations occurring most frequently in rural areas at harvest time and in the informal sector.

ECONOMIC CONDITIONS

Panama's service-based economy has performed well in the last several years, with economic growth rates of 7.2% in 2005, 8.7% in 2006, and 11.2% in 2007. Continuing to be one of the fastest growing economies in Latin America, the estimate for 2008 is 8.6% growth.[16] With a per capita income level of $4,890 in 2006, Panama is classified by the World Bank as an upper-middle-income developing country. Yet income distribution remains highly skewed with large disparities between rich and poor, with about one third of the population living in poverty.[17] In October 2005, the Torrijos government launched an anti-hunger and anti-poverty program targeting the rural population and an indigenous community in a central rural province. The government has also begun providing direct monthly subsidies to poor families that can demonstrate that their children attend school regularly.[18] As noted above, the government announced earlier this year that the monthly subsides would be extended to elderly living in extreme poverty. Unemployment fell from 10.3% in 2005 to 6.4% in 2007, but the forecast for 2008 is just a slight decrease to 6.3%.[19]

The administration of President Pérez Balladares (1994-1999) implemented an economic reform program that included liberalization of the trade regime, privatization of state-owned enterprises, the institution of fiscal reform, and labor code reform. Tariffs were reduced to an average of 8%. The Moscoso government partially reversed the trade liberalization process by raising tariffs on some agricultural products, some of which reached the maximum rate allowed under Panama's World Trade Organization obligations.[20]

Although Panama has traditionally eschewed economic linkages and integration schemes with its Central American neighbors (largely because of its privileged relationship with the United States), it has joined with Mexico and Central American states in a regional economic project known as the Puebla-Panama plan. The plan, which has the goal of spurring development in the region, will improve highways, standardize customs procedures, and join power grids to improve the quality of life in the region.

As part of its strategy of increasing its global trade and investment links, and accentuating its role as a global transportation hub, Panama has pursued free trade agreements (FTAs) with several countries, including the United States (see "U.S. Trade Relations and a Potential Free Trade Agreement" section below). In June 2003, an FTA with El Salvador entered into force, and more recently signed agreements with Costa Rica, Honduras, Nicaragua, and Guatemala. In June 2006, Panama signed an FTA with Chile. Beyond the Western Hemisphere, Panama negotiated an FTA with Taiwan that entered into force in January 2004, and in April 2005, Panama and Singapore announced the conclusion of talks for a free trade agreement that was ratified in June 2006.

U.S. RELATIONS

Background on the 1989 U.S. Military Intervention

The December 20, 1989, U.S. military intervention in Panama, known as Operation Just Cause, was the culmination of almost two and a half years of strong U.S. pressure, including economic sanctions, against the de facto political rule of General Noriega, Panama's military commander. Political unrest had erupted in mid-1987 when a high-ranking Panamanian military official alleged that Noriega was involved in murder, electoral fraud, and corruption, which prompted the formation of an opposition coalition that challenged his rule. The regime nullified the results of May 1989 national elections, which international observers maintain were won by the opposition by a 3-1 margin. It also harassed U.S. citizens in Panama, including the killing of a U.S. Marine lieutenant. President George H. W. Bush ultimately ordered U.S. forces into combat to safeguard the lives of Americans in Panama, to defend democracy, to combat drug trafficking, and to protect the operation of the Panama Canal.

In early January 1990, with the restoration of democracy and Noriega's arrest to face trial in the United States on drug charges, President Bush announced that the objectives of the U.S. intervention had been achieved. In terms of casualties, 23 U.S. soldiers and three U.S. civilians were killed, while on the Panamanian side, some 200 civilians and 300 Panamanian military were killed. While Congress was not in session during the intervention, in general, Members were strongly supportive of the action. In February 1990, the House overwhelmingly approved a resolution, H.Con.Res. 262, stating the President acted appropriately to intervene in Panama after substantial efforts to resolve the crisis by political, economic, and diplomatic means.

Overview of Current U.S.-Panamanian Relations

Since the 1989 U.S. military intervention, the United States has had close relations with Panama, stemming in large part from the extensive history of linkages developed when the Panama Canal was under U.S. control and Panama hosted major U.S. military installations. Today, about 25,000 U.S. citizens reside in Panama, many retirees of the former Panama Canal Commission, and there are growing numbers of other American retirees in the western part of the country.[21]

The current U.S. relationship with Panama is characterized by extensive cooperation on counternarcotics efforts, U.S. assistance to help Panama assure the security of the Canal, and efforts to complete a bilateral free trade agreement (FTA). Panama is seeking an FTA as a means of increasing U.S. investment in the country, while the Bush Administration has stressed that an FTA with Panama, in addition to enhancing trade, would further U.S. efforts to strengthen support for democracy and the rule of law.

U.S.-Panamanian negotiations for a bilateral FTA began in April 2004, and were completed in December 2006, although at the time U.S. officials stated the agreement was subject to additional discussions on labor and that the Administration would work with Congress to ensure strong bipartisan support. Subsequently, congressional leaders and the Bush Administration announced a bipartisan deal on May 10, 2007, whereby pending FTAs, including that with Panama, would include enforceable key labor and environmental standards. The United States and Panama ultimately signed the FTA on June 28, 2007, which included the enforceable labor and environmental provisions. Panama's Legislative Assembly overwhelmingly approved the agreement on July 11, 2007, by vote of 58 to 3, with 1 abstention. The U.S. Congress had been likely to consider implementing legislation for the agreement in the fall of 2007, but the September 1, 2007, election of Pedro Miguel González to head Panama's legislature for one year delayed consideration of the FTA. González is wanted in the United States for his alleged role in the murder of a U.S. serviceman in Panama, U.S. Army Sergeant Zak Hernández, in June 1992.

The United States turned over control of the Canal to Panama at the end of 1999, according to the terms of the 1977 Panama Canal Treaty, at which point Panama assumed responsibility for operating and defending the Canal. All U.S. troops were withdrawn from Panama at that time and all U.S. military installations reverted to Panamanian control. However, under the terms of the Treaty on the Permanent Neutrality and Operation of the Panama Canal, or simply the Neutrality Treaty, the United States retains the right to use military force if necessary to reopen the Canal or restore its operations. U.S. officials congratulated Panama on the success of the October 2006 Canal expansion referendum, but also asserted that the challenge for the government is to ensure that the expansion project is conducted with transparency and without any hint of corruption.[22]

In recent years, U.S. foreign assistance amounted to $19 million in FY2005, $10.5 million in FY2006, and $12.2 million in FY2007. For FY2008, about $7.7 million will be provided through the regular foreign aid funding measure, while Panama also could receive up to almost $4 million in FY2008 supplemental appropriations assistance under the Mérida Initiative (P.L. 110-252). That program provides assistance to Mexico and Central to combat drug trafficking, gangs, and organized crime. For FY2009, the Administration's FY2009 foreign aid request for Panama was for $11.6 million, with $4 million for development assistance, $2.6 million in military assistance, $1 million for assistance under the Andean Counterdrug Program (ACP), and $3.4 million for a Peace Corps program. In addition, Panama could receive an additional $8.9 million of the $100 million requested for Central America in FY2009 for the Mérida Initiative under the Western Hemisphere Regional program. (For additional information, see CRS Report RS22837, *Mérida Initiative: Proposed U.S. Anticrime and Counterdrug Assistance for Mexico and Central America.*)

A number of U.S. agencies provide support to Panama. The State Department, the Drug Enforcement Administration, the U.S. Coast Guard, and the Department of Homeland Security are involved in providing counternarcotics support to Panama. In October 2006, the Centers for Disease Control and Prevention (CDC) helped Panama solve the mystery of deaths ultimately traced to contaminated cough syrup from China (at least 100 deaths have been traced to the contaminant). The Department of Health and Human Services is providing support for a Regional Training Center for health-care workers in Panama City that will train students from throughout Central America. The U.S. Southern Command also provides support to Panama through military exercises providing humanitarian and medical assistance, and at times provides emergency assistance in the case of natural disasters such as floods or droughts. The U.S. Southern Command also has sponsored annual multinational training exercises since 2003 focused on the defense of the Panama Canal.

In February 2007, Panama and the United States signed a declaration of principles intended to lead to Panama's participation in the Container Security Initiative (CSI) operated by the U.S. Customs and Border Protection (CBP) of the Department of Homeland Security, and the Megaports Initiative run by the National Nuclear Security Administration of the Department of Energy. Panama's port of Balboa became operational under the CSI in August 2007, while the ports of Colón and Manzanillo became operational in September 2007. CSI uses a security regime to ensure that containers that pose a potential risk for terrorism are identified and inspected at foreign ports before they are placed on vessels destined for the United States. The Megaports Initiative has the goal of deploying radiation detection equipment to ports in order to detect nuclear or radioactive materials.

A sensitive issue in U.S.-Panamanian relations has been Panama's desire to have the United States clean up three contaminated firing ranges in Panama as well as San Jose Island, which was contaminated with chemical weapons used in training exercises during World War II. With regard to the firing ranges, U.S. officials maintain that the United States has already met its treaty obligations to clean up the ranges. With regard to the cleanup of San Jose Island, Panama rejected a U.S. offer in September 2003 that would have provided equipment and training so that Panama could clean up the island; the Panamanian government maintains that it did not want to sign any agreement releasing the United States from liabilities.

President Bush visited Panama in November 2005, on his way back from the fourth Summit of the Americas held in Argentina. During the visit, he endorsed the concept of widening the Canal and indicated that the two countries were close to completing negotiations for a free trade agreement. While in Panama, the President also rejected Panama's calls to remove unexploded ordnance from former U.S. firing ranges that were returned to Panama in 1999. According to the President, "we had obligations under the treaty, and we felt like we met those obligations." Despite the disagreement, President Bush indicated that Panama and the United States could discuss the issue in a constructive way since the two countries have friendly relations.[23]

In February 2007 and again in May 2008, President Torrijos met with President Torrijos in Washington D.C., with talks focused on the free trade agreement and the Canal expansion project. President Torrijos is expected to visit Washington in mid -September 2008 to promote the approval of the FTA.[24]

Status of Manuel Noriega

In the aftermath of the 1989 U.S. military intervention, General Manuel Noriega was arrested in January 1990 and brought to the United States to stand trial on drug charges. After a seven-month trial, Noriega was convicted on eight out of ten drug trafficking charges in U.S. federal court in Miami in 1992, and sentenced to 40 years in prison. That sentence was subsequently reduced to 30 years, and then to 20 years. With time off for "good behavior," Noriega was scheduled to be released from jail on September 9, 2007, but has remained in U.S. custody pending appeals of his extradition to France.

France is seeking Noriega's extradition, where he faces a 10-year prison sentence for his conviction in absentia in 1999 on money laundering charges, but would be eligible for a new trial. Despite having lost all previous appeals, on May 19, 2008, Noriega's defense filed an appeal on the grounds that the French government would not respect special protections that were granted to him in a 1992 ruling as a "prisoner of war" under the Geneva Conventions. On January 9, 2008, a U.S. federal judge in Miami denied a previous request to block the extradition of Noriega to France.[25]

Noriega wants to return to Panama in order to appeal his convictions in absentia, including for two murders: the brutal killing of vocal critic Hugo Spadafora in 1985; and the killing of Major Moisés Giroldi, the leader of a failed 1989 coup attempt. Panamanian courts sentenced Noriega to at least 60 years in prison, but the law only allows him to serve a maximum sentence of 20 years, and according to some reports, 18 years of Noriega's imprisonment in the United States could be subtracted from his sentence in Panama.[26] Nevertheless, according to Panama's attorney general, there are an additional 15 outstanding cases against Noriega, including his responsibility for the deaths of several members of the Panamanian Defense Forces for their involvement in the failed 1989 coup.[27]

Noriega's attorneys argue that since Noriega has been recognized as a prisoner of war in the U.S. courts, the United States should repatriate him to his native Panama, insisting that this complies with the Geneva Conventions. U.S. officials have argued that France's extradition should be honored because Panama by law does not extradite its nationals.[28] Panama had filed an extradition request for Noriega in 1991.

While Panamanian officials have called for Noriega's extradition to Panama, they have not opposed the possibility of Noriega being extradited to France and have stated that the government would respect the decision of the U.S. courts on this matter. Some observers maintain that the Panamanian government is reluctant to have Noriega extradited to Panama, since some members of the ruling Democratic Revolutionary Party worked with Noriega when he controlled the government and are now reluctant to have Noriega return and revisit cases from the past. Other observers contend that Panamanian officials are reluctant to have Noriega return because of recent changes to the penal code that could allow Noriega to serve little, if any, of his sentence.[29]

Drug Trafficking and Money Laundering

An important concern for U.S. policymakers over the years has been securing Panamanian cooperation to combat drug-trafficking and money-laundering. Panama is a major transit country for illicit drugs from South America to the U.S. market because of its geographic location and its large maritime industry and containerized seaports. Moreover, the country's service-based economy, with a large banking sector and trading center (Colón Free Zone), makes Panama a significant drug money laundering center.

Drug traffickers use fishing vessels, cargo ships, small aircraft, and go-fast boats to move illicit drugs — primarily cocaine, but also heroin and Ecstasy — through Panama. Some of the drugs are transferred to trucks for northbound travel or are placed in sea-freight containers for transport on cargo vessels. Traffickers also utilize hundreds of abandoned or unmonitored airstrips as well as couriers who transit Panama by commercial air flights. There also has been increasing domestic drug abuse, particularly among youth. Addiction has also increased significantly among Panama's Kuna indigenous population, whose lands lie just south of a transit zone for Colombian cocaine.[30] The country is also a small-scale producer of coca leaf in the remote Darien province that borders Colombia. According to the Department of State, security in Darien has improved in recent years, although the smuggling of weapons and drugs across the border continues.

The State Department's March 2008 *International Narcotics Control Strategy Report* (INCSR) states that the Torrijos administration has been "dynamic" in cooperating with the

United States on joint counternarcotics efforts, but maintains that it has been less rigorous in cooperating with neighboring countries. The United States has provided equipment, training, and information to enhance Panama's interdiction and eradication capabilities, and is supporting the restructuring of Panama's law enforcement agencies to enhance their abilities. Looking ahead, the INCSR report encourages Panama to devote sufficient resources to patrol its land borders with Colombia and Costa Rica and its coastline, and to increase the number of arrests and prosecutions in the areas of corruption and money laundering. It also states that the United States will provide expertise and resources to assist Panama develop a new Coast Guard and a border control unit.

Over the past three years, Panamanian cooperation with U.S. law enforcement led to several major successful anti-drug operations. In January 2006, more than 20 people were arrested in New York and Panama in a heroin smuggling operation involving dozens of "swallowers" who transported the drug. In May 2006, law enforcement authorities from the United States, Panama, and several other countries broke up a cocaine smuggling operation that used three islands on Panama's Caribbean coast to refuel fast boats and fishing trawlers carrying drugs. According to the State Department's 2008 INCSR report, in 2007 a record 60 metric tons of cocaine were seized. In March 2007, U.S. and Panamanian authorities cooperated in the interdiction of more than 21 tons of cocaine off the coast of Panama, valued at nearly $300 million, the largest seizure in U.S. history.

Panama has made significant progress in strengthening its anti-money laundering regime since June 2000 when it was cited as a non-cooperative country in the fight against money laundering by the Financial Action Task Force (FATF), a multilateral anti-money laundering body. Subsequently, the government undertook a comprehensive effort to improve its anti-money laundering regime by enacting two laws and issuing two decrees in 2000. As a result of these efforts, the FATF removed Panama from its non-cooperative country list in June 2001.

Nevertheless, the State Department's March 2008 INCSR maintains that Panama "remains vulnerable to money laundering because of its lack of adequate enforcement, personnel, and resources, the sheer volume of economic transactions, its location as a major drug transit country, and corruption." As such, Panama continues to be categorized by the Department of State as a country of primary concern for money laundering. The INCSR report notes that Panama has continued to make progress in strengthening its anti-money laundering regime, and has cooperated with the United States and other countries in investigating money laundering cases involving Panama. Looking ahead, the report called on Panama to consider adopting legislation to allow for civil forfeiture and the freezing of terrorist assets, and to enhance law enforcement actions that address smuggling, abuse of the real estate sector, trade-based money laundering, and the proliferation of nontransparent offshore companies.

U.S. Trade Relations and a Potential Free Trade Agreement

Panama has largely a service-based economy, which historically has run a merchandise trade deficit with the United States. In 2007, the United States had a $3.4 billion trade surplus with Panama, exporting $366 million in goods and importing $3.7 billion. Panama was the 42nd largest U.S. export market in 2007.[31] Panama's major exports include fish and seafood (accounting for one-third of its exports to the United States), sugar, coffee, and other agricultural products. Major imports include oil, consumer goods, foodstuffs, and capital goods. Almost half of Panama's exports are destined for the United States, while almost one-third of its imports are from the United States. The stock of U.S. foreign investment in Panama was estimated at $5.7 billion in 2006, largely concentrated in the financial and wholesale sectors. This surpassed the combined U.S. foreign investment in the five other Central American nations.[32]

With the exception of two years (1988-1989), when the United States was applying economic sanctions on Panama under General Noriega's rule, Panama has been a beneficiary of the U.S. preferential import program known as the Caribbean Basin Initiative (CBI) begun in 1984. The program was amended several times and made permanent in 1990. CBI benefits were expanded in 2000 with the enactment of the Caribbean Basin Trade Partnership Act (CBTPA) (Title II, P.L. 106-200), which provided NAFTA-equivalent trade benefits, including tariff preferences for textile and apparel goods, to certain CBI countries, including Panama, until September 30, 2008.

Panama and the United States began negotiations for a free trade agreement in April 2004. There had been expectations that the negotiations would be completed in early 2005, but continued contention over several issues and a lengthy hiatus prolonged the negotiations until December 2006. These included market access for agricultural products, considered sensitive by Panama; procurement provisions for the Panama Canal Authority regarding expansion activities; and sanitary control systems governing the entry of U.S. products and animals to enter the Panamanian market. Negotiations were suspended for some time in 2006 until after Panama held its Canal expansion referendum in October, but a tenth round led to the conclusion of negotiations on December 19, 2006.

Under the agreement, over 88% of U.S. exports of consumer and industrial goods would become duty-free immediately, while remaining tariffs would be phased out over 10 years. Over 50% of U.S. agricultural exports to Panama would become duty-free immediately, while tariffs on most remaining farm products would be phased out within 15 years. In December 2006, Panama and the United States also signed a bilateral agreement on sanitary and phytosanitary measures in which Panama will recognize the equivalence of the U.S. food safety inspection to those of Panama and will no longer require individual plant inspections. Under the FTA, U.S. companies would be guaranteed a fair and transparent process to sell goods and services to Panamanian government entities, including the Panama Canal Authority.[33]

When the negotiations were concluded, U.S. Trade Representative Susan Schwab stated that the agreement would be subject to additional discussions on labor, and that the Administration would work with both sides of the aisle in Congress to ensure strong bipartisan support before submitting it to Congress.[34] On May 10, 2007, congressional leaders and the Bush Administration announced a bipartisan trade deal whereby pending free trade agreements would include enforceable key labor and environmental standards. This would include an obligation to adopt and maintain in practice five basic internationally recognized labor principles: freedom of association; recognition of the right to collective bargaining; elimination of forced or compulsory labor; abolition of child labor; and elimination of discrimination in respect of employment and occupation.

The United States and Panama ultimately signed the FTA on June 28, 2007, with the enforceable labor and environmental standards outlined in the bipartisan trade deal. Panama's

Legislative Assembly ratified the agreement on July 11, 2007, by a vote of 58 to 3, with 1 abstention.

The U.S. Congress had been likely to consider implementing legislation for the agreement in the fall of 2007, but the September 1, 2007, election of Pedro Miguel González of the ruling PRD to head Panama's legislature for one year delayed consideration of the FTA. González is wanted in the United States for his alleged role in the murder of U.S. Army Sergeant Zak Hernández and the attempted murder of U.S. Army Sergeant Ronald Marshall in June 1992. The State Department issued a statement expressing deep disappointment about the election of González because of his October 1992 indictment in the United States for the murder of Sergeant Hernández. Although González was acquitted in Panama in 1997 for the Hernández murder, observers maintain that the trial was marred by jury rigging and witness intimidation. González denies his involvement, and his lawyer asserts that ballistic tests in the murder were inconclusive. While polls in Panama in 2007 showed that Panamanians believed that González should step down, the case also energized the populist anti-American wing of the ruling PRD.[35]

González has stated he will not seek a second term as president of the Legislative Assembly when his term expires on September 1, 2008. This could increase chances that Congress will consider implementing legislation for the FTA.

For more details on the bilateral FTA, see CRS Report RL32540, *The Proposed U.S.-Panama Free Trade Agreement*, by J.F. Hornbeck.

Operation and Security of the Panama Canal

Historical Background and the Panama Canal Treaties

When Panama proclaimed its independence from Colombia in 1903, it concluded a treaty with the United States for U.S. rights to build, administer, and defend a canal cutting across the country and linking the Pacific and Atlantic oceans. (See **Figure 1**, *Map of Panama*, at the end of this report.) The treaty gave the United States rights in the socalled Canal Zone (about 10 miles wide and 50 miles long) "as if it were sovereign" and "in perpetuity." Construction of the canal was completed in 1914. In the 1960s, growing resentment in Panama over the extent of U.S. rights in the country led to pressure to negotiate a new treaty arrangement for the operation of the Canal. Draft treaties were completed in 1967 but ultimately rejected by Panama in 1970.

New negotiations ultimately led to the September 1977 signing of the two Panama Canal Treaties by President Jimmy Carter and Panamanian head of government General Omar Torrijos. Under the Panama Canal Treaty, the United States was given primary responsibility for operating and defending the Canal until December 31, 1999. (Subsequent U.S. implementing legislation established the Panama Canal Commission to operate the Canal until the end of 1999.) Under the Treaty on the Permanent Neutrality and Operation of the Panama Canal, or simply the Neutrality Treaty, the two countries agreed to maintain a regime of neutrality, whereby the Canal would be open to ships of all nations. The U.S. Senate gave its advice and consent to the Neutrality Treaty on March 16, 1978, and to the Panama Canal Treaty on April 18, 1978, both by a vote of 68-32, with various amendments, conditions, understandings, and reservations. Panama and the United States exchanged instruments of ratification for the two treaties on June 16, 1978, and the two treaties entered into force on October 1, 1979.

Some treaty critics have argued that Panama did not accept the amendments, conditions, reservations, and understandings of the U.S. Senate, including the DeConcini condition to the Neutrality Treaty. That condition states: "if the Canal is closed, or its operations are interfered with, the United States of America and the Republic of Panama shall each independently have the right to take such steps as each deems necessary, in accordance with its constitutional processes, including the use of military force in the Republic of Panama, to reopen the Canal or restore the operations of the Canal, as the case may be." However, others argued that Panama, in fact, had accepted all U.S. Senate amendments. The State Department asserted that Panama expressly accepted all amendments, conditions, and understandings to the two treaties, including the DeConcini condition. The United States and Panama signed the instruments of ratification for both treaties, which incorporated all the Senate provisions. The two countries cooperated throughout the years on matters related to the canal and established five binational bodies to handle these issues. Two of the bodies were set up to address defense affairs and conducted at least sixteen joint military exercises between 1979 and 1985 involving Panamanian and U.S. forces.

Canal Transition and Current Status

Over the years, U.S. officials consistently affirmed a commitment to follow through with the Panama Canal Treaty and turn the Canal over to Panama at the end of 1999. That transition occurred smoothly on December 31, 1999. The Panama Canal Treaty terminated on that date, and the Panama Canal Commission (PCC), the U.S. agency operating the Canal, was succeeded by the Panama Canal Authority (ACP), a Panamanian government agency established in 1997.

Under the terms of the Neutrality Treaty, which has no termination date, Panama has had responsibility for operating and defending the Canal since the end of 1999. As noted above, both Panama and the United States, however, in exercising their responsibilities to maintain the regime of neutrality (keeping the Canal secure and open to all nations on equal terms) independently have the right to use military force to reopen the Canal or restore its operations. This is delineated in the first condition of the Neutrality Treaty.

The secure operation of the Panama Canal remains a U.S. interest since about 13%-14% of U.S. ocean-borne cargo transits through the Canal. The United States provides assistance to Panama to improve its ability to provide security for the Canal and to enhance port and maritime security. U.S. officials have consistently expressed satisfaction that Panama is running the Canal efficiently, and since 2003, the U.S. military has conducted exercises with Panama and other countries to protect the Canal in case of attack.[36]

Headed by Alberto Alemán Zubieta, the Panama Canal Authority has run the Canal for more than seven years and has been lauded for increasing Canal safety and efficiency. In January 2006, the Martín Torrijos government established a social investment fund backed by Panama Canal revenues that will invest in schools, hospitals, bridges, roads, and other social projects. The initiative, according to the government, would show Panamanians that the Canal is contributing to economic development and improving the quality of life for Panamanians.[37]

Canal Expansion Project

On April 24, 2006, the Panama Canal Authority presented to President Torrijos its recommendation to build a third channel and new set of locks (one on the Atlantic and one on the Pacific) that will double the capacity of the Canal and allow it to accommodate giant container cargo ships known as post-Panamax ships. The proposal would also widen and deepen existing channels and elevate Gatun Lake's maximum operating level. According to the proposed plan, the overall project would begin in 2007 and take from seven to eight years to complete. The estimated cost of the project is $5.25 billion, to be self-financed by the ACP through graduated toll increases and external bridge financing of about $2.3 billion that would be paid off in about 10 years. The Panamanian government would not incur any sovereign debt as a result of the project. According to the ACP, the overall objectives of the expansion project are to (1) achieve long-term sustainability and growth for the Canal's financial contributions to the Panamanian national treasury; (2) maintain the Canal's competitiveness; (3) increase the Canal's capacity to capture the growing world tonnage demand; and (4) make the Canal more productive, safe, and efficient.[38]

President Torrijos and his Cabinet approved the expansion project on June 14, 2006, and the Legislative Assembly overwhelmingly approved it on July 10, 2006, with 72 out of 78 deputies voting for the project. Pursuant to Panama's Constitution (Article 319), the project had to be submitted to a national referendum no sooner than 90 days from the date of approval by the Assembly. The Torrijos government chose to hold the referendum on October 22, 2006, close to the anniversary of October 23, 1977, the date when Panamanians approved the two Panama Canal treaties in a national plebiscite by a two-to-one margin. A poll from early September 2006 showed almost 64% public support for the Canal expansion project, but on election day the expansion project received 78% of the vote.

The referendum in part can also be viewed as support for the Torrijos government, which advanced the project as integral to Panama's future economic development. The government maintains that some 7,000 direct jobs will be created by the project, as well as some 35,000 indirect jobs. President Torrijos asserts that increased revenue from the Canal arising from the expansion project will allow the government to launch social development programs and improve living conditions in the country.[39]

There had been some vocal opposition to the Canal expansion project. The organization known as the Peasant Coordinator Against the Dams (CCCE, Coordinadora Campesina Contra los Embalses), consisting of agricultural, civil, and environmental organizations, asserts that the expansion project will lead to flooding and will drive people from their homes. An umbrella protest group known as the National Front for the Defense of Economic and Social Rights (Frenadeso), which was formed in 2005 during protests against social security reforms, called for a "no" vote.[40] Former Presidents Jorge Illueca and Guillermo Endara, as well as former Panama Canal administrator Fernando Manfredo, also opposed the expansion project, maintaining that the price is too high and too much of a gamble. Critics fear that the total price tag could rise considerably and are concerned that toll increases could make alternative routes more economically attractive.[41]

The ACP is moving ahead with the Canal expansion project. In April 2007, Panama announced plans for new toll fees to be implemented gradually beginning in July 2007. In early May, the ACP offered its first construction tender for the project. The Panamanian government officially launched the Canal expansion project on September 3, 2007, with a ceremony led by former President Jimmy Carter whose Administration negotiated the Panama Canal Treaties.

Privatization of Two Panamanian Ports and the China Issue

A controversy that arose in U.S.- Panamanian relations in 1996 and continued through 1999 relates to the privatization of two Panamanian ports at either end of the Panama Canal, Balboa on the Pacific and Cristobal on the Atlantic. In July 1996, the Panamanian government awarded the concession to operate the ports to a Hong Kong company, Hutchison International Port Holdings, one of the world's largest container port operators and a subsidiary of the Hutchison Whampoa Limited Group. The company operates the concession in Panama as the Panama Ports Company, S.A. Then U.S. Ambassador to Panama William Hughes complained about the lack of transparency in the bidding process in which several U.S. companies competed.

The Panamanian government responded with a communique describing the process by which Hutchison was awarded the 25-year concession. Panamanian officials maintain that Hutchison had the highest bid, agreeing to pay Panama $22.2 million annually over the life of the concession. In May 1997, six U.S. Senators charged in a letter to the Federal Maritime Commission that irregularities in the bidding process denied U.S. companies an equal right to develop and operate terminals in Panama.

After a review of the issue, the Commission responded that while the port award processes were unorthodox and irregular by U.S. standards, it saw no evidence that U.S. companies were subjected to discriminatory treatment. A May 1997 Senate Foreign Relations Committee staff report on the issue also concluded that while the bidding process was unorthodox, U.S. officials found no evidence of illegality.[42]

In addition to the privatization process, some press reports in March 1997 raised the issue of Hutchison's relationship with the Chinese government and the China Ocean Shipping Company (COSCO) and suggested that China would gain control of the Panama Canal or threaten the operation of the Canal. Over the years, U.S. officials, however, have consistently confirmed that Hutchison's operations of the ports does not constitute a threat to the Canal. The same May 1997 Senate Foreign Relations Committee staff report mentioned above concluded that legal safeguards in the Panama Canal Treaties and Panamanian law guarantee the continued operation of the Canal and ensures its access to all nations. (Also see CRS Report 97-476, *Long Beach: Proposed Lease by China Ocean Shipping Company (COSCO) at Former Naval Base* by Shirley Kan.)

In early August 1999, Senator Trent Lott raised questions about Chinese influence over the Canal in a letter to Defense Secretary William Cohen. Subsequently, both the State Department and the Department of Defense made statements responding to the concerns raised about potential Chinese influence in Panama. In an August 12, 1999, press briefing, the Department of Defense noted that it does not consider Hutchison's ownership of two port facilities as a threat to U.S. security. DOD asserted that "the company does not have any ability to stop or impede traffic through the Canal" and noted that under the Neutrality Treaty, "the United States has a unilateral right to maintain the neutrality of the Canal and reopen it if there should be any military threat." The State Department, in an August 12, 1999, press briefing, noted that it has seen "no capability or interest on the part of the People's Republic of China, a major user of the Canal, to disrupt its operations."

According to September 29, 1999, congressional testimony by Peter Romero, then Acting Assistant Secretary of State for Western Hemisphere Affairs (before the House International Relations Committee, Subcommittee on the Western Hemisphere), the U.S. intelligence community also studied the question of the influence of China in Panama as a result of the concession. Romero testified that, after reviewing the study, the State Department concluded that the Hutchison concession "does not represent a threat to canal operations or other U.S. interests in Panama."

On October 22, 1999, the Senate Armed Services Committee held a hearing on Canal security. Officials from the Department of Defense, the Panama Canal Commission, the SOUTHCOM, and the Department of State testified, and all concluded that the Hutchison's port operations did not constitute a threat to the Canal. Ambassador Lino Gutierrez, Principal Deputy Assistant Secretary of State for Western Hemisphere Affairs, stated that the Department found no information to substantiate the allegation that Hutchison is a front for the People's Republic of China. He noted that Panama's contract with Hutchison (Law 5) does not give China any role in determining which ships will pass through the Canal or in which order they will travel, and it does not give Hutchison any control over Canal pilots. Alberto Aleman Zubieta, Administrator of the Panama Canal Commission, stated that "Hutchison has no authority whatsoever to interfere with, dictate or influence the operation of the Canal, nor will it ever be allowed to do so." Gen. Charles Wilhelm, SOUTHCOM Commander in Chief, stated: "We are not aware of any current internal or external threats to the Panama Canal, and we have no evidence that it has been targeted by terrorists or foreign governments."

In April 2004, the issue of Hutchison's operations of the ports was raised during a hearing of the Senate Armed Services Committee. In response to a question, General James T. Hill, Commander of SOUTHCOM, asserted that Hutchison's operations of the ports in Panama have not had a negative impact on the security of the Canal.[43]

Contamination of Firing Ranges and San Jose Island

Another issue in relations has been Panama's desire to have the United States clean up three former firing ranges (Empire, Piña, Balboa West) used by the U.S. military for live-fire exercises and testing of ground explosives during its tenure in the country. The Piña range was turned over to Panama in June 1999, while the Empire and Balboa West ranges were turned over in July 1999. Some 60,000 Panamanians live in areas surrounding the ranges, and reportedly at least 24 Panamanians have been killed in the last two decades by coming into contact with the explosives.[44] Estimates of the cost to clean up the unexploded bombs and other contaminants range from $400 million to $1 billion.[45]

U.S. officials maintain that it is not possible to remove the unexploded ordinance without tearing down the rain forest and threatening the Canal's watershed. They also point to a Canal treaty provision which states that the United States is obligated to take all measures "insofar as may be practicable" in order to ensure that hazards to human life, health and safety were removed from the defense sites reverting to Panama. In response to a press question while attending Panama's centennial celebration in November 2003, Secretary of State Colin Powell maintained that the United States had already met its obligations to clean up the ranges.[46]

The controversy over the U.S. cleanup of the ranges at times has been an irritant in the bilateral relationship, but at this juncture appears to be somewhat of a dormant issue. Officials of the Pérez Balladares government (1994-1999) believed that the United States was reneging on its treaty commitment and wanted to press the United States to clean up the firing ranges regardless of economic cost. The Moscoso government raised the issue during her October 19, 1999, meeting with then President Clinton in Washington. At the time, President Clinton stated that the United States had met its treaty obligations to clean up the ranges to the extent practicable, but did say that the United States wanted to stay engaged and work with Panama on the issue. The issue also came up during then Secretary of State Albright's visit to Panama on January 15, 2000. In a December 2001 letter to Secretary of State Colin Powell, Panama's Foreign Minister reiterated his county's call to clean up the three firing ranges.[47] In April 2003, Panamanian Foreign Minister Harmodio Arias asserted that the issue of clearing the firing ranges was not dead.[48] As noted above, during a November 2005 visit to Panama, President Bush reiterated the view that the United States had met its obligations under the treaty.

On another sensitive issue, U.S. Embassy officials in Panama announced in May 2002 that a plan was being prepared to clean up Panama's San Jose Island, which was contaminated with chemical weapons used in training exercises during World War II.[49] The Organization for the Prohibition of Chemical Weapon (OPCW) had confirmed in July 2001 that there were several live chemical bombs on the island, and Panama evacuated residents of the island.[50] In September 2003, however, Panama rejected a U.S. offer for the environmental cleanup of the island that would have reportedly offered more than $2 million in equipment and training so that Panama could clean up the island. According to Foreign Minister Harmodio Arias, Panama rejected the offer because it did not want to sign a document releasing the United States from all liabilities.[51] A provision in the FY2004 Foreign Operations appropriations measure (P.L. 108-199, Division D) would have permitted Foreign Military Financing for the San Jose Island cleanup.

During a November 2004 visit to Panama, Secretary of Defense Donald Rumsfeld indicated that issues involving both the firing ranges and San José Island were considered closed.[52] At the time, Panamanian officials, however, maintained that both were pending bilateral issues.[53]

Former U.S. Military Presence in Panama

Under the terms of the Panama Canal Treaty, all U.S. military forces withdrew from Panama by December 31, 1999, since no mutual agreement was reached to continue their presence. At that time, Panama assumed responsibility for defending as well as operating the Canal. Nevertheless, under the terms of the Treaty on the Permanent Neutrality and Operation of the Canal, often referred to as the Neutrality Treaty, the United States will have the right to use military force to reopen the canal or restore its operations.

Former Role and Presence of U.S. Troops

Over the years, U.S. military forces in Panama had several functions. The primary purpose of the troops was to provide for the defense of the Panama Canal, as set forth in the

Panama Canal Treaties, until December 31, 1999. Another function served by the presence of the U.S. military in Panama stemmed from its activities throughout Latin America. Until late September 1997, Panama served as the headquarters of the U.S. Southern Command (SOUTHCOM), a unified command responsible for all U.S. military operations south of Mexico. In March 1995, President Clinton announced that SOUTHCOM headquarters, located at Quarry Heights in Panama, would be moved to Miami. The move began in June 1997 and was completed by the end of September 1997. U.S. bases in Panama provided assistance to Latin American nations combating drug trafficking with aerial reconnaissance and counter-narcotics training. Howard Air Force Base in Panama provided secure staging for detection, monitoring, and intelligence collecting assets. Panama also provided unique opportunities and facilities for military training, including the Jungle Operations Training Center (which was deactivated on April 1, 1999) at Fort Sherman, Panama.

By the end of December 1999, all U.S. forces had withdrawn from Panama, and all of the U.S. bases and facilities had reverted to Panamanian control. Ten major installations were returned to Panama over a four-year period: Fort Davis and Fort Espinar in early September 1995; Fort Amador, at the Pacific entrance to the Canal, on October 1, 1996; Albrook Air Force Station on October 1, 1997; Galeta Island (a former U.S. Naval Security Group Activity that passed to Army control in 1995) on March 1, 1999; Rodman Naval Station on March 11, 1999; Fort Sherman, on the Atlantic side, on June 30, 1999; and Howard Air Force Base, which ceased air operations in May 1999, was officially turned over to Panama on November 1, 1999, along with Fort Kobbe. Finally, Fort Clayton and was turned over on November 30, 1999.

Failed Negotiations

In September 1995, President Clinton and President Pérez Balladares met in Washington and announced that the two countries would begin informal discussions to determine if there was mutual interest in the United States maintaining a military presence in Panama beyond the end of 1999. Those talks never materialized, but instead there were a series of bilateral talks regarding a U.S. contribution to a Multinational Counternarcotics Center (MCC). President Pérez Balladares had announced in July 1996 that Panama would be willing to allow the United States to use Howard Air Force Base, at no cost, as an international drug interdiction center. He stated that Panama would "provide the facility free of charge as part of our contribution to the drug war."

Talks on a potential MCC began in late November 1996 and ultimately led to a tentative agreement, announced December 24, 1997, on the establishment of a MCC with the United States contributing troops for the center. Despite the tentative accord, progress on a final agreement was stymied during 1998, and on September 25, 1998, both countries announced that they were ending the MCC talks without a final accord.

As described in the press, the MCC would have involved about 2,000 U.S. troops operating at Howard Air Force Base, Rodman Naval Station, and Fort Kobbe on the Pacific side of the Canal. Other facilities reportedly to be utilized would have been communication facilities at Galeta Island and Corozal. Panama would have provided free use of the bases, while the United States would have been expected to pay for such facilities as housing. The MCC reportedly would have been established for a 12-year period, renewable for additional five-year periods, with the potential participation of other Latin American nations. Reportedly the MCC would have had a Directors' Council made up of the foreign ministers of participating countries and presided over by Panama's foreign minister. If the United States and Panama had agreed on the MCC, the next step would have been for Panama's Legislative Assembly to approve the agreement, which then would have been subject to a national referendum in Panama.

As early as April 1998, the Clinton Administration had expressed concern that negotiations would have to be concluded soon, or the United States would be forced to locate the U.S. anti-drug operations elsewhere. Although the text of the draft MCC accord was not made public, press reports indicated that one problem in the negotiations was a provision that would permit U.S. soldiers to engage in other missions beyond counter-narcotics. Panama and several Latin American nations expected to join the MCC expressed reservations about this aspect of the accord, with concerns centered on the potential for U.S. military intervention in the region. U.S. officials, however, maintained that U.S. military activities beyond anti-narcotics work would consist of such benign activities as search and rescue and disaster relief. Another reported problem in the negotiations was the U.S. rejection of Panama's call to allow a change in the agreement, whereby the center could be dissolved after three years if the drug trafficking problem diminished.

Some participants, including former Ambassador Thomas McNamara, the lead negotiator in the talks with Panama, believe that the main reason that an agreement was not reached was Panama's internal politics. While Panamanian opinion polls overwhelmingly favored a continued U.S. military presence, the President appeared concerned about vocal opposition, even from within his own party, to the proposed center. Moreover, President Pérez Balladares was actively seeking a constitutional change for a second term of office, and this appeared to have influenced the MCC negotiations.

In early December 1998, U.S. officials announced that they had begun talks with several Latin American countries to find new bases of operation in Central and South America for the anti-drug missions formerly undertaken in Panama. Short-term interim agreements were concluded in April 1999 to have Forward Operating Locations (FOLs) in Ecuador, Aruba, and Curaçao for U.S. aerial counternarcotics missions. Subsequently, the United States concluded longer-term 10-year agreements with Ecuador and with the Netherlands (for Aruba and Curaçao) for the anti-drug FOLs. An additional FOL site also was being sought in Central America, and on March 31, 2000, a 10-year agreement was signed with El Salvador.

In 1999, some Members of the U.S. Congress and politicians in Panama suggested that there was still an opportunity for the United States to negotiate the use of facilities in Panama for U.S. anti-drug flights, similar to the FOLs negotiated with Ecuador, Aruba, and Curacao. Press reports suggested that President-elect Moscoso was interested in allowing the U.S. military to use Panama as a staging area for antidrug flights. In 2000, however, President Moscoso turned down a request from the United States for a visiting military forces agreement. On September 26, 2000, she announced that Panama would not participate in a visiting forces agreement with the United States.

U.S. Congressional Views on U.S. Military Presence

Before December 1999, Congress had twice gone on record favoring negotiations to consider a continued U.S. presence in Panama beyond the end of 1999, and in the 104th Congress the Senate approved a non-binding resolution on the issue. In 1991, Congress enacted legislation (P.L. 102-190, Section 3505) expressing the sense of Congress that the President should begin negotiations with Panama to consider whether the two nations should allow the permanent stationing of U.S. forces in Panama past 1999. Twelve years earlier, Congress had approved the Panama Canal Act of 1979 (P.L. 96-70, Section 1111) which states that "it is the sense of the Congress that the best interests of the United States require that the President enter into negotiations" with Panama "for the purpose of arranging for the stationing of United States military forces after the termination of the Panama Canal Treaty." And on September 5, 1996, the Senate approved S.Con.Res. 14, expressing the sense of Congress that the President should negotiate a new base rights agreement with Panama, while consulting with Congress regarding any bilateral negotiations that take place.

In the 106th Congress, numerous measures were introduced relating to a continued U.S. military presence in Panama as the Canal turnover approached, but no legislative action was taken on these measures. The measures would have urged the President to negotiate a new base rights agreement with Panama to permit U.S. troops beyond December 31, 1999 (S.Con.Res. 59, S.J.Res. 37, H.Con.Res. 233); expressed the sense of the Congress that the United States should negotiate security arrangements with Panama to protect the Canal and to ensure Panama's territorial integrity (H.Con.Res. 186/S.Con.Res. 61); authorized and directed the President to renegotiate the Panama Canal Treaties to provide for the security of the Canal (H.R. 2244); and expressed the sense of the Senate that the President should negotiate security arrangements with Panama regarding the protection of the Canal and that any attack on or against the Canal would be considered an act of war against the United States (S.Res. 257). One measure (H.R. 3452) would have provided that unpaid balances of the Panama Canal Commission be payable to Panama only upon completion of an agreement that leases half of Howard Air Force Base to the United States.

In the second session of the 106th Congress, H.R. 3673, introduced by Representative Benjamin Gilman, and reported by the House International Relations Committee (H.Rept. 106-803, Part I), would have provided Panama with certain benefits if Panama agreed to permit the United States to maintain a presence there sufficient to carry out counternarcotics and related missions from Panama. The benefits would have been preferential trade access to the U.S. market; a scholarship program for Panamanians to study in the United States; and assistance for infrastructure construction. Supporters argued that the bill offered an opportunity for the United States to regain its traditional military presence in Panama and restore full U.S. military capability to perform anti-narcotics missions in the region. Opponents argued that Panama had not expressed interest in regaining a U.S. military presence in the country and believed that it could jeopardize talks underway with Panama for a "visiting forces" agreement. The State Department expressed opposition to the bill for several reasons. It maintained that there was a lack of credible support in Panama for any agreement to re-establish a U.S. military presence there; that the quid pro quo nature of the offer to Panama would give the appearance of the United States paying rent for the right to establish a military presence, and U.S. policy was not to pay rent for foreign bases or base rights; and that the trade benefits offered for Panama could violate the most-favored-nation obligation of the World Trade Organization. State Department officials also pointed out that trade benefits for Panama and other Caribbean Basin countries had been enacted into law in May 2000 as part of the U.S.- Caribbean Basin Trade Partnership Act (Title II of P.L. 106-200).

In the 107th Congress, just a single resolution was introduced related to the stationing of U.S. troops in Panama, but no legislative action was taken on the measure. H.Con.Res. 296, introduced by Representative Bob Barr on December 20, 2001, would have urged the President to negotiate a new base rights agreement with Panama in order for U.S. Armed Forces to be stationed there for purposes of defending the Canal.

In the 108th Congress, H.Con.Res. 9, introduced by Representative Virgil Goode, is identical to H.Con.Res. 296 introduced in the 107th Congress described above. The resolution would urge the President to negotiate a new base rights agreement with Panama for the purposes of defending the Panama Canal.

Panamanian Views on U.S. Military Presence

Prior to the departure of U.S. troops at the end of 1999, public opinion polls in Panama cited overwhelming support for a continued U.S. military presence. Some Panamanians focused on the importance of continuing a U.S. military presence to help conduct counternarcotics operations in Panama and in the region. They pointed with concern to incursions of Colombian narco-traffickers into the Darien jungle region of Panama. Despite the polls, Panamanian opponents to the MCC were vocal and staged protests at various times. In 1997, there were several protests by student, human rights, and labor groups who opposed a continued U.S. presence. An umbrella organization was formed known as the Organizations Against Military Bases, which included some 30 labor, peasant, and student groups. In early 1998 another umbrella organization against U.S. military presence was formed, the National Movement for the Defense of Sovereignty, consisting of labor, student, and professional organizations. These groups argued for the need to break what they regarded as Panama's dependent relationship with the United States and recover its own national identity.

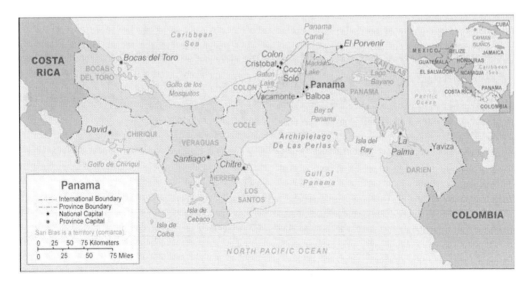

Figure 1. Map of Panama

Source: Map Resources. Adapted by CRS.

END NOTES

[1] "Ex-Leader of Panama Linked to Visa Sales," *Washington Post*, November 27, 1999; Pablo Bachelet, "U.S. Uses Visas to Combat Corruption," *Miami Herald*, February 21, 2006.

[2] "Toss Up Between Torrijos and Endara," *Caribbean and Central America Report*, February 17, 2004.

[3] Frances Robles, "Ex-leader's Son Wins Presidency in Panama," *Miami Herald*, May 3, 2004.

[4] "Panama: Presidential Candidates Remark on FTA with US," *La Prensa* (Panama), January 24, 2004, translated by Foreign Broadcast Information Service.

[5] Marion Barbel, "Panamanian Congress Approves Modified Social Security Reform," *World Markets Research*, December 22, 2005

[6] "Panama: Country Report," *Economist Intelligence Unit*, January 2008, p. 2.

[7] Richard Lapper, "Good Luck, Good Timing," *Financial Times*, July 24, 2007.

[8] "Panama Unveils New Penal Code," *Latin American Weekly Report*, May 29, 2008.

[9] "Panama: Torrijos to Undertake Security Reform by Decree," *Latin American Weekly Report*, July 3, 2008.

[10] "Panama: Country Report," *Economist Intelligence Unit*, July 2008, p. 11.

[11] "Torrijos Growing Unpopular in Panama," *LatinNews Daily*, June 25, 2008.

[12] "Panama: Country Report," *Economist Intelligence Unit*, July 2008, p. 14.

[13] Steven Dudley, "Justice Elusive for Victims of Panama's Ex-Dictators," *Miami Herald*, September 29, 2006.

[14] "Panama: First Indigenous Colombians Get Refuge," *UNHCR Briefing Notes*, December 15, 2006.

[15] "UNHCR Welcomes New Panama Law," *UNHCR Briefing Notes*, April 1, 2008.

[16] "Panama: Country Report," *Economist Intelligence Unit*, July 2008, p. 14.

[17] Ibid, p. 4.

[18] Adam Thomson, "Excessive Wealth Fails to Filter Down to the Poor," *Financial Times*, July 24, 2007.

[19] "Panama: Country Report," *Economist Intelligence Unit*, May 2008, p. 13.

[20] United States Trade Representative, 2006 *National Trade Estimate Report on Foreign Trade Barriers*, p. 501.

[21] U.S. Department of State, Background Note: Panama, February 2007.

[22] U.S. Department of State, U.S. Embassy Panama, "Principal Deputy Assistant Secretary Charles S. Shapiro at Panama Week," and "Ambassador Eaton's Remarks at the Panama Week Power Breakfast," October 2006.

[23] White House, Office of the Press Secretary, "President Bush Meets with President Torrijos of Panama," November 7, 2005; Edwin Chen, "Bush's Trip Ends with Discord," *Los Angeles Times*, November 8, 2005; William Douglas, "Bush's Last Stop: Panama," *Miami Herald*, November 8, 2005.

[24] "Realizará Torrijos Visita a EU Para Cabildear por TLC," *Agencia Mexicana de Noticias*, July 25, 2008.

[25] Kirk Simple, "Noriega Loses Another Round," *New York Times*, January 10, 2008.

[26] Kathia Martinez, "A Homecoming for Noriega after Miami Release? Many Hope Not," *Associated Press Newswires*, August 12, 2007.

[27] "Torrijos on Edge over Noriega Release," *Latin American Regional Report, Carribean and Central America*, August 2007.

[28] Carmen Gentile, "Noriega Court Bid Called a Charade; Aims to Avoid Extradition," *Washington Times*, August 14, 2007.

[29] Marc Lacey, "An Ambivalent Panama Weights Noriega's Debt and Threat," *New York Times*, July 29, 2007.

[30] Chris Kaul, "A New Foe Threatens Tribe's Independent Spirit," *Los Angeles Times*, January 3, 2006; "Panama Tribe Faces Threat as Cocaine Comes Ashore," Reuters, February 18, 2006; "Panama's Kuna Fear Drug Threat," *Latin American Weekly Report*, February 1, 2007.

[31] United States Trade Representative, 2008 National Trade Estimate Report on Foreign Trade Practices.

[32] U.S. Department of Commerce, Bureau of Economic Analysis, "Survey of Current Business," September 2007, p. 93.

[33] Office of the United States Trade Representative, "Free Trade with Panama, Brief Summary of the Agreement," December 19, 2006.

[34] Rosella Brevetti, "Panama, United States Conclude Negotiations on Free Trade Pact," but Labor Issues Remain," *International Trade Daily*, December 20, 2006.

[35] Marc Lacey, "Fugitive from U.S. Justice Leads Panama's Assembly," *New York Times*, November 28, 2007.

[36] Senate Committee on Armed Services, Hearing, "Testimony on United States Southern Command, United States Northern Command, and United States Joint Forces Command in Review of the Defense Authorization Request for Fiscal Year 2008 and the Future Years Defense Program," March 22, 2007, *Federal News Service*.

[37] Rainbow Nelson, "Canal Cash to Pay for Social Development," *Lloyd's List*, January 18, 2006.

[38] Autoridad del Canal de Panama (ACP), "Proposal for the Expansion of the Panama Canal, Third Set of Locks Project," April 24, 2006.

[39] "Panama: Torrijos Wins Backing to Expand Canal," *Latin American Weekly Report*, October 24, 2006; "Panama's Torrijos on Referendum Results: 'Opportunity to Materialize Our Hopes," Open Source Center (*Panama City TVN*), October 23, 2006.

[40] "Torrijos Appeals for Approval of Canal Expansion," *Latinnews Daily*, September 1, 2006.

[41] "Panama: Torrijos Reveals Plans to Expand Canal," *Latinnews Daily*, April 25, 2006; Chris Kraul and Ronald D.White, "Panama is Preparing to Beef up the Canal," *Los Angeles Times*, April 24, 2006; John Lyons, "Panama Takes Step Toward Expanding the Canal," *Wall Street Journal*, April 24, 2006.

[42] Senate Committee on Foreign Relations. *Staff Report on the Privatization of Panamanian Ports*. May 1997.

[43] Hearing of the Senate Armed Services Committee, "Defense Authorization Request for Fiscal Year 2005," April 1, 2004, *Federal News Service*.

[44] "No Home on Panama's Range, U.S. Munitions Scattered Over Canal Training Zones," *Washington Post*, January 10, 2000; Vanessa Hua, "U.S. Weapons, U.S. Mess? Panama," *Bulletin of the Atomic Scientists*, July 1, 2002.

[45] "An Expensive Farewell to Arms: The U.S. Has Abandoned 51 Military Sites in Canada." *The Gazette (Montreal)*, April 28, 2001.

[46] U.S. Department of State. International Information Programs. Washington File. "Colin Powell Hails Panama's 100 Years of Independence," November 3, 2004.

[47] "Panama Asks U.S. Military to Clean Up Former Bases," *Agence France Presse*, December 27, 2001.

[48] Foreign Broadcast Information Service, Highlights: Central America Press, April 8, 2003 ("Panamanian Foreign Minister Says Firing Range Cleanup Not Dead Issue," *La Prensa*)

[49] "U.S. Creates Chemical Weapon Clean-up Plan on Panamanian Island." *EFE News Service*, May 27, 2002.

[50] "Panama-U.S. Panama Clears Isle After Finding World War II Chemical Weapons." *EFE News Services*, September 6, 2001.

[51] Victor Torres, "Foreign Minister Explains Why Panama Rejected U.S. San Jose Island Cleanup Offer," *La Prensa* (Panama), October 12, 2003 (as translated by Foreign Broadcast Information Service).

[52] "Donald H. Rumsfeld Holds Joint News Conference with the Panamanian Minister of Government & Justice," *FDCH Political Transcripts*, November 13, 2004.

[53] "Donald Rumsfeld in Panama Says Contaminated Firing Ranges 'Closed Case,'" *BBC Monitoring International Reports*, November 14, 2004.

INDEX

consumption, 10, 16, 25, 26, 28, 29, 30, 32, 34, 35, 96, 123, 124, 153
consumption patterns, 32
Container Security Initiative, 171, 179
Container Security Initiative (CSI), 171, 179
contaminant, 171, 179
contaminants, 188
continental shelf, 109
contractors, 73, 128, 134
contracts, 11, 70, 71, 72, 73, 76, 78, 92, 98, 133, 155, 157
control, ix, 109, 127, 144, 169, 178, 179, 182, 183, 187, 188, 190
Convention on International Trade in Endangered Species, 90
Convention on International Trade in Endangered Species (CITES), 90
convergence, 168
conversion, 111, 145
conviction, 170, 180
copper, 116
copyrights, 82, 97, 98
corn, vii, 1, 3, 6, 9, 14, 15, 16, 18, 19, 21, 23, 28, 29, 30, 34, 35, 99, 100, 114, 124, 126, 153, 166
corporations, 12
corruption, 92, 95, 148, 173, 174, 176, 178, 179, 182
cost accounting, 153
Costa Rica, 81, 86, 87, 111, 146, 147, 148, 177, 182
costs, 42, 56, 58, 59, 62, 65, 66, 86, 92, 122, 123, 131, 137, 138, 145, 148, 149, 159, 163, 167, 168
cough, 171, 179
counsel, 12, 86, 104, 137, 138
counterfeit, 11, 81, 84, 158
counterfeiting, 84, 99
counternarcotics, ix, 169, 178, 179, 182, 191, 192, 193
country of origin, 152
courts, 54, 79, 80, 157, 177, 181
covering, 17, 50, 60, 67, 94, 163
CP, 194
credit, 148
crime, 175, 179
crimes, 175
criminal activity, 156
criticism, 160
crops, 28, 30, 153
cross-border, 6, 43, 44, 45, 47, 48, 49, 50, 51, 55, 65, 75, 78, 92, 108, 121, 122, 129, 130
cross-border investment, 75
CRS, ix, 86, 87, 128, 131, 132, 133, 142, 143, 147, 166, 167, 168, 170, 179, 184, 187, 193
crude oil, 149
crustaceans, 13

CSS, 174
culture, 11
currency, 45, 71, 123, 138, 148, 167
current account, 147
current account deficit, 147
customers, 41, 50, 51
Customs and Border Protection, 180
Customs and Border Protection (CBP), 180
Customs Union, 138

D

dairy, 10, 12, 17, 32, 62, 63, 100, 153, 154
dairy products, 17, 62, 63, 153
data availability, 6
data processing, 49, 114
data set, 106, 107
database, 81
deaths, 171, 179, 181
debt, 186
decisions, 109
defense, 70, 144, 179, 180, 185, 188, 189
deficit, 146, 147, 182
deficits, viii, 146, 167, 169, 174
definition, 78, 79, 109, 134
degradation, 159, 162, 168
Delaware, 107
delivery, 45, 58, 59, 61, 91, 157
demand curve, 118
democracy, 99, 144, 172, 178
Democratic Party, 173
Democrats, 164, 174
Denmark, 25, 124
Department of Agriculture, 6, 124
Department of Commerce, 6, 9, 13, 18, 23, 112, 114, 116, 117, 123, 125, 128, 129, 149, 150, 166, 167, 194
Department of Defense, 187, 188
Department of Energy, 167, 171, 180
Department of Health and Human Services, 179
Department of Homeland Security, 171, 179, 180
Department of Justice, 94
Department of State, 6, 12, 87, 128, 132, 161, 166, 168, 181, 182, 188, 194, 195
destruction, 158
detection, 180, 190
developed countries, 159, 168
developing countries, 53, 59, 156, 158, 159, 161, 168
developing nations, 85
development assistance, 179
dictatorship, 148
diesel, 40, 97
differential treatment, 77

E

J

K

S

T

U